W9-CPF-742

CLASSICAL PRESENCES

General Editors

LORNA HARDWICK   JIM PORTER

CLASSICAL PRESENCES

The texts, ideas, images, and material culture of ancient Greece and Rome have always been crucial to attempts to appropriate the past in order to authenticate the present. They underlie the mapping of change and the assertion and challenging of values and identities, old and new. Classical Presences brings the latest scholarship to bear on the contexts, theory, and practice of such use, and abuse, of the classical past.

Victorian Women Writers and the Classics: The Feminine of Homer

ISOBEL HURST

OXFORD
UNIVERSITY PRESS

OXFORD
UNIVERSITY PRESS

Great Clarendon Street, Oxford OX2 6DP

Oxford University Press is a department of the University of Oxford.
It furthers the University's objective of excellence in research, scholarship,
and education by publishing worldwide in

Oxford New York

Auckland Cape Town Dar es Salaam Hong Kong Karachi
Kuala Lumpur Madrid Melbourne Mexico City Nairobi
New Delhi Shanghai Taipei Toronto

With offices in

Argentina Austria Brazil Chile Czech Republic France Greece
Guatemala Hungary Italy Japan Poland Portugal Singapore
South Korea Switzerland Thailand Turkey Ukraine Vietnam

Oxford is a registered trade mark of Oxford University Press
in the UK and in certain other countries

Published in the United States
by Oxford University Press Inc., New York

© Isobel Hurst 2006

The moral rights of the author have been asserted
Database right Oxford University Press (maker)

First published 2006

All rights reserved. No part of this publication may be reproduced,
stored in a retrieval system, or transmitted, in any form or by any means,
without the prior permission in writing of Oxford University Press,
or as expressly permitted by law, or under terms agreed with the appropriate
reprographics rights organization. Enquiries concerning reproduction
outside the scope of the above should be sent to the Rights Department,
Oxford University Press, at the address above

You must not circulate this book in any other binding or cover
and you must impose the same condition on any acquirer

British Library Cataloguing in Publication Data

Data available

Library of Congress Cataloging in Publication Data

Hurst, Isobel, 1973–
Victorian women writers and the classics : the feminine of Homer / Isobel Hurst.
p. cm. – (Classical presences)
Based on the author's thesis (doctoral) – University of Oxford, 2003.
Includes bibliographical references and index.

1. English literature–Women authors–History and criticism. 2. English literature–Women
authors–Classical influences. 3. English literature–Women authors–Greek influences. 4. English
literature–19th century–History and criticism. 5. Women authors, English–19th century. 6. Women
and literature–Great Britain–History–19th century. I. Title. II. Title: Feminine of Homer. III. Series.

PR115.H87 2006
820.9'928709034–dc22
2006008191

Typeset by SPI Publisher Services, Pondicherry, India
Printed in Great Britain
on acid-free paper by
Biddles Ltd., King's Lynn, Norfolk

ISBN-13: 978-0-19-928351-4   ISBN-10: 0-19-928351-6

Preface

I would like to thank the Trustees of the E. K. Chambers Bequest and Corpus Christi College, Oxford for financial support during the writing of the D.Phil. thesis on which this book is based. I am grateful to the Institute of Hellenic and Roman Studies, University of Bristol for appointing me to a Junior Postdoctoral Research Fellowship, which enabled me to begin work on the book.
Many people have helped with the writing of this book. I would like to thank Kate Flint for her stimulating and incisive supervision of my thesis. Dinah Birch and Norman Vance examined the thesis and made many valuable suggestions about revising it. I have learnt a lot about the reception of the classics from the members of the Archive of Performances of Greek and Roman Drama at Oxford and am particularly indebted to Fiona Macintosh for her continuing encouragement. I would also like to thank Stephen Harrison, Christopher Stray, Lorna Hardwick, and Charles Martindale for their assistance with the classical side of my work. I am very grateful to Stefano Evangelista, Muireann Ó'Cinnéide, Kirstie Blair, and other Oxford Victorianists for their help and advice. Christine deBlase-Ballstadt, Kurt Ballstadt, Heather Clark, Ruth Gill, Nathan Holcomb, Liz and David Menezes, Pete McDonald, John Mills, and Siobhan McAndrew have contributed to my work in various ways. Most importantly, this book could not have been written without the endless and inspirational support of my parents, John and Cathie Hurst, my sister Charlotte, and my grandparents Elsie Hurst and Bob and Catherine Simpson.

I.H.

Contents

Abbreviations   viii

Introduction   1

1. Encounters with the Ancient World in Nineteenth-
   Century Literary Culture   11

2. Classical Training for the Woman Writer   52

3. 'Unscrupulously Epic'   101

4. Classics and the Family in the Victorian Novel   130

5. Greek Heroines and the Wrongs of Women   164

6. Revising the Victorians   192

Conclusion: 'On Not Knowing Greek'   220

Bibliography   223
Index   247

Abbreviations

BC	*The Brownings' Correspondence*
ELH	*English Literary History*
PMLA	*Proceedings of the Modern Language Association*
RES	*Review of English Studies*
SEL	*Studies in English Literature*
TSWL	*Tulsa Studies in Women's Literature*
UP	University Press
VP	*Victorian Poetry*

Introduction

Maggie found the Latin Grammar quite soothing after her mathematical mortification; for she delighted in new words, and quickly found that there was an English Key at the end, which would make her very wise about Latin, at slight expense. She presently made up her mind to skip the rules in the Syntax,—the examples became so absorbing. The mysterious sentences snatched from an unknown context,—like strange horns of beasts and leaves of unknown plants, brought from some far-off region, gave boundless scope to her imagination, and were all the more fascinating because they were in a peculiar tongue of their own, which she could learn to interpret.[1]

In *The Mill on the Floss* (1860), Maggie Tulliver's imaginative response to the unfamiliarity of Latin vocabulary suggests that encountering the classics as a girl who is not confined by a school curriculum may be an exciting experience. Her brother Tom is engaged in an uncomprehending struggle with a series of dull tasks, with no idea of the reason he is forced to memorize Latin sentences and lacking any awareness of ancient civilization. His experience of classical education is plainly unenviable, yet he pours scorn on Maggie's sense of excitement at encountering the Latin language, her speculations about the lives of the Romans, and her pleasure in the exoticism of these new preoccupations. Tom aligns himself with his dull tutor and mistakenly tries to claim an intellectual superiority based on gender: 'Girls never learn such things. They're too silly' (127). His condescending attitude is a familiar example of the gendering of classical studies as masculine in the nineteenth century, used by men who 'wished to keep women out of the club, which was partly defined by precisely that exclusion; and women ambitious for

---

[1] George Eliot, *The Mill on the Floss* (1860), ed. Gordon S. Haight (Oxford: Clarendon, 1980), 129.

literary accomplishment, just as naturally, yearned to get in'.[2] The
impression which novelists like George Eliot and Charlotte M.
Yonge convey most powerfully is the distress of intelligent girls at being
denied the educational opportunities granted to their brothers, an
impediment which many Victorian women writers lament. Yet in *The
Mill on the Floss*, in Elizabeth Barrett Browning's *Aurora Leigh* (1856),
and in Yonge's *The Daisy Chain* (1856), notions of education as a
process of gender separation are both reinforced and resisted: the
heroines' obvious inclination and potential for learning are painfully
checked by gender constraints, but not entirely suppressed. It was
undeniably more difficult for a girl to study Latin and Greek at home,
or later in the century at school or college, than for a boy who
followed the traditional path from public or grammar school to
university. The ways in which they encountered the ancient languages, in varied environments with differing access to texts and
tuition, made women's responses to the classics distinctive. Even
the most accomplished female classicists did not spend much time
composing prose or verse in the classical languages or analysing
grammar, but concentrated on translating and understanding
Greek and Latin texts. They had to work extremely hard, sometimes
without any support, in order to be able to read classical authors.
Nevertheless, for the Victorian girl Latin and Greek are associated
with empowerment, and a significant number of women with literary
ambitions found the effort worthwhile: the 'mysterious sentences' of
classical literature give 'boundless scope to [their] imagination'.

   In studies of the Victorians and the ancient world a classical
education has been characterized as almost an exclusively male
prerogative.[3] The extent to which women writers actually studied

   [2] Dorothy Mermin, *Godiva's Ride: Women of Letters in England, 1830–1880*
(Bloomington: Indiana UP, 1993), 51.
   [3] The following studies examine the reception of the classics in 19th-cent. culture:
Richard Jenkyns, *The Victorians and Ancient Greece* (Oxford: Blackwell, 1980); Frank
M. Turner, *The Greek Heritage in Victorian Britain* (London: Yale UP, 1981) and
Frank M. Turner, *Contesting Cultural Authority: Essays in Victorian Intellectual Life*
(Cambridge: CUP, 1993); G. W. Clarke (ed.), *Rediscovering Hellenism: The Hellenic
Inheritance and the English Imagination* (Cambridge: CUP, 1989); Simon Goldhill,
Who Needs Greek? Contests in the Cultural History of Hellenism (Cambridge: CUP,
2002); Norman Vance, *The Victorians and Ancient Rome* (Oxford: Blackwell, 1997);

classical texts, and made use of them in their writing, has been seriously underestimated. Yopie Prins remarks that 'the place of women within Victorian Hellenism remains largely unexplored, despite the fact that an increasing number of women were learning Greek in the course of the century'.[4] A more accurate impression of the influence of the classics on women writers, representations of and allusions to female classicists, and the shifts in their relationship to classical texts, influenced by educational reforms, will both illuminate Victorian women's literary culture, and throw new light on an under-examined aspect of women's education. Fictional representations of girls studying the classics tend to stress the difficulties encountered by educated women rather than their achievements, yet if in novels women's desire to learn Latin and Greek like their brothers is usually thwarted, it was not so for writers like Eliot, Barrett Browning, Yonge, and Augusta Webster. Biographical sources reveal that the study of Latin and Greek was not only more widespread among women than previous accounts have suggested, but that those women who did study the classical languages were likely to become writers or be involved in reforming women's education, or both. Examples include Mary Shelley, Sara Coleridge, Anna Jameson, Florence Nightingale, Augusta Webster, Dorothea Beale, and Anna Swanwick.

A considerable number of women writers came from large, isolated households where there were lots of books and periodicals;

Catharine Edwards (ed.), *Roman Presences: Receptions of Rome in European Culture, 1789–1945* (Cambridge: CUP, 1999). The history of classics in schools and universities has been examined by M. L. Clarke, *Classical Education in Britain, 1500–1900* (Cambridge: CUP, 1959) and Christopher Stray, *Classics Transformed: Schools, Universities, and Society in England, 1830–1960* (Oxford: Clarendon, 1998).

[4] Yopie Prins, 'Greek Maenads, Victorian Spinsters', in Richard Dellamora (ed.), *Victorian Sexual Dissidence*, 43. (Chicago: University of Chicago Press, 1999). An interesting exception is Rowena Fowler, ' "On Not Knowing Greek": The Classics and the Woman of Letters', *Classical Journal*, 78 (1983), 337–49. The women writers Fowler discusses demonstrate a variety of reactions to the dominance of the classics in literary culture: 'Some pressed their own claims, forcing themselves into long and solitary courses of study in pursuit of the learning that seemed to confer so much intellectual and psychological power. Others took a less reverent view, suspecting that the classical wisdom quoted at, about and against them was as partial and fallible as its proponents' (337).

'strong, dominating fathers fostered their gifted daughters' talents', and although they 'followed the practice of the time in giving vastly greater freedom and educational opportunity to their sons', they often taught their daughters Latin and sometimes Greek.[5] While women were mainly educated in the home, fathers could control their access to classical texts, and omit controversial authors from their reading. Such censorship went some way to countering the fear that girls would be exposed to the kind of indecencies which boys found in their school classics texts. Women writers were anxious to protect themselves from accusations of unwomanliness, domestic incompetence, and publicity-seeking. A girl who studied the classics alone might encounter exactly these objections, but a father who permitted his daughter to learn Latin and Greek enabled her to step out of rigid gender categories without offending against the family. The licensed acquisition of a kind of knowledge which remained overwhelmingly associated with masculine freedom and authority was a uniquely empowering experience for intelligent girls: this is why some degree of classical education often goes together with successful literary ambitions for women writers in the nineteenth and early twentieth centuries.

Elizabeth Barrett Browning and George Eliot have been granted an exceptional status as female classicists in the nineteenth century. Although they never met, Robert Browning expressed his recognition of their similar intellectual pursuits by showing Eliot his wife's copies of the Greek dramatists, annotated in her own hand. Jennifer Wallace comments that 'Elizabeth Barrett Browning was unusually able to learn Greek with her brother and later to read it with a local scholar—a training which Barrett Browning felt qualified her to become the first serious woman poet.'[6] In fact, both elements of Barrett's 'training' have parallels in the lives of other women: Augusta Webster, Anne Brontë, and Charlotte M. Yonge (among others) learnt Greek with their brothers, and relationships between ambitious young women and older male scholars, based on the study of Greek, were familiar enough to become a recognizable trope in

[5] Mermin, *Godiva*, 3.
[6] Jennifer Wallace, *Shelley and Greece: Rethinking Romantic Hellenism* (Basingstoke: Macmillan, 1997), 16.

fiction. Eliot is the only woman writer discussed at length in Richard Jenkyns's *The Victorians and Ancient Greece* (1980): 'No novelist can compare with George Eliot in fervency of enthusiasm for the ancient world ... without tutors to coax or threaten her into knowledge she acquired a degree of learning which many a university man might have envied.'[7] Greek, noticeably foreign and difficult because of the different alphabet which makes it seem like a secret language to the uninitiated, is central to the narrative of women's exclusion from classical study. The fact that Barrett Browning and Eliot were both dedicated Hellenists and comparatively uninterested in Latin literature—Barrett Browning was greatly influenced by the Romantic aesthetic in which the secondariness of Augustan poetry made it inferior to the folk poetry of Homer—has led to the privileging of Greek in accounts of Victorian women's literary responses to the ancient world. One interesting exception is Norman Vance's discussion of responses to Lucretius by Barrett Browning and Eliot.[8] When Latin literature is considered as well as Greek, women writers' use of classical intertexts covers a remarkable range of themes and images.

By considering Barrett Browning's and Eliot's classical achievements only in relation to those of male scholars and poets, critics endorse the gendered stereotypes associated with the classics: an exceptional woman may study Latin and Greek to a high standard, but only if her intellect is so powerful that it may be described as 'masculine'. Such stereotypes contribute to the preconception that the only three women to participate at any level in nineteenth-century Hellenism were also successful and distinguished writers, one a poet considered for the Laureateship, another a novelist, journalist, translator, and female sage, and the third a professional classical scholar, Jane Ellen Harrison (often invoked because of her influence on Virginia Woolf).[9] In Frank M. Turner's *The Greek Heritage in Victorian Britain* (1981), which focuses on the reception of classical ideas in Victorian intellectual life rather than literary

[7] Jenkyns, *Greece*, 113.

[8] Vance, *Rome*, 98–9.

[9] For Harrison's influence on Woolf, see Sandra D. Shattuck, 'The Stage of Scholarship: Crossing the Bridge from Harrison to Woolf', 278–98; Jane Marcus, *Virginia Woolf and the Languages of Patriarchy* (Bloomington: Indiana UP, 1987).

6 Introduction

responses, Harrison is the only representative of women's involvement in the discourses of Hellenism relating to religion, mythology, politics, and philosophy. She has usually been compared with contemporary male scholars, particularly the Cambridge Ritualists. However, Yopie Prins has interestingly linked Harrison's version of Hellenism with that of Katherine Bradley, another early student at Newnham and one half of the poetic partnership known as 'Michael Field'.[10] Similarly, in *The Invention of Jane Harrison* (2000), Mary Beard focuses on the earlier part of her academic career to 'bring a new cast of characters, friends and intellectual allies into the Harrison legend', and to 're-establish a connection' between Harrison and Eugénie Sellers, a female scholar who has been erased from the history of classics.[11]

Making connections and comparisons with other women writers who studied Latin and Greek does not detract from the distinction of Barrett Browning, Eliot, and Harrison; rather, it emphasizes not only their outstanding attainments in classical studies but also the emulative desire for learning that they inspired in other women. Whether through awareness of predecessors like Mary Shelley, correspondence and friendship like that of Charlotte Brontë and Elizabeth Gaskell, or the example of predecessors and peers at school or college later in the century, women derived encouragement from knowing that their intellectual ambitions were not eccentric and unwomanly, but characteristic of women writers' lives. Eliot's life provided a model for those whose classical reading was mainly undertaken alone. In her novels, the determination to gain access to a source of truth and wisdom forbidden to women, figured in the ability to read Greek and Latin, exemplifies female independence. Her representations of intellectual women whose classical ambitions are thwarted remained influential through half a century of educational reform, for scholars like Harrison and feminist revisers of Greek mythology like Amy Levy and Mary Coleridge. Vera Brittain's belief that she should be able to go to Oxford with her brother was rooted in her childhood identification with Maggie Tulliver. Women of Brittain's generation,

[10] See Prins, 'Maenads', 44–7.
[11] Mary Beard, *The Invention of Jane Harrison* (London: Harvard UP, 2000), 11, 13.

born at the end of the nineteenth century and educated at the schools and universities from which Victorian women writers had been excluded, sought to continue their project of re-evaluating classical literature from a woman's perspective and promoting the novel as a form in which epic and tragic concerns could be expressed.

'THE FEMININE OF HOMER'

There are a few recurrent phrases which act as shorthand for women's relationship to classical culture in the nineteenth and early twentieth centuries. Of these the most popular are variations on 'lady's Greek | Without the accents', from *Aurora Leigh* (276), and 'On Not Knowing Greek', the title of an essay by Virginia Woolf.[12] These phrases focus on the limitations experienced by women in their encounters with the classics, the uncertainty they felt about their linguistic and historical grasp of a subject in which they had little or no formal teaching. This reflects the tendency of Victorian novels to represent knowledge of Greek as an elusive goal—in *Middlemarch* Eliot alludes ironically to Dorothea's 'painful' difficulties with the Greek accents, which cause her to feel that 'here indeed there might be secrets not capable of explanation to a woman's reason'.[13] If a Victorian woman did try to lay claim to an equal share in the classical inheritance, male critics ridiculed her mistakes, such as Aurora Leigh's accentless 'lady's Greek', in order to prove the superiority of their own classical tradition.

A more positive phrase is needed to represent the confidence and skill with which women writers adapted and reworked classical genres and tropes: Elizabeth Barrett's declaration of her childhood dream of being the 'feminine of Homer'.[14] As Dorothy Mermin notes,

[12] e.g. Alice Falk, 'Lady's Greek without the Accents: Aurora Leigh and Authority', *Studies in Browning and his Circle*, 19 (1991), 84–92; Jennifer Wallace, 'Elizabeth Barrett Browning: Knowing Greek', *Essays in Criticism*, 50 (2000), 329–53.

[13] George Eliot, *Middlemarch: A Study of Provincial Life* (1871–2), ed. David Carroll (Oxford: Clarendon, 1992), 64.

[14] *The Brownings' Correspondence*, ed. Ronald Hudson and Philip Kelley (Winfield, Kan.: Wedgestone, 1984–), i. 361.

in the formative years of writers such as Barrett Browning, Charlotte
Brontë, and Anna Jameson, ambitious girls tended to identify themselves with male heroes and to be interested in politics and war.[15]
Barrett, who had written an epic in the style of Pope's Homer by the
age of 14, claimed a place in what was still the most prestigious poetic
genre (also attempted by male contemporaries such as Tennyson). She
moved on from mimicry of Homer and Pope, and in *Aurora Leigh*,
she modernized and feminized the epic. In choosing to be like Homer,
she was rejecting the model of lyric poetry associated with Sappho.
Poets like Felicia Hemans and L.E.L. (Letitia Elizabeth Landon),
important precursors for Victorian women writers because they
wrote about the position of women in a patriarchal world, owed
much to the prevalent image of Sappho.[16] The Greek poet was seen
as the epitome of the creative feminine poetic sensibility, connected
with suffering and the seductive appeal of suicide, a myth which was
reinforced by the death of L.E.L. (the 'English Sappho') in 1838.[17]

The combination of the themes and techniques of the nineteenth-
century novel with forms and archetypes derived from classical
literature appears in the work of many different women writers
examined in the following chapters. In literary histories, novel writing is often identified as a suitable mode for women writers because it
did not require a classical education, and feminist scholars anxious to
establish a tradition of women's literature have tended to accept the
opposition between the novel as a genre in which women excelled
and classical literature as the source and symbol of patriarchal literary culture.[18] Rather than seeing the novel as a form inimical to the
classical heritage of English literature, it is more productive to see it
as a genre which can take up classical narratives and characters and

---

[15] Mermin, *Godiva*, 5.
[16] Studies of the 19th-cent. reception of Sappho include: Ellen Greene, *Re-Reading
Sappho: Reception and Transmission* (London: University of California Press, 1996);
Yopie Prins, *Victorian Sappho* (Princeton: Princeton UP, 1999); Margaret Reynolds
(ed.), *The Sappho Companion* (London: Chatto & Windus, 2000); Margaret
Reynolds, *The Sappho History* (Basingstoke: Palgrave, 2003).
[17] Glennis Stephenson, *Letitia Landon: The Woman Behind L.E.L.* (Manchester:
Manchester UP, 1995), 29.
[18] e.g. Sandra M. Gilbert and Susan Gubar, *The Madwoman in the Attic: The
Woman Writer and the Nineteenth-Century Literary Imagination*, 2nd edn. (New
Haven: Yale UP, 2000), 545–7.

render them comprehensible to a modern readership. George Eliot draws on epic and tragedy in her novels, assimilating the experiences of ancient heroes to those of her protagonists as part of her ongoing novelistic project of the 'comparison of small things with great'.[19] The significance of themes which are subtly incorporated into realist narrative or epic poetry by writers like Eliot and Barrett Browning may become clearer when they are compared with texts which engage more directly with the classics, such as Augusta Webster's *The Medea of Euripides*.[20] Translations of classical texts by women writers reveal critiques of nineteenth-century gender politics, particularly when it comes to such texts as *Prometheus Bound* and *Medea*. Lorna Hardwick focuses on 'three women writers who each demonstrated different kinds of empowerment based on the increasing diversity of translational practices': Augusta Webster, Amy Levy, and Anna Swanwick (who translated Aeschylus' tragedies and wrote introductions and general essays which 'opened up knowledge of classical culture and especially of Athenian democracy').[21] Eliot, Webster, and Levy respond creatively to the 'astonishing wealth of imposing female characters' in Greek tragedy and epic, such as Antigone, Medea, Hecuba, Electra, and Circe, and use them to comment obliquely on the restricted lives of nineteenth-century women, in feminist reworkings of classical characters which draw on novelistic conventions.[22]

To establish the place of classics in the Victorian popular imagination, Chapter 1 examines men's experiences of classical education in schools and universities, and the resources available to those whose

[19] Eliot, *Mill*, 238.

[20] Anthologies of women's poetry are particularly helpful, as they can show a writer choosing to explore a favourite theme through a classical story: Angela Leighton and Margaret Reynolds, *Victorian Women Poets: An Anthology* (Oxford: Blackwell, 1995); Virginia Blain, *Victorian Women Poets: A New Annotated Anthology* (Harlow: Longman, 2001). The feminist rediscovery of women writers like Webster and Levy, whose work was regarded as uncanonical and therefore not reprinted until recently, has enabled the re-examination of women's responses to the classics.

[21] Lorna Hardwick, *Translating Words, Translating Cultures* (London: Duckworth, 2000), 31, 33. Lorna Hardwick, 'Women, Translation and Empowerment', in Joan Bellamy, Anne Laurence, and Gillian Perry (eds.), *Women, Scholarship and Criticism: Gender and Knowledge c.1790–1900* (Manchester: Manchester UP, 2000), 180–203.

[22] Bernard Knox, *The Oldest Dead White European Males and Other Reflections on the Classics* (London: W. W. Norton, 1993), 52.

education had not equipped them to read ancient texts in the original languages, such as translations, popular fiction, and travel. Chapter 2 deals with the shift from solitary women learning classics in the home to formal education in girls' schools and women's colleges in the second half of the nineteenth century. As Latin and Greek became more accessible to women, the prestige of classical study was in decline: Vera Brittain, studying in Oxford during the First World War, remarked that it could safely be left to women because it had become an irrelevance. Chapter 3 emphasizes how a woman who was largely self-taught, Elizabeth Barrett Browning, successfully negotiated gender difficulties by choosing to concentrate on poetry rather than scholarship. Her autobiographical essays demonstrate how a woman whose access to the classics was comparatively easy might imagine herself as the author of a female epic. Chapter 4 looks at fictions about women studying the classics at home: the varied accounts of classical studies in fiction deserve a more prominent place in the analysis of nineteenth-century reception of the classics. The negative representation of the selfish scholarly heroine is contrasted with the compliant girl whose access to patriarchal culture is controlled by her own father. Chapter 5 looks at the use of Greek heroines such as Medea, Aspasia, and Alcestis to explore feminist issues in the work of George Eliot, Eliza Lynn Linton, Augusta Webster, and Amy Levy. Chapter 6 focuses on women writers in the early years of the twentieth century, who had to learn the classical languages quickly in order to prove that they could compete with men. Their responses to the classics are mediated by English literature, particularly Victorian women's novels. In conclusion, Woolf's ironic attitude to the classics in 'On Not Knowing Greek' is examined not as the bitterness of a woman who has been excluded from patriarchal culture, but as a fascinating and idiosyncratic response to Greek, which owes much to her female predecessors.

1

Encounters with the Ancient World in Nineteenth-Century Literary Culture

> I abhorr'd
> Too much, to conquer for the poet's sake,
> The drill'd dull lesson, forced down word by word
> In my repugnant youth, with pleasure to record
>
> Aught that recalls the daily drug which turn'd
> My sickening memory ... [1]

Gazing at Mount Soracte, Byron's Childe Harold refuses to adopt the characteristic pose of the Grand Tourist, to 'quote in classic raptures, and awake | The hills with Latian echoes'. He considers it a 'curse' that he can 'understand, not feel' and 'comprehend, but never love' the 'lyric flow' of Horace's renowned Soracte Ode (*Odes* 1. 9) because he associates the verse with the tedious Latin lessons he endured at school.[2] What is remarkable here is Byron's forceful denunciation of the educational methods which leave his hero equipped to repeat Horace's ode from memory, but prevent his appreciating it as poetry. He expanded on these ideas in a prose comment which was described by John Nichol in his 1880 biography of the poet as still relevant to 'recent educational controversies':[3]

I wish to express that we become tired of the task before we can comprehend the beauty; that we learn by rote before we get by heart; that the freshness is

---

[1] Byron, *Childe Harold's Pilgrimage*, 4. 672–7: George Gordon Byron, *Poetical Works*, ed. Frederick Page, 3rd edn. (London: OUP, 1970).

[2] Ibid. 4. 671–2, 686–8.

[3] John Nichol, *Byron* (London: Macmillan, 1880), 26.

worn away, and the future pleasure and advantage deadened and destroyed, by the didactic anticipation, at an age when we can neither feel nor understand the power of compositions which it requires an acquaintance with life, as well as Latin and Greek, to relish, or to reason upon.[4]

Since women did not have to memorize and construe Latin and Greek on a daily basis, did not attempt competitive examinations, and were not awarded degrees, only those who were exceptionally diligent could attain the level of familiarity with ancient texts that any intelligent schoolboy would possess. Women who studied the classics, especially Greek, concentrated on reading rather than composition or rote-learning. They were patronized by male scholars for mistakes in Greek accents or Latin quantities. Yet they had one advantage over those who found the excessive repetition and grammatical analysis in the classroom dull and sickening: they did not experience the kind of alienation from classical literature described by Byron, but could 'feel', 'relish', and 'love' poetry.

Before looking at the availability of classical discourses to a wider readership in this period, it is important to establish what and how the (relatively few but disproportionately influential) men who studied the classics in schools and universities learnt, since women who chose to study the classics measured their progress against the achievements of fathers, brothers, or mentors. Byron's allusion to the Soracte Ode reflects Horace's status in the nineteenth century as 'the common possession of well educated men':[5] those who had attended public schools and the ancient universities would have memorized, parsed, construed, and imitated the *Odes*, perhaps several times at different stages of their careers. His abhorrence of a poet so closely associated with the repetitiveness of nineteenth-century classical studies was shared by men like Tennyson and Anthony Trollope, who only overcame their antipathy to Horace when they rediscovered the poet later in life. Tennyson recalled that 'the author "thoroughly drummed" into him [was] Horace; whom he disliked in proportion', and wrote: 'It was not till many years after boyhood that I could like Horace. Byron expressed what I felt, "Then

[4] Byron, *Poetical Works*, 204.
[5] Vance, *Rome*, 175.

farewell Horace whom I hated so". Indeed I was so over-dosed with Horace that I hardly do him justice even now that I am old.'[6] Despite this hostility, *In Memoriam* (1850) and 'To the Rev. F. D. Maurice' (1854) contain allusions to the *Odes* which demonstrate that the Horatian themes of *amicitia* and conviviality 'provided Tennyson with a literary model' for writing about friendships between men.[7] Trollope saw his twelve years of Latin and Greek lessons at public schools (he attended both Harrow and Winchester) as a 'waste of time', since 'no attempt was made to teach [him] those languages'; he prided himself on the pleasure he derived from his own self-directed classical studies in adulthood (although he acknowledged that he was 'aided' by the 'groundwork' he had put in at school).[8] This 'groundwork' included learning by rote Horace's *Odes*, Virgil's *Aeneid*, and the *Iliad* and *Odyssey* of Homer; that these texts remained in his memory is confirmed by numerous allusions in his novels (in English or Latin, but not in Greek).[9]

Horace's elegantly condensed and aphoristic style meant that lines from his poems could be recalled with comparative ease in later life: in *Adam Bede* (1859), when Arthur Donnithorne hopes to retain just enough Latin to be used on appropriate occasions he thinks of Horace as the poet who will 'adorn my maiden speech in Parliament six or seven years hence. "Cras ingens iterabimus aequor," and a few shreds of that sort, will perhaps stick to me, and I shall arrange my opinions so as to introduce them.'[10] Trollope quotes aphorisms from

[6] Hallam Tennyson, *Alfred, Lord Tennyson: A Memoir* (London: Macmillan, 1897), i. 16.

[7] Norman Vance, 'Horace and the Nineteenth Century', in Charles Martindale and David Hopkins (eds.), *Horace Made New: Horatian Influences on British Writing from the Renaissance to the Twentieth Century*, (Cambridge: CUP, 1993), 208–9.

[8] Anthony Trollope, *An Autobiography* (1883), ed. Michael Sadleir and Frederick Page (Oxford: OUP, 1980), 17–18.

[9] Robert Tracy, '*Lana Medicata Fuco*: Trollope's Classicism', in John Halperin (ed.), *Trollope Centenary Essays* (London: Macmillan, 1982), 6. The fairly limited number of Latin quotations employed by Victorian novelists may suggest that they are often derived from the widely used *Eton Latin Grammar* rather than memorized from the original texts. An especial favourite was Terence's *amantium irae amoris integratio est* (lovers' quarrels are the renewal of love: *Andria* 555), which appears in Thackeray's *Vanity Fair*, Trollope's *Framley Parsonage* and *Phineas Finn*, and Meredith's *The Egoist*, usually in abbreviated form as *amantium irae.*

[10] George Eliot, *Adam Bede* (1859), ed. Carol A. Martin (Oxford: Clarendon, 2001), 158–9. *Cras ingens iterabimus aequor* (tomorrow we shall sail the vast sea

Terence, Juvenal, Horace, and Virgil in his fiction, but his self-con-
sciousness contrasts with the gentlemanly ease with which Thackeray
(educated at Charterhouse and Cambridge) assimilates classical allusions into his text: in *Vanity Fair* (1847) he refers to Horace in his
description of 'all the *fumum* and *strepitus* of a German inn in fair-
time'.[11] Such gestures towards a shared cultural possession, in order
to define one's own social position, are familiar in the context of
nineteenth-century reception of the classics.

By the mid-nineteenth century a defence of classical studies 'as an
indispensable element in every liberal system of education' was no
longer 'superfluous', as it would have been fifty years earlier, but
'[ran] counter to the selfish and material tendencies of the age ...
always in danger of being undermined by ... modern educational
reform'.[12] Yet although the classical curriculum was attacked by
utilitarians and supporters of scientific education, wealthy merchants
and manufacturers had learnt to value its social desirability. Many of
those who had made their money by practical skills were well aware
that classical studies acted as a social marker, providing 'access to
culture and power, to which ... Greek with its exotic alphabet, held
the magic key', and they wanted to buy their sons a place in the
established order.[13] This did not necessarily mean that they had any
real admiration for classical learning: Latimer, the narrator of George
Eliot's 'The Lifted Veil', describes how his father (a banker) chooses to
send his eldest son, 'his representative and successor', to Eton and
Oxford

for the sake of making connections, of course: my father was not a man to
underrate the bearing of Latin satirists or Greek dramatists on the attainment of an aristocratic position. But, intrinsically, he had slight esteem for

again) is from Horace, *Odes* 1. 7. 32. Latin quotations were a familiar feature of
parliamentary discourse, especially in the early decades of the 19th cent (*Adam Bede*
is set *c.*1800). For the decline in classical allusions in Parliament during the century,
see Stray, *Classics Transformed*, 65–8.

[11] Horace, *Odes* 3. 29. 12—*fumum ... strepitumque Romae* (the smoke ... and
noise of Rome). William Makepeace Thackeray, *Vanity Fair: A Novel Without a Hero*
(1847), ed. John Sutherland (Oxford: OUP, 1998), 842.

[12] H. M. Wilkins, 'Latin Versification', *Blackwood's Edinburgh Magazine*, 76 (1854),
560.

[13] Mermin, *Godiva*, 51.

'those dead but sceptred spirits'; having qualified himself for forming an independent opinion by reading Potter's 'Æschylus', and dipping into Francis's 'Horace'. To this negative view he added a positive one ... that a scientific education was the really useful training for a younger son.[14]

The frequency with which the topic of education appears in Victorian fiction is a reminder of its importance in nineteenth-century society and literary culture. Although gender has traditionally been regarded as the determining factor in access to classical education, Victorian novelists help us to understand that class is always significant. Christopher Stray comments that 'relatively fluid social boundaries' in England made education 'a crucial status marker, the battleground of class identification'.[15] The futility of attempting social advancement on the basis of a boy's ability to learn Latin is a popular theme, explored in *Dombey and Son* (1846–8) and *Vanity Fair* as well as *The Mill on the Floss*. Contrasting the levels of classical education offered to or achieved by characters offers novelists the opportunity to depict class tensions: an impoverished cleric uses his Latin to patronize the ignorant aristocrats or merchants on whom he is financially dependent; a self-made industrialist who studies the classics as a recreation clashes with his family, who cannot understand his high opinion of a tutor whose learning barely enables him to support his wife and daughter. In *Vanity Fair*, the merchant John Osborne gradually adjusts to the social expectations which accompany his increasing prosperity, when he plans his grandson's future:

He saw him in his mind's eye, a collegian, a Parliament man, a Baronet, perhaps ... A few years before, he used to be savage, and inveigh against all parsons, scholars, and the like declaring that they were a pack of humbugs, and quacks that weren't fit to get their living but by grinding Latin and Greek, and a set of supercilious dogs that pretended to look down upon British merchants and gentlemen, who could buy up half a hundred of 'em. He would mourn now, in a very solemn manner, that his own education had been neglected, and repeatedly point out, in pompous orations to Georgy, the necessity and excellence of classical acquirements.   (707–8)

[14] George Eliot, *The Lifted Veil; Brother Jacob*, ed. Helen Small (Oxford: OUP, 1999), 5–6.
[15] Stray, *Classics Transformed*, 27.

The value of a classical education in social and political terms is memorably stated by those who were outside the system and could see its flaws, especially Charles Dickens, George Eliot, and Thomas Hardy. In *The Mill on the Floss*, Eliot's satire is clearly directed against the mismatch between ability and the gendered educational system— it quickly becomes clear that Maggie could easily outstrip Tom—but it is also significant that learning Latin is futile for both of them, ultimately offering neither social advancement nor intellectual satisfaction. Tom is educated according to the conventions of the class of gentlemen his father wishes him to join, and not the one to which he is later confined by the need to pay off the family's debt. Mr Tulliver hopes 'to give Tom a good eddication: an eddication as'll be a bread to him', but classical studies turn out to be a positive hindrance in terms of earning money. Even before he starts to learn Latin Tom is already well educated enough to become a miller, but his father would prefer him to become 'a sort o' engineer, or a surveyor, or an auctioneer', someone who would be able to argue a case with Lawyer Wakem (8–9). Eliot suggests in *Middlemarch* that classical studies are an inappropriate training for such a career: Fred Vincy obtains a degree, which qualifies him to become a clergyman (again, an example of misdirected paternal ambition, since it is a vocation for which Fred is clearly unfitted) but the more practical occupation he eventually chooses requires him to relearn everything, including how to write neatly. Tulliver recognizes that Maggie is better suited to learning than Tom but regards her cleverness as a disadvantage: 'an over 'cute woman's no better nor a long-tailed sheep—she'll fetch none the bigger price for that' (11). This is an astute comment on Maggie's social environment, in which education is not valued for its own sake but for what it can buy, and marriage is the only possible career for a girl. When Maggie later shares her cousin Lucy's education she encounters a different world in which women can at least support themselves through teaching, but her relatives do not accept the distinction between governesses and servants which made teaching acceptable to the daughters of more genteel but impoverished families. Eliot observes that too much education can be socially awkward even in the upper classes, when it is associated with earning money. Sir Hugo Mallinger sends Daniel Deronda to public school and university but warns him not to go too far into classical scholarship, because all he needs is 'a passport in life', and 'unless a man can get the prestige and income of a Don and write donnish books, it's hardly worth while for him to make a Greek and Latin machine of himself and be able to spin out pages of the Greek dramatists at any verse you'll give him as a cue'.[16]

'THE DRILL'D DULL LESSON'

Eton, Winchester, Rugby, and other public schools founded during the Renaissance with a humanist curriculum based on Latin and Greek remained key institutions for educating men of the Victorian aristocracy, gentry, and clergy. A cheaper alternative for the middle classes was the endowed grammar schools, which provided a very similar education: grammar school pupils included Coleridge, de Quincey, Wordsworth, and Tennyson. The *Eton Latin Grammar* (based on William Lily's sixteenth-century textbook and revised in 1758) was the most famous classical textbook for much of the nineteenth century, used by clerical tutors, governesses preparing pupils for school and other home-based learners, as well as in public and grammar schools.[17] The beginning of the rules for the genders of nouns ('Propria, quae maribus tribuuntur mascula dicas') and for verbs ('As in praesenti') are often assumed to be so familiar that they act as a metonym not only for the grammar book, but for the system of classical education.[18] When Thackeray describes William Dobbin's unhappiness at school, he comments that parents and teachers

[16] George Eliot, *Daniel Deronda* (1876), ed. Graham Handley (Oxford: Clarendon, 1984), 161.

[17] See *An Introduction to the Latin Tongue, 1758* (Menston, Ill.: Scolar Press, 1970). As 'the leading public school', Eton opposed 'attempts to establish new standard Latin and Greek grammars, but in the 1860s the Clarendon Commission asked the head-master of Shrewsbury to prepare a standard Latin grammar—Kennedy's *Public School Latin Primer* (1866)': Stray, *Classics Transformed*, 56.

[18] 'Propria *proper names* quae *which* tribuuntur *are assigned* maribus *to the male kind*, dicas *you may call* mascula *masculines*'. 'As in praesenti *a verb making as in the present tense* format *forms* perfectum *the preterperfect tense* in avi'. W. F. Mavor, *The Eton Latin Grammar, Or An Introduction to the Latin Tongue*, 11th edn. (London: 1822), 139.

should 'leave children alone a little more,—small harm would accrue, although a less quantity of *as in praesenti* might be acquired'.[19] The grammar book appears with surprising frequency in fiction: for example, in the sensation novel *Lady Audley's Secret* (1862), Mary Elizabeth Braddon uses the book to help create the genteel background against which bigamy, murder, and blackmail appear all the more shocking. When Robert Audley examines Talboys's possessions for clues to his disappearance, he finds the grammar along with a Greek Testament; the choice of texts and the implication that he has read very little since leaving school emphasize that Talboys is a gentleman.[20]

Memorizing prose and verse texts—'the wholesale committing to memory of books of the *Aeneid*, the odes of Horace, or even speeches of Cicero'—played a large part in the public school classical education; in many cases this feat of memory was all that was tested, and no care was taken to check whether pupils could 'construe accurately a single passage therein'.[21] In 1830, the *Edinburgh Review* published details of a typical week's work for the fifth form at Eton: seventy lines of the *Iliad* and the same of the *Aeneid*, a few pages of the anthologies of prose authors *Scriptores Graeci* and *Scriptores Romani*, a few pages to be memorized from the grammar book and some Latin translation exercises.[22] Lessons consisted of recitation of lines in the original language, translation, parsing, and questions about grammar and syntax. 'Every word was translated literally and the whole then rendered into elegant English. With dutiful assistance from Lily's *Grammar* the schoolboy puzzled out every tense so that the grammar and syntax of the poems were implanted in his memory.'[23] Boys prepared for their lessons by studying in groups, or with an older student acting as tutor, and, as Trollope complained, there was little teaching in the classroom: the 'masters' responsibility was

---

[19] Thackeray, *Vanity Fair*, 51.

[20] Mary Elizabeth Braddon, *Lady Audley's Secret* (1862), ed. David Skilton (Oxford: OUP, 1987), 156.

[21] Wilkins, 'Latin Versification', 566.

[22] 'Public Schools of England—Eton', *Edinburgh Review*, 51 (1830), 68; Wallace, *Shelley*, 23.

[23] R. M. Ogilvie, *Latin and Greek: A History of the Influence of the Classics on English Life from 1600 to 1918* (London: Routledge & Kegan Paul, 1964), 40.

not to instruct but to hear recitations and to punish failure'.[24] Reading whole poems or plays was not necessarily more stimulating than learning from the grammar book: since there was no commentary on the literary or historical nature of the texts, they were largely forgotten once their usefulness as sources of grammatical examples was over, or reread year after year for the same purpose.

In *Tom Brown's School Days* (1857), Thomas Hughes describes a class which recalls Byron's 'drill'd dull lesson': the lower fourth, pupils between the ages of 9 and 15, expend 'such part of their energies as was devoted to Latin and Greek upon a book of Livy, the Bucolics of Virgil, and the Hecuba of Euripides, which were ground out in small daily portions'.[25] The texts are not regarded as literature, but as an exercise to be completed with as little effort as possible: the pupils deliberately waste lesson time, resisting any attempt on the part of the master to go beyond the regulation forty lines they have prepared in small groups. According to the schoolboy code, masters and boys are on opposing sides in the classroom—'like a match at football or a battle'—an approach which is understandable given the emphasis in the curriculum on texts based on war and competition:

We're natural enemies in school—that's the fact. We've got to learn so much Latin and Greek, and do so many verses, and they've got to see that we do it ... I don't tell the master I've learnt it. He's got to find out whether I have or not. What's he paid for? If he calls me up and I get floored, he makes me write it out in Greek and English. (365)

Dr Arnold emphasized Greek epic, prose history, and philosophy in the curriculum at Rugby School because the heroes in Homer and Thucydides exemplified ideals of masculinity on which his pupils could model their conduct; he wanted to produce gentlemen noted for manly virtue rather than the aristocratic style which earlier educators had seen as characteristic of a classical education.[26] *Tom*

---

[24] Tracy, 'Trollope's Classicism', 5.

[25] Thomas Hughes, *Tom Brown's School Days* (Cambridge: Macmillan, 1857), 177.

[26] See James Bowen, 'Education, Ideology and the Ruling Class: Hellenism and English Public Schools in the Nineteenth Century', in G. W. Clarke (ed.), *Rediscovering Hellenism: The Hellenic Inheritance and the English Imagination* (Cambridge: CUP, 1989), 170.

Brown's School Days suggests that most boys would identify with scenes of combat and heroic victory rather than Homer's sympathy for the victims of war. Arthur, who reads the text for his own pleasure, is ridiculed by his peers for weeping over an episode in the last book of the *Iliad*, Helen's lament over the body of Hector. The narrator's praise is reserved not for Arthur's diligence or sensitivity but for the physical courage of Tom Brown, who takes Arthur's place in a fight against the bully Slogger Williams.

The composition of original verses in Latin or Greek, usually on a set theme and imitating the style of ancient authors, was more controversial than the linguistic drilling based on classical texts. Books like the *Gradus ad Parnassum* and *Musae Etonenses*, both of which went through several editions in the nineteenth century, gave the quantities which would enable the student to select a word which would fit the allocated metre, and also suggested synonyms. The purpose of such a task was to train the faculties and cultivate a pure taste; one Oxford don defended the 'habit of classical composition' because it 'supplies the only effective antidote to the predominance of mere learning over intellect and taste'.[27] The success of this exercise is questionable, since weaker students notoriously copied verses written by previous generations in order to meet the requirements of grammatical and metrical correctness. A similar theme would probably have been set before: 'one hundred and fourteen subjects every year, two hundred and twenty-eight every two years, and so on ... it will not be wondered that the masters gave the same subjects sometimes over again after a certain lapse of time', comments the narrator of *Tom Brown's School Days*.[28] It is appropriate that this criticism of Latin verse composition comes from a novel set in Rugby School, since Arnold was particularly opposed to a practice he had described as 'one of the most contemptible prettinesses of the understanding'.[29]

[27] Wilkins, 'Latin Versification', 566.

[28] Hughes, *Tom Brown*, 287.

[29] Arthur Penrhyn Stanley, *The Life and Correspondence of Thomas Arnold* (London: Ward Lock, 1844), i. 131. Arnold's contempt for 'prettiness' (elegance, especially in composition) recalls a conversation between Dr Johnson and Boswell: 'BOSWELL "A good scholar, sir?" JOHNSON. "Why, no, sir." BOSWELL. "He was a pretty scholar." JOHNSON. "You have about reached him" ': James Boswell, *Journal of a Tour to the Hebrides with Samuel Johnson, LL.D., 1773*, ed. Frederick A. Pottle and Charles H. Bennett (London: Heinemann, 1963), 308.

Verse composition exercises gradually gave way to the translation of English poetry into Latin verse, a gentlemanly pursuit which could be continued by men whose formal education was over, since similar effusions were published in the *Gentleman's Magazine* until the 1860s, and in *Blackwood's Magazine.* Writing in *Blackwood's* in 1854, H. M. Wilkins commends the practice of translating English verse, and gives examples of poems by Wordsworth and Coleridge translated into Latin.[30] From articles such as this, readers could form an idea of the principles and practice of the dominant educational system, and of its drawbacks—when nineteenth-century women lament their lack of classical knowledge, they are not talking about the ability to translate Wordsworth into Latin. Those who did not personally experience the public or grammar school classical curriculum did not always envy the boys who seemed to have no idea that what they were studying was anything but an exercise created to cause them difficulty—like Tom Tulliver, who comes 'to a dim understanding of the fact that there had once been people upon the earth who were so fortunate as to know Latin without learning it through the medium of the Eton Grammar' only through Maggie's questions (133). What they did miss out on was what Trollope called 'groundwork': reading a wide range of authors was more difficult for those who started later in life but still wanted to study Homer and Virgil in the original before moving on to less canonical texts.

UNIVERSITIES

If the lack of a classical schooling was not necessarily to be regretted, the idea of the university remained particularly attractive to aspiring writers and intellectuals, who felt that 'the truly intelligent person will naturally gravitate towards the University, as a means of ... finding communion with like minds'.[31] The autodidact who acquires sufficient learning to be worthy of admission to the ancient universities,

---

[30] Wilkins, 'Latin Versification', 566.
[31] Janice Rossen, *The University in Modern Fiction: When Power is Academic* (Basingstoke: Macmillan, 1993), 13.

proving that he or she could rival men with a classical education, is a notable fantasy figure in the nineteenth century. Although the most famous fictional embodiment is Hardy's Jude Fawley, a lower-class male, his failure to achieve the required level of scholarship and the harsh admonitions he receives for his ambition represent fears shared by middle-class women and working men as outsiders seeking to enter the privileged world of the university. The absence of women and working-class men from Oxford and Cambridge for much of the nineteenth century was eventually ended by the establishment of colleges for women and cheaper alternatives for men, such as Keble College, founded in 1870 to offer the advantage of an Oxford education combined with plain and economical living.

Oxford did not greatly resemble the ideal community of scholars imagined by outsiders but was, as Matthew Arnold privately acknowledged, a glorified finishing school.[32] The university was recovering from the low point it had reached in the eighteenth century, when scholars were largely 'content with an empirical knowledge of the ancient languages based on the reading and imitation of the best authors, and did not encourage a more profound and critical study'.[33] Undergraduates often ended up rereading the texts they had studied at school, with very little formal tuition, and did not have to prepare for examinations. In the early part of the nineteenth century Oxford education continued on the traditional model: little teaching was undertaken by the university; the quality of 'lectures and prescribed exercises ... in effect construing lessons like those at school' varied widely at different colleges.[34] Given the wide range of ability and experience within college classes, 'those who had been taught the classics well before arriving at Oxford were apt to become hopelessly bored', and the best students relied on private tutors.[35] If those who were already accomplished linguists became more

---

[32] Chris Baldick, *The Social Mission of English Criticism, 1848–1932* (Oxford: Clarendon, 1987), 46.

[33] M. L. Clarke, 'Classical Studies', *The History of the University of Oxford*, v. *The Eighteenth Century*, ed. L. S. Sutherland and L. G. Mitchell (Oxford: Clarendon, 1986), 525.

[34] Ibid. 517.

[35] M. G. Brock, 'The Oxford of Peel and Gladstone, 1800–1833', *The History of the University of Oxford*, vi. *Nineteenth-Century Oxford, Part 1*, ed. M. G. Brock and M. C. Curthoys (Oxford: Clarendon, 1997), 33.

proficient in Latin and Greek it was largely as a result of self-directed study: while at the university, Percy Shelley went to very few lectures but spent up to sixteen hours a day reading.[36] He favoured authors who were not taught at school, such as Aeschylus, Aristophanes, Pindar, Lucretius, and Lucan, and Hogg observed that he read them 'if not as readily as an English author, at least with as much facility as French, Italian, or Spanish'.[37]

Oxford underwent a gradual but comprehensive process of reform in the Victorian period, prompted by public criticism, the Royal Commissions of 1837 and 1851, challenges from Scottish and Continental universities, and an increasing enthusiasm for classical studies, particularly Greek.[38] A notable change was the creation of the Literae Humaniores or 'Greats' course in 1850, so that students concentrated on language and literature until the first public examination in the fifth term ('Moderations', or 'Mods'), and then ancient history and philosophy (particularly Plato and Aristotle) for the remainder of their studies.[39] A remarkably narrow range of authors was required, including Homer, Greek dramatists and orators, and (rarely) Pindar; for Latin Cicero, Virgil, Horace, and Juvenal. Richard Jenkyns comments that the most frequently studied authors were considered to be the greatest intellects of antiquity: a reaction against Regency taste led to the omission of those who were seen as minor artists, such as the Roman elegists Catullus, Propertius, and Ovid. This changed in 1872, when the first selection of set authors for Mods included Theocritus, Propertius, and some Catullus, as well as the 'big four' Homer, Virgil, Demosthenes, and Cicero. Students would not have time to read the complete works of these four main authors, and they were tested on the ability to translate, but they could apply their critical skills to 'lesser authors'.[40]

[36] Richard Holmes, *Shelley: The Pursuit*, 2nd edn. (London: Flamingo, 1995), 39.

[37] Thomas Jefferson Hogg, *The Life of Percy Bysshe Shelley* (London, 1858), i. 86, quoted in Timothy Webb, *The Violet in the Crucible: Shelley and Translation* (Oxford: Clarendon, 1976), 14.

[38] Bowen, 'Education', 169.

[39] See Richard Jenkyns, 'The Beginnings of Greats, 1800–1872: Classical Studies', *The History of the University of Oxford*, vi. *Nineteenth-Century Oxford, Part 1*, ed. M. G. Brock and M. C. Curthoys (Oxford: OUP, 1997), 513–20.

[40] Richard Jenkyns, 'Classical Studies, 1872–1914', *The History of the University of Oxford*, vii. *Nineteenth-Century Oxford, Part 2*, ed. M. G. Brock and M. C. Curthoys (Oxford: Clarendon, 2000), 327.

Despite their many similarities, Oxford and Cambridge exemplified different approaches to classical study. Cambridge focused on language skills so that undergraduates could translate any unseen text, and was concerned with 'close linguistic analysis of texts' rather than 'broader cultural resonance'. The strong links between classics and mathematics (compulsory until the 1850s) in Cambridge may have contributed to this problem-solving approach, in which any tendencies towards literary criticism were firmly suppressed.[41] Advocates of this 'masculine' and 'pure' style of scholarship despised Oxford's preoccupation with the content of ancient literature, history, and philosophy and with contemporary politics and society. Professional classical scholars 'regarded their chief task as the establishment of authentic Greek and Latin texts, with the writing of interpretive studies or essays very much a secondary task', so that 'the endeavour of interpretation and commentary' was largely left to amateur scholars, who were often involved in public life.[42] Prominent examples include Matthew Arnold, who spoke in his inaugural lecture as Oxford Professor of Poetry (later published as 'On the Modern Element in Literature', 1857) of the literature of ancient Greece as 'a mighty agent of intellectual deliverance', which might help to solve the problems of Victorian Britain as it had solved those of fifth-century Athens.[43] Gladstone applied political and religious principles derived from authors such as Aristotle and Homer to the problems of his own age: Mrs Humphry Ward recalled him saying 'There are still two things left for me to do ... One is to carry Home Rule—the other is to prove the intimate connection between the

[41] Stray, *Classics Transformed*, 120–2. Flora Mayor, the daughter of Cambridge-educated Joseph Bickersteth Mayor, Professor of Classical Literature at King's College London, satirizes the rivalry in her novel *The Rector's Daughter* (1924). The heroine's father, Canon Jocelyn, who prides himself on his scholarship (for him the Cambridge University Calendar holds the same importance as the Peerage for Austen's Sir Walter Elliot), criticizes a clergyman who 'had no depth; the foundations had not been securely laid—more what one might call the Oxford stamp. There have no doubt been certain eminent and really sound scholars among them, but I think it is fair to say the Oxford mind is superficial.' F. M. Mayor, *The Rector's Daughter* (1924; Harmondsworth: Penguin, 1985), 30.

[42] Turner, *Contesting Cultural Authority*, 286–7.

[43] Matthew Arnold, *On the Classical Tradition*, ed. R. H. Super (Ann Arbor: University of Michigan Press, 1960), 20–1.

Hebrew and Olympian revelations!'[44] Unlike the ancient historians Niebuhr and Grote, who read the Homeric poems as myths, Gladstone considered them to be a source for archaic Greek history, the closest available approximation to prelapsarian life, offering 'a full account of "religion, ethics, policy, history, arts, nature, and the entire circle of human action and experience." '[45]

There were some notable exceptions to the focus on textual criticism in the universities, and the contemporary scholars who were most attractive to female classicists and other autodidacts were those like Benjamin Jowett and R. C. Jebb, who undertook major works of translation and interpretation. Jowett, whose pupils included Pater and Swinburne, was instrumental in establishing a new ethos of university education, moving 'away from the narrowly grammatical emphasis in reading ancient texts and toward a powerfully engaged mode of reading which insisted on the vivid contemporaneity and philosophical depth of these works'.[46] He discussed the classics with friends like George Eliot and Robert Browning, and corresponded with Florence Nightingale, asking her for some of her translations and criticism of Plato when he was working on his edition of the *Republic*. He wrote to her: 'In some places I think that you will find remarks wh. have been suggested by you' and 'You are a first-rate Critic & you keep me up to a higher standard'; the suggestion that she might comment on contemporary politics in Platonic terms in a way that would be useful to Jowett must have been very flattering.[47] In Cambridge Eliot visited Jebb, who edited and translated Sophocles' tragedies with introductions suitable for the general reader and 'wrote on literature and Hellenism in a style more familiar in Oxford'.[48] Gilbert Murray, Jebb's successor as Professor of Greek at Glasgow University, promoted the teaching of classical texts in translation and proclaimed in his 1889 inaugural lecture, *The Place of*

[44] Mrs Humphry Ward, *A Writer's Recollections* (London: W. Collins, 1918), 238.
[45] D. W. Bebbington, *The Mind of Gladstone: Religion, Homer, and Politics* (Oxford: OUP, 2004), 146–8.
[46] Linda C. Dowling, *Hellenism and Homosexuality in Victorian Oxford* (London: Cornell UP, 1994), 64.
[47] *Dear Miss Nightingale: A Selection of Benjamin Jowett's Letters to Florence Nightingale*, ed. Vincent Quinn and John Prest (Oxford: Clarendon, 1987), 204, 258.
[48] Stray, *Classics Transformed*, 142.

Greek in Education: 'There is more in Hellenism than a language ... It is quite possible for a man who cannot read a single page of Plato intelligently to acquire a tolerable proportion of the Greek spirit.'[49] Murray made important contributions to contemporary literature both through his popular translations of Greek plays and his readiness to assist author friends with details of ancient history and literature—he helped George Bernard Shaw with *Caesar and Cleopatra* and *Major Barbara* (which draws on Murray's translation of Euripides' *Bacchae*) and Rudyard Kipling with *Puck of Pook's Hill*.[50]

As Professor of Greek at Oxford, Murray opposed 'compulsory Greek' (the Greek section of a preliminary examination—'Responsions'—which was required for a degree) which caused difficulties for women and other non-traditional students; he wanted classical studies to be chosen by students rather than imposed on them. Compulsory Greek was also a problem at Cambridge, where it was part of the Previous Examination or 'Little-Go'. The examination was not considered particularly difficult, with only two set books, a Gospel and one other text: Judith Raphaely claims that the arguments which were made 'for such a paltry requirement as fundamental either to other studies or to the understanding of religion stretch credibility'.[51] Nevertheless, it was a significant obstacle for those who began their Greek studies at university, since they had to spend a long time in preparation for what was supposed to be a preliminary to studying for a degree. Candidates often learnt the set texts by heart and reformers argued that such a test did not add much to the linguistic training already derived from Latin. Opposition to the ending of compulsory Greek was strong among clergymen, most of them non-resident MAs who travelled in large numbers to exercise their votes: 'The clergy, traditionally so integral to the University but also to its

[49] Gilbert Murray, *The Place of Greek in Education: An Inaugural Lecture* (Glasgow, 1889), quoted in Duncan Wilson, *Gilbert Murray, OM, 1866–1957* (Oxford: Clarendon, 1987), 44.

[50] Wilson, *Gilbert Murray*, 92–6, 108–9. See also Fiona Macintosh, 'The Shavian Murray and the Euripidean Shaw: *Major Barbara* and the *Bacchae*', *Classics Ireland*, 5 (1998), 64–84.

[51] Judith Raphaely, 'Nothing But Gibberish and Shibboleths? The Compulsory Greek Debate 1870–1919', in Christopher Stray (ed.), *Classics in 19th- and 20th-Century Cambridge: Curriculum, Culture and Community* (Cambridge: Cambridge Philological Society, 1999), 88.

conservatism, came to be seen as a minority inappropriately med-
dling in affairs more properly of wider interest.'[52] At both universities
the question of the Greek requirement arose in the late nineteenth
century and was revived at intervals before and after the First World
War, ending in a relatively uncontroversial abolition at Cambridge in
1919. In Oxford the same result was achieved in 1920, a few weeks
after the statute which settled the other great controversy of the
period by awarding women full membership of the university.

EXTENDING ACCESS

The reforms which made education more accessible to women and
working-class men contributed to the downfall of classics. From the
1870s onwards university men undertook extension lectures in provincial cities to supplement their incomes. Thirty thousand students
attended Oxford Extension Lectures in 1894–5, a number which
decreased as local universities and technical colleges took over the
task of providing for students. Extension teaching was originally seen
as a 'philanthropic venture aimed at benefiting the poor' but was
enthusiastically received by women who were 'hungry for education
and academic challenge, and eager to escape from the drawing
room'.[53] These 'sisters of university men' formed about two thirds of
the audience for such lectures, whereas the male students were from 'a
non-university class'.[54] Vera Brittain attended extension lectures on
economics in her home town, Buxton, and was encouraged by the
lecturer to apply to Oxford.[55] The universities which were founded
in the nineteenth century, such as London (UCL, 1826; King's,
1828), Durham (1832), Bristol (1876), and Liverpool (1881) offered
a wider range of academic subjects than Oxford and Cambridge, and

---

[52] Ibid. 92.
[53] Christina S. Bremner, *The Education of Girls and Women in Great Britain*
(London: Sonnenschein, 1897), 158–9.
[54] Annabel Robinson, *The Life and Work of Jane Ellen Harrison* (Oxford: OUP,
2002), 35.
[55] Vera Brittain, *Testament of Youth: An Autobiographical Study of the Years 1900–
1925* (1933; London: Virago, 1978), 60–3.

contributed to the development of English Literature as an alternative to Classics. English scholars offered courses on ancient literature in translation to remedy students' lack of knowledge about the classical sources of canonical English texts. John Churton Collins opened his Birmingham University lectures to the public, hoping to contribute to a second Renaissance:

Experience has shown that such poems as the 'Iliad,' the 'Odyssey' and the Attic Dramas ... can be rendered as intelligible and instructive to the many as they are to the few ... If it shall be found that the attainment of such a knowledge of the Greek language exacts so much time and labour that it is practically impossible except for the few, can we not do something, nay do much, by judicious use of the best translations?[56]

Lectures given at Mechanics' Institutes and Working Men's Colleges include Samuel Butler's series on 'The Humour of Homer' (1892). Extension lecturers tended to talk about authors in biographical terms, and Butler exemplifies this tendency when he speculates on the identity of the author of the *Iliad* and develops his idea that the *Odyssey* was written by a 'fascinating brilliant girl, who naturally adopts for her patroness the blue-stocking Minerva; a man-hatress, as clever girls so often are'. Butler seems to open up the field of Homeric interpretation when he challenges the universities' monopoly on the criticism of classical texts: 'Of course in reality the work must be written by a man, because they say so at Oxford and Cambridge ... but I venture to say that if the *Odyssey* were to appear anonymously for the first time now ... there is not a professional critic who would not see that it is a woman's writing and not a man's.'[57] However, Butler's interpretation of Homer is strongly idiosyncratic, focusing on the comic tone of episodes which deal with gender, and it works better as a provocation to readers already familiar with Homer than as an introduction. Jonathan Rose suggests that working-class autodidacts wanted to read 'great books' because canonical texts 'offered artistic excellence, psychological insights, and penetrating philosophy to the governing classes' and therefore 'the

[56] John Churton Collins, *Greek Influence on English Poetry*, ed. Michael Macmillan (London: I. Pitman, 1910), 3–5.
[57] Samuel Butler, *The Humour of Homer and Other Essays*, ed. R. A. Streatfeild (London: A. C. Fifield, 1913), 79.

politics of equality must begin by redistributing this knowledge to the governed classes'.[58] Butler does not point out such awe-inspiring qualities in the Homeric poems, but domesticates them: 'though woman in the *Iliad* is on one occasion depicted as a wife so faithful and affectionate that nothing more perfect can be found either in real life or fiction, yet as a general rule she is drawn as teasing, scolding, thwarting, contradicting'. He extends this far from reverential tone to his paraphrases of episodes: 'First [Hera] bolted herself inside her own room on the top of Mount Ida and had a thorough good wash. Then she scented herself, brushed her golden hair, put on her very best dress and all her jewels. When she had done this, she went to Venus and besought her for the loan of her charms.'[59] Butler's lectures attracted hostile responses from commentators such as the classical scholar Jane Ellen Harrison, including a review entitled 'How to Vulgarize Homer'.[60]

An article from the *Oxford Magazine* in 1920 about the Working Men's College in London shows how teaching Greek literature in translation raised questions about the ways in which the classics had become associated with a public school education, so that 'Theocritus or Plato or Thucydides signify, above all, English playing-fields, English class-rooms, and the scent of English limes'.[61] The writer recognizes that 'in such an atmosphere much evaporates ... There is even absurdity in the way in which some story of perverted passion is pleasantly droned through a drowsy summer afternoon' and wonders whether the experience could or should be 'reproduced for my little group of tired city clerks, telephone operators, and mechanics in Camden Town?' He finds that the students have 'a profound curiosity about Greek civilization, Greek literature, the Greek point of view', often derived from their extensive reading in English poetry and prose, and many had tried reading translations of the classics alone but found that 'the fact of working with a teacher who had before him the original text somehow or other contributed unmistakably to

---

[58] Jonathan Rose, *The Intellectual Life of the British Working Classes* (London: Yale UP, 2001), 4.

[59] Butler, *Humour*, 60, 70.

[60] Robinson, *Life*, 115.

[61] A.H.S., 'A Note on the Teaching of Greek in Translations', *Oxford Magazine*, 38 (5 Mar. 1920), 259–60.

the feeling of direct contact with the author studied'. In these classes, the Greek text was read aloud first, followed by a very literal translation, then 'the class would be shown the actual order of the words in the Greek, and it would be pointed out how words calling up certain images were juxtaposed and so forth'. Struck by the curiosity of the working men, he concludes:

Delightful as may be the process of gradually absorbing classical learning permeated with the most English of English atmospheres, there is something to be said for the value of the sharp contact of comparatively mature minds with an unknown literature and civilization. The excitement and zest of discovery is something for which it would not always be easy to find a parallel in the classical education of the average public-school boy.

It is worth noting that the experience of a conventional classical schooling such as that of Thackeray at Charterhouse and Cambridge or Matthew Arnold at Rugby and Oxford was not shared by all Victorian writers—even Tennyson (whom Stuart Gillespie describes as 'the last great English classicist among the poets') had what his son Hallam considered 'a good but not a regular classical education' at home and at Louth grammar school before going to Cambridge.[62] Such notable contributors to Victorian Hellenism as Thomas Hardy and Robert Browning relied on self-education as a supplement to or substitute for school classics or private tutorials. The difficulties involved in studying classics outside the formal education system are poignantly represented in Hardy's *A Pair of Blue Eyes* (1872) and *Jude the Obscure* (1895).[63] Male autodidacts (especially those whose exclusion from classical studies could be represented as a marker of their social inferiority) were vulnerable to attacks by the kind of

[62] Stuart Gillespie (ed.), *The Poets on the Classics: An Anthology of English Poets' Writings on the Classical Poets and Dramatists from Chaucer to the Present* (London: Routledge, 1988), 12; Tennyson, *Alfred, Lord Tennyson*, i. 16.

[63] Hardy's mother chose his school because its headmaster, Isaac Last, was known as a good teacher of Latin; he studied Latin there for four years, but no Greek. After leaving school he read Latin (Horace, Ovid, and Virgil) with a fellow architectural pupil, consulting a local schoolmaster (the philologist and poet William Barnes) on points of difficulty. He taught himself Greek, with assistance from the classical scholar Horace Moule, starting with the *Iliad*. Classical Greek was abandoned in favour of the New Testament dialect to settle a debate over infant baptism, and he could not read Greek easily but had to rely on translations. Jeremy Steele, 'Classics', *Oxford Reader's Companion to Hardy*, ed. Norman Page (Oxford: OUP, 2000), 58–66.

critics who mocked George Eliot's mistakes in Greek accents, and they were well placed to understand the problems facing women who tried to study classical texts at home. Browning corresponded with Elizabeth Barrett about her translation of Aeschylus before their marriage, and after her death he showed her copies of Greek texts to admirers like George Eliot, Vernon Lee, and Katherine Bradley and Edith Cooper (Browning's 'two dear Greek women', who wrote poetry together under the name of 'Michael Field'). He encouraged female students of the classics such as Julia Wedgwood and Countess Cowper (to whom he dedicated *Balaustion's Adventure*) mostly through the medium of correspondence. He helped Mrs Thomas FitzGerald to study Greek in her seventies: she did the grammar exercises from Joseph B. Mayor's *Greek for Beginners* and sent them to him for marking.[64] His own Greek was described by the classicist Benjamin Jowett as 'homespun', and an American scholar noted that he read 'in a genial way and with less grammatical consciousness than do many Greek professors. His scholarship was extensive and, I would add, *vital*, it not having been imposed upon him at a public school and a university.'[65]

CLASSICS IN TRANSLATION

Those who did not have the opportunity to read extensively in ancient literature could read translations, look at works of art, watch Greek drama, and study mythology. Textbooks and dictionaries of quotations were widely available, as well as famous reference works such as Keats' favourite, Lemprière's *Classical Dictionary* (1788).[66] Keats was

[64] Edward McAleer (ed.), *Learned Lady: Letters from Robert Browning to Mrs Thomas FitzGerald* (Cambridge, Mass.: Harvard UP, 1966), 13–14.

[65] Hiram Corson, 'A Few Reminscences of Robert Browning', *Elizabeth Barrett Browning and Robert Browning: Interviews and Recollections*, ed. Martin Garrett (Basingstoke: Macmillan, 2000), 136–7.

[66] John Lemprière, *Bibliotheca Classica; or, A Classical Dictionary* (Reading, 1788). Byron complained in a letter to John Murray that Keats 'took the wrong line as a poet ... versifying Tooke's Pantheon and Lempriere's Dictionary': George Gordon Byron, *Byron's Letters and Journals*, ed. Leslie A. Marchand, viii (London: John Murray, 1978), 102.

an encouraging example for those who could not afford the time to read Greek literature in the original language: Gilbert Highet describes him as 'the Shakespeare of the revolutionary period: in his stimulating but incomplete education, ... in his determination to write poetry ... and in the rich fertility with which his mind developed themes taken from classical literature and legend'.[67] In 'Ode on a Grecian Urn' (1819), Keats uses the device of ekphrasis to represent an encounter with the ancient world; his sonnet 'On First Looking into Chapman's Homer' (1816) 'dramatizes—and exposes—an engagement with Homer' by a reader who does not have the classical training of a Shelley or a Byron.[68] Although merely 'looking into' a translation, Keats confidently acclaims Chapman for allowing him to breathe the 'pure serene' of 'deep-brow'd Homer'. That his enthusiasm for the 'loud and bold' Elizabethan rendering of Homer was intended at least partly as a denigration of Alexander Pope's elegant Augustan couplets is reinforced by Charles Cowden Clarke's comment on their reading of Chapman's translation: 'to work we went, turning to some of the "famousest" passages, as we had scrappily known them in Pope's version'.[69] In their translations of Virgil and Homer, Dryden and Pope attempted to convey the spirit of the ancient texts in the language which their authors would use if they were writing in England in the eighteenth century: Susan Bassnett remarks that the 'right of the individual to be addressed in his own terms, on his own ground' was crucial to these poets' conceptualization of translation. Victorian translators, on the other hand, were concerned to convey 'the remoteness of the original in time and place'.[70]

An encounter with a major classical text in translation is a common event in biographies of nineteenth-century women writers. It is interesting that Pope's translations of the *Iliad* and *Odyssey* are frequently cited, as from their first publication they 'directly addressed the female reader, inviting her into what had hitherto been an

[67] Gilbert Highet, *The Classical Tradition: Greek and Roman Influences on Western Literature* (London: OUP, 1949), 415.

[68] Goldhill, *Who Needs Greek?*, 190–1.

[69] Charles Cowden Clarke and Mary Cowden Clarke, *Recollections of Writers* (London: Sampson Low Marston Searle & Rivington, 1878), 129.

[70] Susan Bassnett, *Translation Studies*, 3rd edn. (London: Routledge, 2002), 65, 71.

exclusively masculine cultural realm. Women made up 8 per cent of the subscribers to his *Iliad* and 13 per cent for his *Odyssey*.[71] It was Pope's Homer which convinced Elizabeth Barrett of the necessity of studying the text in the original language (a similar progression from Pope to Homer is described in Robert Browning's poem 'Development'). Anna Jameson recalled that after reading the *Odyssey* she particularly remembered 'the picture of Nasicaa [*sic*] and her maidens going down in their chariots to wash their linen ... The Syrens and Polypheme left also vivid pictures on my fancy'.[72] Frances Power Cobbe read in translation 'the Iliad, Odyssey, Aeneid, Pharsalia, and all or nearly all, Aeschylus, Sophocles, Euripides, Ovid, Tacitus, Xenophon, Herodotus, Thucydides, &c.' This was part of her plan to read 'as many of the great books of the world as [she] could reach; making it a rule always (whether bored or not) to go on to the end of each'.[73] Mary Russell Mitford (who was learning Latin) read Dryden's *Aeneid*, and preferred Pope's *Odyssey* to the *Iliad*, declaring the *Odyssey* 'beautiful beyond comparison'.[74]

In periodicals such as *Blackwood's Edinburgh Magazine*, long and detailed reviews with substantial passages quoted from a variety of works, including translations of classical texts, gave readers 'access to books and knowledge which were otherwise beyond their reach'.[75] *Blackwood's* (familiarly known as *Maga*) appears to address readers with a sound classical education, and articles about the future of British education take for granted a readership which largely approves of the dominance of classics in the curriculum. Nevertheless, those who are outside this educational system are not excluded as readers by lengthy passages of unreadable quotation—everything is translated into English, often by several different authors, so that the reader may participate in the process of comparing and analysing different translations. A reader with no Latin or Greek could become

---

[71] Rose, *Intellectual Life*, 18.

[72] Valerie Sanders (ed.), *Records of Girlhood: An Anthology of Nineteenth-Century Women's Childhoods* (Aldershot: Ashgate, 2000), 85.

[73] Ibid. 196.

[74] W. J. Roberts, *Mary Russell Mitford: The Tragedy of a Bluestocking* (London, 1913), 56–7.

[75] Juliet Barker, *The Brontës* (London: Phoenix, 1995), 149. See also Christine Alexander, 'Readers and Writers: *Blackwood's* and the Brontës', *Gaskell Society Journal*, 8 (1994), 54–69.

familiar with non-canonical texts such as the pseudo-Homeric 'Batrachomyomachia' ('Battle of the Frogs and Mice'), through the medium of a verse translation, and might also learn from reviews. For example, 'Christopher North' criticizes a book of Latin translations by John Dunlop, quoting a passage from Ennius' *Annales* in Latin, Dunlop's translation, and then other versions by William E. Aytoun, William Hay, and Charles Neaves.[76] As the article proceeds, Dunlop's work is subjected to a detailed and almost invariably negative critique: his translation of a three-line speech from Ennius is held up to ridicule, then 'Christopher North' adds six different versions, then fourteen of another brief passage, and twenty of another, all ostensibly superior to Dunlop's. By this stage, impartial judgement of the accuracy of individual versions is difficult since the reader is so involved in the article's competitive rhetoric, and the rapid accumulation of varying interpretations leaves the non-classical reader almost as well equipped to make a judgement as anyone else.

As the nineteenth century progressed, the number of those whose classical education had been inadequate or non-existent but who wanted to obtain access to the content of ancient texts (especially Greek history and literature) increased considerably. Many readers wanted reliable introductions to canonical works, such as A. J. Valpy's Family Classical Library (1830–6) or Bohn's Classical Library (1848–1913) which provided translations of Greek and Roman authors with notes and explanations.[77] Women were amongst those who undertook this kind of work: Anna Swanwick's versions of the *Oresteia* (1865), and the complete works of Aeschylus (1873) 'enabled people who did not know Greek to read the tragedies and so opened up knowledge of classical culture and especially of Athenian democracy'.[78] In the 1870s Blackwood's started a series of *Ancient Classics for English Readers* for those who had no classics or whose education had been incomplete—like that of Anthony Trollope, who reviewed the series shortly after the first volumes were issued, and wrote: 'it will afford an easy means of removing very common and

[76] John Wilson, 'The Latin Anthology', *Blackwood's Edinburgh Magazine*, 43 (1838), 521–64.

[77] Vance, *Rome*, p. viii.

[78] Hardwick, *Translating Words*, 33–6.

very dense ignorance as to authors whose names are common in our mouths'.[79] These volumes combined translations of selected passages with commentary on the whole work, and included Pliny, Euripides, Herodotus, Demosthenes, Sophocles, Aristophanes, Pindar, Hesiod, Juvenal, Tacitus, Plautus and Terence, Livy, Virgil, Cicero, and Horace; Trollope himself contributed a volume on Julius Caesar later in the series. Trollope finds W. Lucas Collins's volumes on Homer 'remarkably successful' and thinks they will extend the poet's audience considerably beyond 'the comparatively few in number who have read Greek, or the hardly more numerous class who have made themselves acquainted with the poems by means of translation' (664). The *Iliad* and *Odyssey* are ideal for beginners, Trollope suggests, because each has 'a tale to tell ... which, from its marvellous incidents, can be made almost as interesting in prose to the ordinary reader of English, as it has been in verse' (664). He is evidently thinking of a readership accustomed to the novel when he says that works with a strong narrative like Homer's (including histories such as those of Herodotus and Greek tragedies) would be successful, but is doubtful about translations of Horace, Cicero, and Juvenal. Trollope makes it clear that reading in translation should not be regarded as an easy way of studying the classics but as the best possible alternative for those who cannot obtain knowledge in the traditional way, 'by study, till from long study enjoyment and knowledge will come' (665). He envisages a readership made up of women, and men like himself whose education has not really equipped them to read the classics, as well as the new readers whose numbers are constantly increasing. To such people 'the names of the classic authors become almost painfully familiar' because Homer, Virgil, and other authors are spoken of as if everyone has read them (665–6). Trollope argues forcefully against the snobbery which suggests that it is only worth reading ancient literature in the original language and also points out that full-length translations rarely succeed in making works popular. He encourages his readers by claiming that

---

[79] Anthony Trollope, 'Ancient Classics for English Readers', *Saint Pauls*, 5 (1870), 664. Further references are given parenthetically in the text. See also Margaret Oliphant, 'The Ancient Classics', *Blackwood's Edinburgh Magazine*, 116 (1874), 365–86.

they are already, to some extent, acquainted with the classics: 'we must all have heard at least something' of the 'delightful little story' of Ulysses' return home, when he 'revenges himself upon the suitors of his wife, Penelope' (668). Alluding to the popular theatre, he says that Homer's 'feeders on ambrosia' will be familiar to those who have seen the 'tinsel absurdities' of classical burlesques (667). He sets out further inducements in his description of Collins's Homer volumes as 'very pleasant reading;—as good as a novel we might say ... were it not that they are very much better than most novels' (667).

Victorian poets and scholars (amateur and professional) continued the tradition of 'literary' translation 'for those with appropriate taste and interest'.[80] Apart from the complete translations published in the period, surviving fragments in the collected works of poets suggest that translation was a popular amusement, and it is likely that many examples were never written down. Tennyson, for example, 'is said to have regularly taken with him on his travels a copy of Homer, to have translated aloud the *Odyssey* to Mrs Tennyson'.[81] Edward FitzGerald claimed that his 'Version—or Per-Version' of Aeschylus' *Agamemnon* (privately printed in 1865, published in 1876) was 'originally printed to be given away among Friends, who either knew nothing of the Original, or would be disposed to excuse the liberties taken with it by an unworthy hand'.[82] A verifiably accurate translation of an ancient text could improve a writer's reputation. Augusta Webster's translations of *Prometheus Bound* (1866) and *Medea* (1868) impressed contemporary critics with their fidelity to the Greek plays, and lent authority to her contributions to the debate on translation exemplified by Arnold's 'On Translating Homer'. In 'A Transcript and a Transcription', a review of versions of Aeschylus' *Agamemnon*, she contrasts Robert Browning's 'dogged fidelity as a translator' favourably with that of another translator who 'adds himself to Æschylus', yet the qualities of obscurity and harshness with which Browning's readers were familiar in his own poetry seem to Webster to exceed what is necessary to convey a

[80] H. MacL. Currie, 'English Translations of the Classics in the Nineteenth Century', in H. D. Jocelyn (ed.), *Aspects of Nineteenth-Century British Classical Scholarship* (Liverpool: Liverpool Classical Monthly, 1996), 53.

[81] John A. Scott, *Homer and his Influence* (London: G. G. Harrap, 1925), 148.

[82] Edward FitzGerald, *Selected Works* (London: Hart-Davis, 1962), 386.

true idea of Aeschylus' play (although they are not entirely inappropriate in a rendering of a tragedy by the most stylistically difficult of
the Greek tragedians).[83] She argues that translators cannot claim to
represent the 'spirit' rather than the 'letter' of a poem: a poet's
'implement is the letter, and he knows it. His result is the letter, and
he knows it' (62). Webster is impressed by Browning's adherence to
the standard which she also set herself in translation, that of an exact,
'line by line' rendering: 'He has added nothing, altered nothing,
omitted nothing. He has done by Æschylus as he would have had
Æschylus do by him if each had been the other. And no poet will
dispute his theory of translation' (71). However, Browning's 'dogged
fidelity' is seen as excessive when his sentences reproduce the form of
the Greek line at the expense of the English sense: 'the reader who
knows no Greek at all will be left bewildered and incredulous. For Mr
Browning's translation ... needs the Greek text to explain it' (72).
Webster ends by expressing a wish that 'Mr Browning, having translated the Agamemnon of Æschylus, should go on to translate the
Agamemnon of Robert Browning' (79). Her rejection of the attempt
to force English to equal the concision of the ancient languages is
expressed with a forceful metaphor which Victorian novelists used to
denote the social and physical constrictions to which women were
subject: 'Chinese feet', painful and deformed. It seems unlikely that
many women would possess sufficient familiarity with Greek to use
the Aeschylean text to explicate Browning's 'transcript', but Webster's
authoritative review implicitly claims that a woman has the right to an
intellectual training which would enable her to judge such texts
competently.

HISTORICAL FICTION AND POETRY

Many nineteenth-century readers learnt about the ancient world
from contemporary poetry and fiction, reframed to suit Victorian
tastes. Novelists seem to have been unwilling to represent a pagan

---

[83] Webster, *Housewife's Opinions*, 66. Further references are given parenthetically
in the text.

hero or heroine without allowing for a conversion to Christianity at some point in the narrative, so nineteenth-century fiction about the ancient world is rarely set in fifth-century Athens or Augustan Rome. Most historical novels about the ancient world are set in the first five centuries after the birth of Christ; the decline of pagan religions and the rise of Christianity towards its eventual triumph are hinted at even in those novels which end with death for the Christian characters. The genre proved fertile for those who wished to represent a fictionalized yet easily recognizable sectarian argument about the validity of particular practices within the nineteenth-century Church. The Oxford Movement and the Catholic Church placed a high value on the early Church, which therefore became a target for Charles Kingsley in *Hypatia: New Foes With Old Faces* (1853). John Henry Newman's *Callista: A Tale of the Third Century* (1855) was written in response to Kingsley's novel. Each has a Greek heroine who converts to Christianity and is martyred for her faith. Kingsley's ideal Christianity is concerned with civilization and obedience to institutional authority (in nineteenth-century terms, that of the established Church); Newman perceives a conflict between temporal and spiritual allegiances which forces the individual to make a choice between them.[84] The popularity of the conversion pattern from *The Last Days of Pompeii* (1834) to *Quo Vadis?* (1896) suggests that readers continued to find it satisfying, and its absence may help to explain why Wilkie Collins's *Antonina: Or the Fall of Rome* (1850) never achieved the same status. *The Last Days of Pompeii* was inspired by the rediscovery of the city in the late eighteenth century. Bulwer-Lytton included footnotes and comments on the archaeologists' findings in his narrative, and the didacticism of his tone sometimes makes the novel seem like a textbook. Some novelists attempt to create a realistic atmosphere by featuring historical personages such as various Roman emperors and biblical figures like St Paul and St Peter. Wilkie Collins chose to avoid this kind of realism, claiming that it was better to create characters who were well adapted to the situations in the novel. He also mocked the expectations of 'experienced readers', who would be anticipating 'long rhapsodies on those

---

[84] See Susann Dorman, '*Hypatia* and *Callista*: The Initial Skirmish between Kingsley and Newman', *Nineteenth-Century Fiction*, 34 (1979), 173–93.

wonders of antiquity, the description of which has long since become absolutely nauseous to them by incessant iteration'. Collins asserted that his narrative would concentrate on 'the living, breathing, actions and passions of the people of the doomed Empire'.[85] Yet in her study of Collins, Dorothy L. Sayers finds *Antonina* 'impossibly melodramatic and impossibly dull', commenting that 'the historical sense' is missing: 'Goths and Romans alike hail from Wardour Street; the fifth-century Christians are nineteenth-century Protestants'.[86] This is a familiar complaint about Victorian images of the classical world, applied to the paintings of Alma-Tadema as well as the dramatic monologues of poets like Browning.

Conversion narratives set in the ancient world against a background of persecution and martyrdom figure prominently in Charlotte M. Yonge's recommendations of children's books for parish work, *What Books to Lend and What to Give* (1887). One of these is Emma Marshall's *No. XIII: Or, the Story of the Lost Vestal* (1885), set during the reign of Diocletian. The story of the thirteenth Vestal is tied in with a discovery among the statues in the Roman Forum, recalling Bulwer-Lytton's linking of fiction about the ancient world with archaeology in *The Last Days of Pompeii*. Hyacintha, the daughter of a noble Roman family, is sent to Rome as a disciple to the Temple of Vesta. A Vestal entered the order between the ages of 6 and 10, and was sworn to thirty years of chastity and service, ten in training, ten as a priestess, and ten training others. Hyacintha is seen as fortunate because her religious obligations free her from the 'deadening' atmosphere of the fashionable Roman lady. Interestingly, the only other way in which women can escape this atmosphere is by studying 'their own Latin authors and the Greek tongue'.[87] Already the reader may suspect that this conversion narrative contains lightly disguised protest about the limited lives of Victorian women; this is confirmed when Hyacintha muses on her sense of vocation and the empty social life she has left behind. The narrator

---

[85] Wilkie Collins, *Antonina: Or, The Fall of Rome* (London: Richard Bentley, 1850), 39.

[86] Dorothy L. Sayers, *Wilkie Collins: A Critical and Biographical Study*, ed. E. R. Gregory ([Toledo, Ohio]: Friends of the University of Toledo Libraries, 1977), 64, 66.

[87] Emma Marshall, *No. XIII; Or, The Story of the Lost Vestal* (London: Cassell, 1885), 40.

didactically underlines the point with reference to the inanity of the
London season: 'The human heart, with all its joys and sorrows, is
the same in the nineteenth as it was in the fourth century ... The
woman's heart then, as now, often sent up a cry for something that
could satisfy it.'[88] Since she makes it clear that Hyacintha will end her
life as a Christian, Marshall is not interested in discrediting her pagan
faith or ridiculing ancient beliefs. Instead, the narrative represents the
Vestal Virgins as women granted an unusual degree of influence by a
patriarchal society. The Vestals guarded state documents and tended
a flame which originally symbolized the hearth, but later came to
stand for the Roman state. Although unmarried, Vestals were emancipated from their fathers' power and free to administer their own
affairs. In this context of political influence and independence from
the family, Hyacintha's ambition to become the *Vestalis Maxima*
seems gratifyingly ambitious in comparison to the possibilities for a
nineteenth-century girl. Hyacintha's election causes jealousy among
her fellow Vestals, who attempt to use her inclination towards Christianity to discredit her. The dying Hyacintha is permitted to resign
her office and live in retirement, but when she dies as a Christian the
Pontifex Maximus refuses to acknowledge it and proceeds as if her
change of faith had never happened. Hyacintha's conversion is not
emphasized as a pivotal moment in the narrative; the crucial event
occurs after her death when her successor has Hyacintha's name
erased from the statue of her which stands with those of the other
Vestales Maximae, leaving only 'no. XIII'. Marshall's fiction purport-
edly restores the erased inscription and the history of women other
than virtuous wives and evil murderesses in the ancient world.

A prominent source for stories and allusions based on Roman
history is T. B. Macaulay's hugely popular *Lays of Ancient Rome*
(1842). The book became 'a school classic' in the late nineteenth
century but it was the appreciation of non-academic readers which
maintained its popularity.[89] So successful were these poems that by

---

[88] Emma Marshall, *No. XIII; Or, The Story of the Lost Vestal* (London: Cassell,
1885), 84.

[89] Donald J. Gray, 'Macaulay's *Lays of Ancient Rome* and the Publication of
Nineteenth-Century British Poetry', in James R. Kincaid and Albert J. Kuhn (eds.),
Victorian Literature and Society: Essays Presented to Richard D. Altick (Columbus:
Ohio State UP, 1983), 80, 82.

1912 Longmans had published 'more than 293,000 copies in seven different editions at prices ranging from six pence to a guinea'. Macaulay places his text within a Romantic aesthetic which privileges primitive folk ballads and reads the *Iliad* and the *Odyssey* as the best examples of that tradition. He dismisses Augustan poetry as a 'feeble echo' of Greek literature, and writes of an ancient native Latin literature further back than the acknowledged ancestors of the Roman literary tradition, claiming that historians like Livy were drawing on the ancient ballads for their accounts of Roman history.[90] The influence of Sir Walter Scott's novels as well as his ballads is unmistakable, especially in the framing techniques which ground the main narrative in a domestic setting. Macaulay creates a background and invents a speaker for each poem: in 'Horatius', the speaker sings his ballad more than a century after the battle and ends by describing the surroundings in which he is singing. Macaulay, refusing to Christianize the heroes he depicts, displays a historical awareness that is not always matched by his imitators. He pays tribute to Roman virtues such as fortitude, respect for legitimate authority, and patriotism, whilst acknowledging that chivalric notions should not be projected back onto the Romans. The virtues celebrated in the *Lays* made them suitable reading for children, yet they seem also to have had a strong impact on adults. Their energetic rhythms, rapid narrative movement (the longest is around six hundred lines), the certainty of their morals, and their focus on action made them remarkably 'vigorous' and 'manly' in contrast to the dominant poetic culture of the period.[91] They were attractive to readers who were troubled by the reflection, introspection, moral difficulties, and problematic relationships characteristic of Victorian poetry.

The continuing popularity of the *Lays of Ancient Rome* can be seen in Rudyard Kipling's *Puck of Pook's Hill* (1906), in which two children meet characters from different periods in British history; one of these is 'A Centurion of the Thirtieth' who tells them about Roman Britain. Dan and Una have named their favourite place 'Volaterrae' because of the *Lays*, and as the first story begins, Dan has 'come to grief over his Latin', so Una takes his catapult and prepares 'to meet Lars

[90] Thomas Babington Macaulay, *Lays of Ancient Rome* (London: Longman Brown Green, 1842), 8–9.
[91] Gray, 'Macaulay's *Lays*', 82.

Porsena's army'.[92] Kipling challenges stereotypical views of boys' and girls' education by having Dan's formal instruction in Latin act as an obstacle to his appreciation of Roman history; Una is free to 'shout bits of the *Lays*' and use the catapult, so she meets Parnesius and learns about Britain's Roman past while Dan is still learning grammar. Parnesius' narrative begins with his childhood, and is expressed in terms familiar to Victorian children—he learns ancient history, classics, and arithmetic from a Greek 'governess'. However, this is not the story of a typical Roman childhood; Parnesius is a Roman whose family has lived on the Isle of Wight for generations, and he has only ever seen Rome in a picture:

> Now, like many of our youngsters, I was not fond of anything Roman. The Roman-born officers and magistrates looked down on us British-born as though we were barbarians. I told my father so. 'I know they do,' he said; 'but remember, after all, we are the people of the Old Stock, and our duty is to the Empire.'[93]

Parnesius is sent to join the garrison at Hadrian's Wall, and tells the story of a journey north, away from the social centres of Roman Britain and into a wilder landscape; the narrative is reminiscent of Kipling's fascination with life on the frontiers of British India. Comparisons of the Roman and British Empires were by no means rare, but Kipling illuminates an unfamiliar aspect of empire—emphasized by the change in Britain's position from colonized to colonizer, tensions between Anglo-Indians and British-born men in India clearly lie behind this analysis of Roman Britain.

MYTH AND HISTORY

Books which moulded pagan heroes into models for Christian conduct were an important way of introducing children to the Greeks and Romans: Charlotte M. Yonge suggests that 'classical history is remembered at an earlier age than modern history, probably because

---

[92] Rudyard Kipling, *Puck of Pook's Hill and Rewards and Fairies*, ed. Donald Mackenzie (Oxford: OUP, 1993), 83.

[93] Ibid. 89.

the events are simple, and there was something childlike in the nature of all the ancient Greeks'.[94] In *Aunt Charlotte's Stories of Greek History for the Little Ones* (1876), she retells Greek myths and history with rationalizing explanations, simplified narratives and an emphasis on the inferiority of Greek religion to Christianity. One of the clearest parallels between Greek myth and the scriptures is in the story that the degeneration and wickedness of men led to a divine resolution to drown the population of the earth, an event which is survived by a few virtuous people who have been warned to build a boat. Yonge's commentary on the story of Deucalion and Pyrrha casts it as a later and garbled version of the 'true' story of Noah's Ark, but she argues that it is worth telling because of its beauty as a narrative. She repeatedly distinguishes between the 'true' Christian version and 'not true' Greek myths, but, perhaps to forestall criticism from teachers and parents who might question why children should be exposed to what was 'not true', she represents the stories as an essential foundation course in cultural appreciation: 'nobody can understand anything about art or learning who has not learnt these stories' (12). The historical position of the ancient Greeks enables a final judgement which places them at the summit of purely human achievement: 'The Greeks had more power of thought and sense than any other people have ever had. They always had among them men seeking for truth and beauty ... The history of the Jews shows what God does for men; the history of the Greeks shows what man does left to himself' (108–9).

A Book of Golden Deeds (1864) is a conventional translation of pagan legends into models for Christian conduct. 'What is a Golden Deed?' asks the narrator, before answering 'a story of battle and adventure' and 'forgetfulness of self'.[95] The second of these is the standard for female heroism: women's 'golden deeds' involve self-sacrifice, even to the extent of self-mutilation or suicide. There is a disturbing illustration of 'golden silence' (a quality to be commended

---

[94] Charlotte M. Yonge, *Aunt Charlotte's Stories of Greek History for the Little Ones* (London: Marcus Ward, 1876), 3. Further references are given parenthetically in the text.

[95] Charlotte M. Yonge, *A Book of Golden Deeds of All Times and Lands* (London: Macmillan, 1864), 1–2. Further references are given parenthetically in the text.

in women) in the story of Leæna, an Athenian woman who, tortured for her part in a conspiracy against the Pisistratids, 'fearing that the weakness of her frame might overpower her resolution, actually bit off her tongue, that she might be unable to betray the trust placed in her' (5). Antigone, a figure of rebellion against authority and the family for George Eliot, is blandly represented as a good daughter who cares for her aged father and paired with Alcestis, who died to save her husband's life and was rescued from the Underworld by Heracles. Yonge is preoccupied with the question of how far the true story behind the fable can be recovered from the literary versions in which they exist for a modern readership, 'solemn religious tragedies ... the noble poetry in which they were recounted by the great Greek dramatists' (10). She imposes rationalizing interpretations on her readers' understanding of myth: 'Later Greeks tried to explain the story by saying that Alcestis nursed her husband through an infectious fever, caught it herself, and had been supposed dead, when a skilful physician restored her' (11).

Yonge's various retellings of Greek myth and history are essentially the same narratives, adapted to the needs of readers of different ages. The most idiosyncratic example is her novel *My Young Alcides: A Faded Photograph* (1875). The preface interestingly suggests a more selfish motive for writing than Yonge usually permitted herself, a genuine pleasure in devising the labours which might confront a modern Heracles: 'I could not help going on, as the notion grew deeper and more engrossing.'[96] She describes her creation not as an allegory but a response to the spirit of the myth rather than the letter: Harold is represented as conquering himself, committing a crime and expiating it, choosing between virtue and vice, and finally attaining immortality. The narrative concentrates on the most famous legend connected with Heracles—that of the twelve labours imposed on the hero by Eurystheus of Argos, who is represented in Yonge's narrative by the hero's cousin Eustace, the owner of the Arghouse Estate. One of the creative challenges which made this project 'engrossing' for Yonge was evidently the invention of names for places

---

[96] Charlotte M. Yonge, *My Young Alcides: A Faded Photograph* (1875) (London: Macmillan, 1889), p. v. Further references are given parenthetically in the text.

and people which would recall the Greek originals and yet sound appropriate in a novel about England. Nemea, for example, becomes Neme Heath; the Augean Stables are Ogden's Buildings. In the chapter called 'The Birds of Ill Omen' the monstrous Stymphalian birds whose feathers are poisonous arrows become the Stympsons, one of whom is nicknamed Birdie. Her sister Avice (Yonge mentions the Latin tag *rara avis*—a rare bird—so that the significance of her name cannot be missed) is described as a 'bird whose quills are quills of iron dipped in venom, and her beak a brazen one, distilling gall on all around' (173). The danger represented by the Stympsons is that of malicious gossip. As in the 'Aunt Charlotte' histories, Yonge imposes a rationalizing explanation on the ancient myths, and adds modernizing touches which render the Greek stories into the language of the Victorian novel. Many of Yonge's translations into the terms of realist narrative are very successful: 'The Champion's Belt' turns Heracles' battle with the Amazons into a recognizably Victorian social occasion, an archery contest. That a jocular association between lady archers and the mythical warriors was a familiar element of such amusements is suggested by the narrator's remark, 'Wit about the Amazonian regiment with the long bow was current all the time we ladies were shooting' (221). Using the labours of Heracles as the structure for the novel made it possible for Yonge to venture to write about drunkenness and insanity, which Keble expunged from her decorous Tractarian fictions. Harold has a troubled past—he killed his wife and children while drunk, as Heracles did when Hera sent a madness upon him. His fear of the power of alcohol is vividly evoked: the Hydra becomes a pub called the Dragon's Head, which the teetotal Harold transforms into a coffee shop, only to find that 'To destroy one is to produce two' (86). This is one labour in which the modern, realistic Heracles cannot achieve the same success as his mythic predecessor. In the end, Harold's victory over the menace of alcohol is a posthumous achievement, when the workmen who wish to subscribe for a memorial window are told that only moderate drinkers will be allowed to commemorate their hero. They, like Harold, are encouraged towards the Christian goal of '*self* conquest, just where a great Greek hero would have failed' (337).

CLASSICAL IMAGES IN FICTION

It is clear that a knowledge of Latin and Greek was by no means necessary for a writer who wished to allude to mythological or historical figures, events, or places, or even to classical texts. Indeed, the large number of references suggest that it would be difficult for a novel reader not to acquire some information simply through reading fiction set in the nineteenth century. Those whose curiosity was stimulated by, say, the ongoing mock-Iliadic theme in the characterization and setting of *Barchester Towers* (1857) could read Pope's *Iliad* and *The Rape of the Lock,* and after 1870, they could read a translation and commentary on the *Iliad* which Trollope himself had commended. In 'Schoolboy Latin and the Mid-Victorian Novelist: A Study in Reader Competence', David Skilton observes that classical references may be 'directly gratifying to those who ... are predisposed by reason of inclination or training to welcome them' but they do not necessarily cause difficulties for other readers since 'many references are easy to absorb even if one does not habitually move in the literary universe to which they belong'.[97] Allusions to the classics could 'grant the reader the temporary illusion that she is part of a social and cultural milieu ... in which literary and artistic references are freely shared'.[98]

Novel readers may not have been able to recognize every classical allusion in the works of Trollope and Thackeray, any more than they could necessarily translate the Latin tags which these authors introduced into their narratives, yet it seems likely that novelists would mainly have used easily recognizable allusions. The recurrence of a few characters and stories suggests a small stock of information which most readers would be able to call upon. One such story, condensed into a single iconic image by painters, is employed by Dickens and Gaskell: in a picture known as *Roman Charity* (1625), Rubens depicted an old man, Cimon, starving in a prison, whose daughter, Pero, keeps him alive by breastfeeding him. This image,

[97] David Skilton, 'Schoolboy Latin and the Mid-Victorian Novelist: A Study in Reader Competence', *Browning Institute Studies,* 16 (1988), 39–40.

[98] Kate Flint, *The Woman Reader, 1837–1914* (Oxford: Clarendon, 1993), 258.

taken from the Roman historian Valerius Maximus, became an exemplary scene of a daughter's selfless devotion to her father, and was popular with seventeenth-century artists. The 'Roman daughter' or 'classical daughter' was thus an allusion which could be understood by the majority of readers who would never read Valerius Maximus, and novelists were able to explore the disturbing subtext of this tale of filial piety. In *North and South* (1855), Margaret Hale provides support for her father while her mother is dying: 'she had to act the part of a Roman daughter, and give strength out of her own scanty stock to her father'.[99] Here the nourishment Margaret provides for her father is obviously emotional rather than physical, but the narrator conveys a sense of shock at the unnatural reversal of a parent so dependent on his child that he does not protect but weakens her. In *Little Dorrit* (1857), the image is again translated into emotional sustenance, but Dickens directly refers to the ancient story and then claims that what his heroine does is more noble:

There was a classical daughter once—perhaps—who ministered to her father in his prison as her mother had once ministered to her. Little Dorrit, though of the unheroic modern stock, and mere English, did much more, in comforting her father's wasted heart upon her innocent breast, and turning it to a fountain of love and fidelity that never ran dry or waned, all through his years of famine.[100]

Dickens may well have been influenced by Gaskell's use of the image, since he had edited *North and South* for serialization in his magazine *Household Words*. It is interesting that he chose to explain the story more fully, and to make explicit the complicated relationship between father, daughter, and (dead) mother; clearly the prison setting of the legend also resonates more strongly in Dickens's narrative, although the dark, cramped house of the Hales might be seen as a domestic prison. Dickens's treatment of the trope of daughterly devotion is more sharply ironic than Gaskell's—Mr Dorrit is a selfish parasite whose heart does not become 'a fountain of love and fidelity', however much he feeds off his daughter's self-sacrificing devotion.

[99] Elizabeth Gaskell, *North and South* (1854–5), ed. Angus Easson (Oxford: OUP, 1982), 243.
[100] Charles Dickens, *Little Dorrit* (1857), ed. Harvey Peter Sucksmith (Oxford: Clarendon, 1979), 222.

There are also simpler allusions, as in Mary Elizabeth Braddon's sensation novel *Aurora Floyd* (1863). Braddon is not addressing the kind of readership which enjoyed Trollope's Latin tags, yet her allusions 'establish her narrative as belonging to the "official" middle-class masculine world'.[101] She herself was not part of this genteel society, and her range of reference seems to be representative of the kind of allusions available to most women readers. There are a surprising number of brief references including the battle of Thermopylae, the 'Spartan youth [who] nursed a bosom-devouring fox', lotus-eaters, Apollo, Aphrodite, and 'Penelope's embroidery'. Talbot Bulstrode wonders if Aurora was forced into marriage like 'some white-robed Iphigenia, led a passive victim to the sacrificial shrine'.[102] The image clearly fits neither Aurora's character nor her marriage, and this suggests that a mind which is trained to fit women into such categories will painfully misunderstand them. Interestingly, Braddon, a former actress whose literary career concentrated on profit rather than high culture, actually learnt Greek when her writing career was over. Ford Madox Ford, who visited her just before the First World War, commented, 'She was then reading the "Iliad". I hope she finished the "Odyssey" too before she died.'[103]

WOMEN AND THE GRAND TOUR

Once the Napoleonic Wars were over, Italy became more accessible to female travellers, who could then visit sites which were familiar from history books, translations, or works of art. In 1818 and 1819 Percy and Mary Shelley travelled in the countryside around Naples, visiting the Sibyl's cave and other places associated with the *Aeneid*, such as Cape Miseno, the Elysian Fields, and Lake Avernus; they also viewed the Roman ruins in Pompeii and Herculaneum, although the

---

[101] Skilton, 'Schoolboy Latin', 51.

[102] Mary Elizabeth Braddon, *Aurora Floyd* (1863), ed. P. D. Edwards (Oxford: OUP, 1996), 152.

[103] Robert Lee Wolff, *Sensational Victorian: The Life and Fiction of Mary Elizabeth Braddon* (London: Garland, 1979), 11.

excavations had not progressed very far. On 30 November 1818 they
visited the bay of Gaeta, which Mary Shelley described as 'sanctified
by the fictions of Homer', although it actually appears in the *Aeneid*
as the burial place of Aeneas' nurse Caieta. Despite her enthusiasm
for Homeric associations, she was reading Livy and visited the tomb
and villa of Cicero.[104] She also read the *Georgics*—'in many respects,
the most beautiful poem I ever read'—and was thrilled to find herself
so close to the source of Virgil's inspiration: 'looking at almost the
same scene that he did—reading about manners little changed since
his days, [which] made me enjoy his poem, more, I think, than I ever
did any other'.[105] This experience informs the idyllic scene of reading
in her short story 'Valerius: The Reanimated Roman' (1819), when
the hero and heroine sit among ruins (in Rome) and read the
Georgics together. The description of reading 'sunny beautiful poetry'
under 'the brilliant sun' evokes the enjoyment which rewarded Mary
Shelley's own hard studies, and is a pleasant counter-example to the
prevalent images of exclusion, frustration, and censure associated
with women's classical studies:

We used to visit an obscure nook of the Coliseum, where we scrambled with
difficulty, and few would be inclined to follow us; or, on the walls of the
baths of Caracalla or more frequently at the foot of the tomb of Cestius ...
We read the Georgics here, and I felt a degree of happiness in reading them
that I could not have believed that words had it in their power to bestow. It
was an intoxicating pleasure, which this fine climate and the sunny beautiful
poetry which it inspires can give and which in a clouded atmosphere I am
convinced I never should have felt.[106]

In the *Diary of an Ennuyée* (1826) by Anna Brownell Murphy (later
Jameson, 1794–1860), references to classical sites are usually supplied
by a male travelling companion. The narrator is intensely preoccupied with her own emotions and judges the places she visits in terms
of her own sensibility. Although she refers to classical writers when

[104] *The Journals of Mary Shelley, 1814–1844*, ed. Paula R. Feldman and Diana
Scott-Kilvert (Oxford: Clarendon, 1987), i. 241–2.

[105] M.W.S. to Maria Gisborne, 22 Jan. 1819. *The Letters of Mary Wollstonecraft
Shelley*, ed. Betty T. Bennett (London: Johns Hopkins UP, 1980), i. 85.

[106] Mary Shelley, 'Valerius: The Reanimated Roman', in *Collected Tales and Stories*,
ed. Charles E. Robinson (London: Johns Hopkins UP, 1976), 343.

visiting sites associated with them—'the shores of Baia, where Cicero, Horace, Virgil, Pliny, Maecenas, lived ... the Sybil's Cave, Lake Acheron, and the fabled Lethe', Byron's more congenial influence over female travellers to Italy is already established in this narrative—the tomb of Cecilia Metella and the Fountain of Egeria are valued more for their Byronic interest than their classical associations.[107] At the site of the battle of Thrasymene, the narrator subverts the masculine narrative of war. As she listens to the story of the battle, taken from a Roman historian, she focuses not on heroism in past combat but on peace and continuing life: 'While we traversed the field of battle at a slow pace, V. who had his Livy in his pocket, read aloud his minute description of the engagement; ... from an olive tree which grew close to the edge of the lake I snatched a branch as we passed by, and shall preserve it—an emblem of peace, from the theatre of slaughter' (130–1).

Florence Nightingale's letters show how an appreciation of Italy was inflected by moral judgements about the Romans; visiting the Colosseum, she is repelled by 'the contrast between the blue sky, the type of the goodness of God, shining through the rents of that type of the ugliness of man'. Nightingale's letters also show the extent to which her view of Rome had been shaped by her reading of Byron. Having seen the statue then known as the 'Dying Gladiator', she remarked: 'I do not care about seeing it again—it is so stamped in my mind—and Lord Byron is sufficient to recall it'. Another text which she refers to, and relates to sites in Rome, is Macaulay's *Lays of Ancient Rome*: 'When one looks ... up at Horatius' bridge, how one feels the lines, "And he saw on Palatinus, The white porch of his home, And he spake to the noble river Which flows by the towers of Rome."—I have said them 500 times to myself on beautiful Palatinus.'[108] However, unlike many female tourists, Nightingale could also understand the Latin inscriptions she found in places like

[107] Anna Jameson, *Diary of an Ennuyée* (London: Henry Colburn, 1826), 232. See James Buzard, *The Beaten Track: European Tourism, Literature, and the Ways to Culture, 1800–1918* (Oxford: Clarendon, 1993), 114–30.

[108] Mary Keele (ed.), *Florence Nightingale in Rome: Letters Written by Florence Nightingale in Rome in the Winter of 1847–1848* (Philadelphia, Pa.: American Philosophical Society, 1981), 43–4, 94, 83.

the Catacombs and she comments on her fascination with this burial place with reference to the Sibyl's advice to Aeneas in book 6 of the *Aeneid*: 'Now we are going into the Tombs, my dear people, and once in I assure you it is no easy matter to get me out ... Easy is the descent, as my Virgil used to say, less easy the coming out—but once in and I don't care how I come out'.[109] Nightingale's relaxed tone contrasts with fictions such as *Middlemarch*, *Little Dorrit*, and George Gissing's *The Emancipated*, which stress how impossible it is for an inadequately educated woman to come to terms with a country which is constructed in Victorian culture as a mound of texts. Women writers, better educated than their heroines, could confidently employ their knowledge of classical art and literature, mediated by more recent writings like Madame de Staël's combination of guidebook and fiction *Corinne, or Italy* (1807) and Byron's poems. They found it possible and enjoyable to emulate the Grand Tourists and relate classical poetry to the beauty of the Italian landscape, free from the kind of intellectual fatigue which made Byron associate Mount Soracte with dull lessons.

[109] Ibid. 245. 'Easy is the descent ... less easy the coming out' is an allusion to the lines *facilis descensus Auerno:* | *... sed reuocare gradum superasque euadere ad auras,* | *hoc opus, hoc labor est* (*Aeneid* 6. 126, 128–9). These lines acquired the force of a proverb, as Dryden's translation suggests: 'The gates of hell are open night and day; | Smooth the descent, and easy is the way: | But to return, and view the cheerful skies, | In this, the mighty task and labour lies.' John Dryden, *Dryden's Aeneid: A Selection with Commentary*, ed. Robin Sowerby (Bristol: Bristol Classical Press, 1986), 6. 192–5.

2

Classical Training for the Woman Writer

For a woman writer seeking acceptance from a predominantly masculine literary establishment in which classical education was the norm, the improvement of her English style through the study of Latin and Greek was a significant element of her literary training. In *Female Writers: Thoughts on their Proper Sphere, and on their Powers of Usefulness* (1842), Mary Ann Stodart advised literary women that the 'style of a person well acquainted with the Latin classics will always be found in force and richness far to surpass that of the mere modern linguist' and '[s]ufficient knowledge of Greek for the New Testament, will also be found a most desirable acquirement'.[1] Thackeray wrote of the anonymous author of *Jane Eyre* (1847): 'if a woman she knows her language better than most ladies do, or has had a classical education'.[2] At Oxford University nearly seventy years later the aspiring writer Vera Brittain agreed to begin learning Greek and to improve her hard-won knowledge of Latin, since 'they say the Classical training would be of inestimable value to me, & of course I know it would to my English'.[3] There were dramatic changes in educational provision for Victorian women, from the home education or ladylike seminaries experienced by Charlotte Brontë, Elizabeth Gaskell, and George Eliot, to the academic girls' schools or Oxbridge women's colleges attended by May Sinclair, Amy Levy,

[1] M. A. Stodart, *Female Writers: Thoughts on their Proper Sphere, and on their Powers of Usefulness* (London: R. B. Seeley & W. Burnside, 1842), 36–7.

[2] W. M. Thackeray to William Smith Williams, 23 Oct. 1847. Quoted in Barker, *Brontës*, 147.

[3] Vera Brittain, *Chronicle of Youth: Great War Diary, 1913–1917* (1981), ed. Alan Bishop (London: Phoenix, 2000), 116.

and Vera Brittain, yet women with literary ambitions consistently chose to pursue classical studies, whether encouraged by tuition and easy access to books, tacitly supported under the conventional excuse of helping out younger brothers, or shamed into keeping their desire for erudition a secret. In her book *On Becoming a Writer* (1947), Brittain concludes that the 'scales of opportunity still tend to be weighted against women, and any extra educational asset that a woman can acquire helps to redress the balance': for the women writers examined here that 'extra educational asset' is a knowledge of the classics.[4]

The question of a classical literary training is related to social status for women as well as men: those who learnt Latin and Greek were usually the daughters or sisters of educated men. Potential classical scholars needed to own copies of grammar books and ancient texts, or borrow them from male relatives, and a significant investment of time was required for an attempt to study those texts in the original languages. The classics were an irrelevance to working-class women who came from an environment where the struggle to learn to read the Bible or English literature was difficult enough and 'autodidact culture was an overwhelmingly male territory'.[5] Stodart remarks that the combination of 'a certain degree of talent' with 'the possession of or prospect of fortune sufficient to exempt from the heavy pressure of domestic cares might justify the application of the mind to these beautiful studies'.[6] Economic prosperity had allowed previously aristocratic ideals of womanhood to permeate lower down the social scale, so middle-class families were able to display their status through the accomplishments of their daughters, to show that the women of the family passed their days with genteel leisure pursuits (modern languages, music, and art) and not domestic work; in these aspirational circles classical education was often reserved for boys. Parents could see that Latin or maths might help to gain their sons 'remunerative employment, or ... University preferment', but were of no obvious use to a girl since 'reading the Latin

---

[4] Vera Brittain, *On Becoming a Writer* (London: Hutchinson, 1947), 29.
[5] Rose, *Intellectual Life*, 18.
[6] Stodart, *Female Writers*, 57.

poets will not make her more attractive'.[7] This was not necessarily the case for more socially secure Victorian gentlewomen, who 'displayed their classical learning by peppering their letters with Greek phrases'.[8] As the appearance of gentility became increasingly available to those who owed their leisured status to trade and manufacturing rather than land, upper-middle-class women needed to find new markers of their superior rank. The classical languages, already seen as an indicator of social standing for men, were an obvious choice:

the necessary investment of spare time supposedly required for girls to achieve high standards in the Classics, coupled with the presumption that the necessary mental equipment was most usually to be associated with fine breeding, soon marked it out as desirable for families with talented daughters and the money to support a concentration on more esoteric study.[9]

The aristocratic associations of classical studies for women were well established. In the Renaissance, reading and writing Latin prose and verse was considered 'necessary training for a ruler'; a daughter of the aristocracy such as Jane Seymour might learn Latin to fit her for a royal marriage and 'the Latinity of royal women and the high aristocracy created a potential window of opportunity for other women', especially the daughters of humanist scholars.[10] Victorian commentators like John Churton Collins praised the 'high-born ladies who seized on Greek with as much avidity as the men, and became excellent scholars', including Sir Thomas More's daughter Margaret Roper 'who translated Eusebius into Latin', Henry VIII's sixth wife Catharine Parr, and 'the mother of Francis Bacon', a daughter of Edward VI's tutor Sir Anthony Cooke.[11] Elizabeth I was remembered as 'the Queen who could read Greek; the learned

---

[7] Charles Eyre Pascoe, *Schools for Girls and Colleges for Women: A Handbook of Female Education Chiefly Designed for the Use of Persons of the Upper Middle Class* (London: Hardwicke & Bogue, 1879), 75.

[8] See M. Jeanne Peterson, *Family, Love, and Work in the Lives of Victorian Gentlewomen* (Bloomington: Indiana UP, 1989), 54–5.

[9] Judith Rowbotham, *Good Girls Make Good Wives: Guidance for Girls in Victorian Fiction* (Oxford: Blackwell, 1989), 117.

[10] Jane Stevenson, 'Women and Classical Education in the Early Modern Period', in Yun Lee Too and Niall Livingstone (eds.), *Pedagogy and Power: Rhetorics of Classical Learning* (Cambridge: CUP, 1998), 103–5.

[11] Collins, *Greek Influence*, 49.

woman', whose example, comments Simon Goldhill, 'led some other privileged women to study Greek, in a way which will find parallels later with some remarkable Victorian intellectual women's attempts to break through the gendered boundaries of education'.[12] Contemporary observers made similar connections between aristocratic female scholars of the Renaissance and the nineteenth-century pioneers of women's higher education: in 'Literature and Science' (1882), Matthew Arnold writes 'Women will again study Greek, as Lady Jane Grey did; I believe that in that chain of forts, with which the fair host of the Amazons are now engirdling our English universities ... they are studying it already.'[13]

There is one significant change from the Renaissance ideal of scholarship to the Victorian equivalent: Jane Stevenson evaluates the classical learning of early modern women by looking at the poetry they wrote in Latin and Greek, because 'the ability to compose metrical poetry is the nearest possible thing to an unequivocal indication that the writer in question had received an education comparable to that of a man'.[14] In the nineteenth century the practice of verse composition was controversial even in the context of men's education and while a few girls briefly attempted to emulate their brothers' verse-making, women writers did not choose this way to practise or display their knowledge of the classical languages. The efforts of previous generations of scholarly women in this direction may have seemed a waste of time—in her 'History of England from the Reign of Henry the 4th to the death of Charles the 1st: by a Partial, prejudiced and ignorant Historian', Jane Austen's satirical account of Lady Jane Grey has the young queen's reign ending bathetically in a self-imposed classical task on her way to her own execution, when 'she wrote a

---

[12] Goldhill, *Who Needs Greek?*, 56.

[13] Matthew Arnold, *Philistinism in England and America*, ed. R. H. Super (Ann Arbor: U of Michigan P, 1974), 71.

[14] Stevenson, 'Women and Classical Education', 83–4. The anthology *Early Modern Women Poets* includes a Greek poem by Mildred Cecil, Lady Burleigh (like Lady Anne Bacon, a daughter of Sir Anthony Cooke), and Latin poems by Elizabeth Hoby and Katherine Killigrew (two more of Cooke's daughters), Elizabeth I, Lady Jane Grey, Elizabeth Jane Weston, Bathsua Rainolds, and Rachel Jevon: Jane Stevenson and Peter Davidson (eds.), *Early Modern Women Poets 1520–1700: An Anthology* (Oxford: OUP, 2001).

Sentence in Latin and another in Greek on seeing the dead body of her Husband accidentally passing that way'.[15]

Making the content of classical texts available to a wider audience held more appeal for the nineteenth-century woman writer, and here too exemplary women could be found, since the 'derivative nature of translation' made it 'one of the very few cultural activities open to women in the early modern period'.[16] Translating ancient texts or theological works (often written in Latin) offered women a chance to publish and to write about ideas without having to defend the content. Lucy Hutchinson (1620–81) wrote the first complete English translation of a classical epic—the Epicurean atheist Lucretius' *De Rerum Natura (The Nature of the Universe)*.[17] More famous in the nineteenth century was the 'bluestocking' Elizabeth Carter (1717–1806), translator of the Stoic philosopher Epictetus, who was considered by Samuel Johnson to be 'possibly the best Greek scholar in the land' and 'achieved European celebrity for her scholarly acquisitions'.[18] She was accepted as an intellectual equal by literary men such as Johnson and Richardson, and contributed poetry to the *Gentleman's Magazine* from the age of 17, including translations of odes by Anacreon and Horace, and poems in English and Latin.[19] She undertook the translation of Epictetus for her friend Catherine Talbot's family reading group, which included the Greek, Latin, and Hebrew scholar, Thomas Secker (later archbishop of Canterbury). Talbot encouraged her to publish the translation since she 'knew that her very talented but husbandless friend would not long survive without a reliable income' and made her own mark on the text by suggesting that Carter warn her readers 'against the potentially dangerous influence of Epictetus's doctrines, especially his lack of belief in an afterlife,

---

[15] Jane Austen, *Catharine and Other Writings*, ed. Margaret Anne Doody and Douglas Murray (Oxford: OUP, 1993), 139.

[16] Mirella Agorni, 'The Voice of the "Translatress": From Aphra Behn to Elizabeth Carter', *RES* 28 (1998), 181.

[17] Lucy Hutchinson, *Lucretius: De Rerum Natura*, ed. Hugh De Quehen (London: Duckworth, 1996).

[18] Norma Clarke, *Dr Johnson's Women* (London: Hambledon & London, 2000), 26–7.

[19] Sylvia Harcstark Myers, *The Bluestocking Circle: Women, Friendship, and the Life of the Mind in Eighteenth-Century England* (Oxford: Clarendon, 1990), 48.

and apparent recommendation of suicide. Carter ... added an introduction and footnotes stressing the superiority of Christianity.'[20]

'Epictetus Carter' acted as a model and a warning for female
scholars, since she overcame her initial slowness in studying languages and ended up learning Latin, Greek, Hebrew, French, Italian,
Spanish, German, Portuguese, and Arabic, but injured her health by
studying. Like a significant number of Victorian women writers, she
was a clergyman's daughter: the clergy could educate their daughters
to a remarkably high standard at home, and perceived scholarship as
a marker of social status. Carter's reputation is also influential in
another respect, contradicting those 'moralizers' who depicted
'women with intellectual or literary ambitions ... as slatternly if
not licentious'.[21] Dr Johnson famously remarked of his friend that
she could make a pudding as well as translate Epictetus. Variations on
his praise of her combination of accomplishments in learning and
domestic duties are regularly employed to commend studious
women, such as Richard Garnett's description of Mary Shelley as 'a
hard student ... [who] read incessantly without any neglect of
domestic duties', or Virginia Woolf's mental picture of her tutor
Janet Case 'read[ing] Greek with one hand, while she slices potatoes
with the other'.[22]

STUDYING AT HOME

The 'community-building of educated women, and the enabling of
well-disposed men' are vital factors in Jane Stevenson's account

[20] Michele Valerie Ronnick, 'Epictetus' Liberation of Elizabeth Carter', *Res Publica Litterarum* 18 (1995), 169; Judith Hawley, 'Carter, Elizabeth (1717–1806)', *Oxford Dictionary of National Biography* (Oxford: OUP, 2004), <http://www.oxforddnb.com/view/article/4782>, accessed 3 June 2005.

[21] Roger Lonsdale (ed.), *Eighteenth-Century Women Poets: An Oxford Anthology* (Oxford: OUP, 1989), p. xxiii.

[22] Richard Garnett, 'Shelley, Mary Wollstonecraft (1797–1851)', *Dictionary of National Biography on CD-ROM* (Oxford: OUP, 1995); V.W. to Janet Case, 4 Nov. [1920], *The Letters of Virginia Woolf*, ed. Nigel Nicolson and Joanne Trautmann Banks, ii (London: Hogarth Press, 1975), 446, quoted in Rowena Fowler, 'Moments and Metamorphoses: Virginia Woolf's Greece', *Comparative Literature*, 51 (1999), 219.

of early modern female scholars;[23] their Victorian counterparts also relied on the support of male mentors and a community of cultured women, either within the family or belonging to a network maintained by correspondence. The extent to which isolated women writers might derive support from friendships with other female intellectuals has often been underestimated. They did not enter London literary society on the same terms as men, but they wrote to each other, sent copies of their books, and sometimes arranged meetings which led to friendships like that of Charlotte Brontë and Elizabeth Gaskell. They might also discuss their classical reading informally in letters, like Elizabeth Barrett and Mary Russell Mitford. Women looked to their predecessors (such as the female scholars discussed above) to prove that their intellectual interests had not always been considered unfeminine. A more recent example was Mary Shelley, who enjoyed unusual freedom to spend her time in studying, access to a wide range of texts (even in Italy when obtaining new books was expensive), and the enabling assistance of male classicists.[24] Perhaps most importantly, during the time she spent in Italy she was (like Barrett Browning and Eliot at the time of their most intensive reading and writing) removed from the kind of bourgeois social and domestic pressures which prevented women from serious study, and which are eloquently described in Florence Nightingale's *Cassandra*. The unconventional standards of a literary household, where intellectual endeavour might be valued at least as highly as household comforts, could be particularly conducive to classical study for women.

In Victorian fiction the ideal of a relationship in which a husband is a kind of tutor, who will help the heroine to escape from the narrowness of the conventional feminine education, usually turns

---

[23] Stevenson, 'Women and Classical Education', 90.

[24] Percy and Mary Shelley, living abroad, both pursuing literary careers and both reading classical texts in the original languages, provided an inspirational model for Robert Browning and Elizabeth Barrett, and also for G. H. Lewes and Marian Evans (the name used by Mary Ann Evans when she began her literary career in London, before she invented the pseudonym George Eliot). U. C. Knoepflmacher, 'On Exile and Fiction: The Leweses and the Shelleys', *Mothering the Mind: Twelve Studies of Writers and their Silent Partners*, ed. Ruth Perry and Martine Watson Brownley (London: Holmes & Meier, 1984), 114.

to disaster, but Mary Shelley (1797–1851) is a very positive model for
female readers of the classics. She learnt Latin and Greek from her
husband, and listened to or wrote down his translations of difficult
Greek texts, although she also undertook a great deal of classical
reading alone.[25] Her journal and reading lists, with their unusually
full record of texts, act as evidence of what a woman could achieve at
home in a fairly intensive course of classical study, given a favourable
environment and access to books.[26] Studying Latin (for the most
part) independently, she appears to have read widely, mainly canonical texts: Augustan poetry such as Horace's *Odes*, Virgil's *Georgics*
and *Aeneid*, Ovid's *Metamorphoses*; prose history, biography, and
letters including thirty books of Livy's *History of Rome*, several of
Cicero's speeches, the letters of Pliny the Younger, Suetonius' life
of Julius Cæsar. Other texts are less predictable: Quintus Curtius'
life of Alexander the Great, Petronius' *Satyricon*—'a most detestable
book'—and Terence's comedies. Unfortunately she rarely records any
comments on her reading, and does not indicate why she chose
particular texts, but some of her preferred authors may be deduced
from her fiction and poetry, which includes responses to the Latin
and Greek texts she read in Italy. Ovid's *Metamorphoses* inspired two
short mythological dramas, *Proserpine* and *Midas*, written in 1820.
Percy Shelley read and translated difficult Greek texts such as
Prometheus Bound for her; this tragedy influenced Mary Shelley's
Frankenstein, or, The Modern Prometheus (1818) as well as his own
lyric drama *Prometheus Unbound* (written after the novel's publication). In 1821, having read many of the major Latin texts, she resumed
her study of Greek despite some practical difficulties: 'I have now
very seriously begun Greek ... now I may boast that I know perfectly

---

[25] Greek was bound up with their elopement from the first: '[Percy] Shelley's
relationships with women tended to be pedagogic', and the 'illicit' reading of classical
texts with women 'lent the subject an extra frisson' for the tutor. He also taught
Mary's stepsister Claire Clairmont, and had taught his first wife Latin so that
she could read Horace and Ovid's *Metamorphoses*. Wallace, *Shelley*, 34; Holmes,
Shelley, 184.

[26] See 'The Shelleys' Reading List', *M.W.S. Journals*, ii. 631–84. The journal entries
and reading lists of the Shelleys and Claire Clairmont from 1814 to 1822 include a
wide range of classical texts, and the differences in the repertoire of texts studied by
each of these three readers are illuminating.

sixty lines of Homer's Odyssey. I am much teazed for the want of a good grammar—S. wanted to persuade me to have Jones's sent out in sheets: but ... a whole box would cost less than that'.[27] Her attempt to study Greek by memorizing poetry recalls the methods of public schools, although on a smaller scale. She continued to read Greek texts at a faster pace with her husband, and had lessons from Prince Alexander Mavrocordato (the dedicatee of Percy Shelley's *Hellas*) from January 1821.[28] After the death of her husband in 1822, she continued to read and engage with classical texts; by March 1823 she had got halfway through the *Odyssey*. She was reading Homer in the evenings, with constant encouragement from Hogg by letter.[29] She wrote that reading Greek made her feel closer to her husband: 'in the company of Homer I am with one of his best friends—and in reading the books he best loved I collect his acquaintances about me.' Her gradual regeneration was traced in terms of her reading, so that she later wrote, in a muted echo of her joy in reading in the Italian sunshine: 'I bask in the sun on the grass reading Virgil, that is, my beloved Georgics ... I begin to live again'.[30]

The attitude of male relatives was crucial to girls' access to learning. In contrast to the forbidding images in nineteenth-century fiction of the unhappiness and familial hostility suffered by women who are learned or desire to become so, the women writers who studied Latin and Greek were helped and supported by at least one male relative or friend. The kind of assistance offered might be tutoring or simply providing money for books or schooling, or at the very least it might be tolerating a daughter's or wife's reading habits, not attacking such pursuits as unwomanly. To take one example, Sara Coleridge (1802–50) encountered varying degrees of encouragement from members of her family: she grew up in the

[27] M.W.S. to Maria Gisborne, 19 July 1820. *M.W.S. Letters*, i. 155. The book she refers to is John Jones, *A Grammar of the Greek Tongue, on a New Plan* (London, 1808).

[28] Mavrocordato was an important figure in the Greek War of Independence in the 1820s. He wrote the Greek Declaration of Independence and later became Prime Minister of Greece. It was at Mavrocordato's request that Byron went to Missolonghi, where he died in 1824.

[29] *M.W.S. Journals*, i. 471, n. 1.

[30] M.W.S. to Leigh Hunt, [26 Oct. 1823]. *M.W.S. Letters*, i. 398. M.W.S. to Leigh Hunt, 8 Apr. [1825]. Ibid. i. 476.

house of her uncle, Robert Southey, who allowed her access to a wide range of books in his library of 14,000 volumes, taught her Greek and Latin, and advised her to translate the medieval Latin text on which he based his 'Tale of Paraguay'. *An Account of the Abipones, an Equestrian People of Paraguay: From the Latin of Martin Dobrizhoffer* (1822) was a very different project from the translation of a classical Latin text, for which there might be previous versions which could help with difficult passages, and Charles Lamb was impressed by the linguistic feat she had accomplished: he wrote to Southey, 'How she Dobrizhoffered it all out puzzles my slender latinity to conjecture.'[31] The work of translation was at first to be shared by Sara's brother Derwent, and the proceeds were to fund his education at Cambridge; she continued the project alone when a relative offered to pay Derwent's expenses, and gave him her earnings. Her brothers exemplified contrasting attitudes to women's education: Derwent was sympathetic to her interests, and they read Tacitus, Livy, Virgil, and Cicero together; Hartley discouraged his sister's studies, warning that for a woman '*Latin & celibacy* go together'.[32] Sara remained painfully aware that she could not have the kind of scholarly career which was available to her brothers: 'I should have been happier, with my taste, temper, and habits, had I been of your sex … The thing that would suit me best of anything would be the life of a country clergyman—I should delight in the studies necessary to the profession'.[33] Samuel Taylor Coleridge had little involvement in his daughter's education, but was proud of her achievements, and planned to present her with his copy of William Sotheby's polyglot edition of the *Georgics* (1827) as 'the most splendid way, that I can command, of marking my sense of the Talent and Industry that have made her Mistress of the Six Languages comprized in the volume'.[34]

---

[31] C.L. to Robert Southey, 19 Aug. 1825. *The Letters of Charles Lamb*, ed. T. N. Talfourd (London, 1837), ii. 189. Quoted in Edith Coleridge (ed.), *Memoir and Letters of Sara Coleridge*, 3rd edn. (London: Henry S. King & Co, 1873), i. 35.

[32] Kathleen Jones, *A Passionate Sisterhood: The Sisters, Wives and Daughters of the Lake Poets* (London: Virago, 1998), 202.

[33] S.C. to Derwent Coleridge, 6 June 1825: unpubl. letter, quoted in Bradford Keyes Mudge, *Sara Coleridge: A Victorian Daughter* (London: Yale UP, 1989), 37.

[34] See *Collected Letters of Samuel Taylor Coleridge*, ed. Earl Leslie Griggs, vi (Oxford: Clarendon, 1956), 691–2. Although he ignored his other children, Samuel

Her protected and studious youth contrasts with her struggle to maintain her intellectual interests as a wife and mother, when ill health and the demands of housekeeping interrupted her studies to devastating effect. Nevertheless, teaching her children offered her the opportunity to read Latin and Greek without seeming to neglect her duties, and to publish a book which drew on her classical learning: *Pretty Lessons in Verse, for Good Children; with Some Lessons in Latin, in Easy Rhyme* (1834).

When there were no sons in the family, a father was perhaps more likely to indulge a daughter who wanted to study the classics. Jane Welsh (later Carlyle, 1801–66) quarrelled with her mother, who 'wanted her daughter to learn subjects more in keeping with the usual pursuits of her sex'. She found a Latin grammar at home and persuaded one of her male contemporaries to help her learn the language; studying late at night and early in the morning (she tied a weight to her ankles to wake her), she convinced her father to let her 'learn Latin like a boy' by demonstrating that she had already learned to decline the noun *penna*. She was then allowed to attend Latin classes at the local grammar school.[35] Like Annie Thackeray (who did not, however, study the classics), she had the 'dual sense of self as simultaneous daughter and son [which] lies at the heart of the achievement of many women writers, and of professional women in general'.[36] That it was possible for a Victorian girl to think of herself as 'simultaneous daughter and son' within the home (especially if she had no brothers) complicates established notions of strictly 'separate spheres'. Sometimes these roles were divided between two daughters: although her feminist writings lament the lack of mental stimulation offered to middle-class women, Florence Nightingale (1820–1910)

Taylor Coleridge tested his educational theories on his eldest son, Hartley, teaching him Greek without Latin as a preliminary. In 1806 he wrote a new Greek grammar which used English rather than Latin as a medium of instruction: see Samuel Taylor Coleridge, *Shorter Works and Fragments*, ed. H. J. Jackson and J. R. de J. Jackson (London: Routledge, 1995), i. 157–200.

[35] Lawrence Hanson and Elisabeth Hanson, *Necessary Evil: The Life of Jane Welsh Carlyle* (London: Constable, 1952), 6.

[36] Katherine Hill-Miller, ' "The Skies and Trees of the Past": Anne Thackeray Ritchie and William Makepeace Thackeray', *Daughters and Fathers*, ed. Lynda E. Boose and Betty S. Flowers (London: Johns Hopkins UP, 1989), 361.

studied philosophy, history, and languages, including classical Greek, with her father, 'a serious private scholar', while her sister Parthenope became her mother's companion.[37]

In families with sons, the boys came first: Elizabeth Barrett and Charlotte Yonge did not receive any classical training until it was time for their younger brothers to begin Latin or Greek, and their learning was not regarded in the same way as a boy's.[38] Girls often learnt Latin and Greek for more practical reasons than their brothers, or at least made use of utilitarian explanations for their studies: they could save money for the family by passing on their learning to younger siblings (and later to their own children), or stimulate lazy brothers by providing competition for them. From the age of 11 Yonge shared the lessons which were intended to prepare her younger brother for the classical curriculum of a public school: 'we went on until I was some years past twenty, and had worked up to the point of such Greek, Euclid, and Algebra as had furnished forth the Etonian and soldier of sixteen'. She stresses that the lessons were arranged around her brother's educational needs, and determinedly erases the question of her own interests, representing herself as a secondary tutor who helped her brother to prepare for the lessons with their father. Her description of their lessons emphasizes that for her imparting the classics was part of her identity as a model daughter and intellectual companion to her father and that she continued to serve the next generation in the same way:

So we worked through Latin Grammar with the old 'Propria quae maribus' and 'As in praesenti,' and through [Plato's] Phaedrus and [the Roman historian] Cornelius Nepos. (Our old copy of Phaedrus has served me again with one of his boys.) Then I went on to Virgil, and selections from Horace, but all this work was spread over a good many years.[39]

Like Yonge, Augusta Webster (1837–94) represented her classical education as a family duty. She learnt Latin and Greek 'with the

[37] Deborah Gorham, *The Victorian Girl and the Feminine Ideal* (London: Croom Helm, 1982), 128.

[38] Mermin, *Godiva*, 52.

[39] Christabel Coleridge, *Charlotte Mary Yonge: Her Life and Letters* (London: Macmillan, 1903), 107, 110.

ostensible aim of helping a younger brother ... to give a feminine touch to such an undertaking.'[40]

A boy might begin Latin with a tutor at home and share his lessons with a sister, or be taught by a governess, probably the daughter of a clergyman, but most boys did go to school at some point and for 'the middle-class Victorian girl, the departure of a brother for school was a painful awakening to her inferior status'.[41] Some brothers wrote to their sisters about their new studies. Maria Rossetti 'tried single-handedly to master the classics by an improvised correspondence course, via her brothers' but could not keep it up without proper lessons; she turned to learning and teaching Italian and 'religious devotion and study'.[42] Rossetti's attempt to keep pace with her brothers is similar to Elizabeth Barrett's relationship with her brother Edward, and strikingly anticipates the story of Ethel May in Yonge's *The Daisy Chain*, who is persuaded to give up her Greek studies and focuses her energies on religion and teaching her younger siblings.

Whereas educated fathers might be willing to pass on their classical learning or brothers share their lessons, mothers often questioned the purpose of classical studies for girls, mindful of the necessity of teaching their daughters practical subjects or attractive accomplishments. Learning which was usually identified as masculine was often seen as a risk to matrimonial prospects or as simply useless: Sarah Stickney Ellis suggested in *The Women of England* (1839) that a husband would place no great value on his wife's ability 'to read Virgil without the use of a dictionary'.[43] Most mothers were undoubtedly hampered by their own inadequate education, although some were able to undertake the relatively passive task of 'hearing' sections from the Latin grammar book, or to teach basic Latin. Women who were educated by their mothers were likely to have a

[40] Petra Bianchi, ' "Hidden Strength": The Poetry and Plays of Augusta Webster', D.Phil., University of Oxford, 1999, 38.

[41] Elaine Showalter, *A Literature of their Own: British Women Novelists from Brontë to Lessing* (1977), rev. edn. (Princeton: Princeton UP, 1999), 41.

[42] Susan Elkin, 'Rossetti, Maria Francesca (1827–1876)', *Oxford Dictionary of National Biography* (Oxford: OUP, 2004), <http://www.oxforddnb.com/view/article/24142>, accessed 3 June 2005.

[43] Sarah Stickney Ellis, *The Women of England: Their Social Duties and Domestic Habits* (London: Fisher, Son & Co., 1839), 71.

better grounding in modern languages rather than ancient; Margaret Oliphant (1828–97), the editor of Blackwood's series of *Foreign Classics for English Readers*, was probably educated at home by a mother 'whose reading habits … ran from the novels to be borrowed at circulating libraries, through the more serious periodicals of the day'.[44] Mary Elizabeth Braddon (1835–1915) was taught by her mother for up to two hours a day: she 'did not have to memorize, but took dictation and wrote "little bits" of history and geography', including Roman history, which she found 'dry' and Greek, which was 'delightful', but both were surpassed in interest by Sir Walter Scott's *Tales of a Grandfather*. When she found a literary patron, John Gilby, a 'Maecenas' who published a volume of her verses at his own expense, he wished that she would read Greek and Latin to improve her poems.[45] Despite her disappointing lack of classical attainments, however, Braddon's mother provided her with an education which was probably no worse than that offered to many pupils at the small seminaries discussed later in this chapter.

INDEPENDENT WOMEN

Some female classicists found mentors outside their families: the figure of a fatherly scholar who helps a young woman to improve her Greek, and at the same time sees her as an amanuensis and disciple, is an important one for Victorian women writers. Elizabeth Barrett read Greek with Hugh Stuart Boyd, Eliza Lynn (Linton) with Walter Savage Landor, and Marian Evans (George Eliot) with Dr Brabant. With the prominence in Victorian women's fiction of the idealized lover who is also father and tutor, it is not surprising that Brabant's wife saw the tutor–pupil relationship, which the participants characterized as a filial bond, as a sexual threat. Linton argued that Brabant was the original of Casaubon in *Middlemarch*: his 'fastidiousness made his work something like Penelope's web. Ever

---

[44] Elisabeth Jay, *Mrs Oliphant: 'A Fiction to Herself'* (Oxford: Clarendon, 1995), 12.
[45] Wolff, *Sensational Victorian*, 35, 81, 92.

writing and rewriting, correcting and destroying, he never got farther than the introductory chapter of a book which he intended to be epoch-making.'[46] In her autobiography, Linton describes how Walter Savage Landor read Greek to her and encouraged her writing. Casting him as a benevolent father, who called her his 'dear daughter', she writes that she never contradicted him.[47] This familial relationship is highlighted in order to counteract the effect of Lynn's status as an independent woman of letters, living alone in London with grudging support from her father. Like the Brontës, Eliza Lynn grew up in a country vicarage with access to a wide range of books, including Latin and Greek texts. She had a 'passion for reading' and taught herself French, Italian, German, Spanish, and some Greek, Latin, and Hebrew. Her favourite authors were Plato, Goethe, and Coleridge; she hated Sappho, Pindar, Schiller, and Byron.[48] In *The Autobiography of Christopher Kirkland* (1885), Linton fictionalized her experience of learning at home and attributed it to her hero, the son of a clergyman and grandson of a bishop. Julia Wedgwood commented: 'She translates a woman's into a man's experience ... the only sign that we are reading the story of a female life is the fact that Christopher Kirkland grew up without any education.'[49] He does not go to school and has no formal tuition at home, so he teaches himself one language a year until he has acquired all the languages Eliza Lynn taught herself. Through her hero, Linton elaborates on a familiar pattern for literary autodidacts—learning languages in order to read, not to parse sentences or compose Latin verses. 'I scamped the grammar and devoted myself to translation—that is, I neglected rules and learnt only words ... I learnt without method, and I have never been able to disentangle my mind from the false order of the start.'[50] Kirkland moves to London and reads at the British Museum, as Eliza Lynn did every day. There he meets 'one of the vanguard of the independent women' who 'did her life's work

---

[46] Eliza Lynn Linton, *My Literary Life* (London: Hodder & Stoughton, 1899), 43.

[47] Ibid. 47.

[48] Herbert Van Thal, *Eliza Lynn Linton: The Girl of the Period* (London: George Allen & Unwin, 1979), 9–11.

[49] Ibid. 147.

[50] Eliza Lynn Linton, *The Autobiography of Christopher Kirkland* (London: Richard Bentley, 1885), i. 71.

without blare or bluster, or help from the outside; and without that weakness of her sex which makes them cry out when they are hustled in the crowd they have voluntarily joined'.[51] When she went to London to begin her literary career, Lynn Linton had been proud of being one of the first independent women, yet she is most famous for a series of articles attacking modern womanhood, 'The Girl of the Period'; she regretted her own lack of formal education, yet strenuously opposed higher education for women. It had been 'an extraordinary venture for a young provincial clergyman's daughter in mid-Victorian England to live independently in London', and the kind of risk from which she claimed her later anti-feminist writings were designed to protect young women.[52]

NEW WOMEN AND GRECIAN LADIES

The resources available to prominent academic and literary families made formal education largely irrelevant for those of their daughters who had serious intellectual interests. Unmarried women who could afford to prolong their education enjoyed an unprecedented degree of liberty to pursue artistic and intellectual interests in the 1870s and 1880s, playing 'an important role in the transition from mid-Victorian Old Maid to fin-de-siècle New Woman'.[53] Despite the reforms which were taking place in the wider context of women's education, some families preferred more traditional methods: pooling resources in educational communities which resembled small and exclusive private schools, and offering access to a wide range of books at home, so that the most ambitious children could teach themselves. This is the kind of education that Sara Coleridge received in Robert Southey's household, and something similar was offered to her great-niece, who learnt Hebrew from her father, began reading Homer and Euripides on her own, and studied the classics as one of a group of

[51] Ibid. i. 253.
[52] Nancy F. Anderson, *Woman against Women in Victorian England: A Life of Eliza Lynn Linton* (Bloomington: Indiana UP, 1987), 35.
[53] Prins, 'Maenads', 46.

ladies taught by William Cory. Mary Elizabeth Coleridge (1861–1907), protected by a supportive and financially secure family, could continue to study and write without domestic responsibilities. Nevertheless, she was painfully aware that outside her cultured milieu learning was equated with a lack of femininity: in Coleridge's poem 'A Clever Woman', the speaker rebukes the object of her unrequited love for seeing her as masculine because of her intellect: 'woman's woman, even when | She reads her Ethics in the Greek' (5–6).[54] Although she published essays on literary topics, most of Mary Coleridge's commentary on classical literature is (like Sara Coleridge's) to be found in private letters or diary extracts, collected after her death, rather than in the work she published during her lifetime.[55]

Cory had been a classics master at Eton until forced to resign after a scandal about a letter he had written to a pupil, and in some ways, he was offering his female students access to public school learning. There was a basic timetable for the fourteen pupils in this very select academy: 'They do ninety minutes Plato, then tea; eighty minutes Sophocles.' The group's reading also included Virgil, Thucydides, Euripides, Xenophon, Ovid, and Catullus. The eccentricity of making Victorian girls read Catullus is emphasized by Cory's account of a pupil who 'became speechless over a very innocent poem, hid her face and wept for several minutes'.[56] They discussed the texts as well as translating them, and seem to have liked tragedy and characters such as Dido. Cory was more interested in cultivating Hellenism than teaching Latin grammar, as his references to his pupils as 'my lady

---

[54] *The Collected Poems of Mary Coleridge*, ed. Theresa Whistler (London: Rupert Hart-Davis, 1954).

[55] Coleridge contributed to a number of journals, including the *Monthly Review*, *Times Literary Supplement*, and the *Cornhill Magazine*. Most of her poetry was available only to her family and friends during her lifetime, but Robert Bridges encouraged her to publish a volume of poetry, *Fancy's Following* (1896), which appeared under a pseudonym because she feared tarnishing the illustrious Coleridge name. See Alison Chapman, 'Mary Elizabeth Coleridge, Literary Influence and Technologies of the Uncanny', in Ruth Robbins and Julian Wolfreys (eds.), *Victorian Gothic: Literary and Cultural Manifestations in the Nineteenth Century* (Houndmills: Palgrave, 2000), 111–13.

[56] Faith Compton Mackenzie, *William Cory: A Biography* (London: Constable, 1950), 128.

Greeks', 'discipulae', and 'Grecian ladies' suggest.[57] Mary Coleridge
kept records of the lessons, which are included in her *Gathered Leaves*
as 'Notes of the Table Talk of William Cory at some Greek Classes
which he gave for Mary Coleridge and Others'. This 'Table Talk' gives
a remarkable sense of the pace and range of Cory's teaching, and
covers modern history (particularly the seventeenth century), contemporary politics, literature, and science as well as classical poetry
and history. Unlike many nineteenth-century classicists, Cory does
not consider the novel an inferior genre, and frequently compares
novels to the prestigious ancient genres of tragedy and epic: 'Ladies
should be interested in Antigone and Ismene, because they are the
forerunners of Minna and Brenda—of Caroline, the most delightful
of all heroines, and Shirley.'[58]

Mary Coleridge was a regular reader in the British Museum Reading Room, as were other New Woman writers and journalists like
Amy Levy, Eleanor Marx, Olive Schreiner, and Beatrice Potter (later
Webb). They benefited from a greater freedom of movement than
earlier generations, which made it easier for women with similar
interests to form alliances outside the home. The Reading Room
was an important resource for literary women in London by the
1880s and 1890s, a professional space, a literary factory, an environment in which the need to produce new articles and books for an
increasing readership overshadowed the study of ancient literature.[59]
In 1884 about a fifth of the readers at the British Museum were
women, and despite some complaints from male readers, the library

[57] *Extracts from the Letters and Journals of William Cory*, ed. Francis Warre Cornish
(Oxford: privately printed, 1897), 523, 552; Mackenzie, *William* Cory, 134. The group
included Margaret Warre Cornish, daughter of the Provost of Eton, and Janet
Bartrum, who became a governess.
[58] Mary Elizabeth Coleridge, *Gathered Leaves from the Prose of Mary E. Coleridge*,
ed. Edith Sichel (London: Constable, 1910), 318. Minna and Brenda are the heroines
of Scott's *The Pirate* (1821), Caroline and Shirley are from Charlotte Brontë's *Shirley*
(1849).
[59] In *New Grub Street*, Marian Yule sits among the 'toilers' in the Reading Room
and feels that she is 'exhausting herself in the manufacture of printed stuff which no
one even pretended to be more than a commodity for the day's market ... She herself
would throw away her pen with joy but for the need of earning money. And all these
people about her, what aim had they save to make new books out of those already
existing...?' George Gissing, *New Grub Street* (1891), ed. Bernard Bergonzi (Harmondsworth: Penguin, 1985), 137–8.

offered access to a far larger number of women than the universities. Friendships among the New Women who regularly used the library alleviated the strain of leading a non-traditional life.[60] The British Museum coterie was more convenient and more visible than the mid-century networks of women writers which had been established and maintained largely by correspondence, and provided an alternative model for ambitious girls who could not afford to go to college and might support themselves by writing.

FORMAL EDUCATION

The schooling available to women born in the first half of the nineteenth century, such as Elizabeth Gaskell and George Eliot, was that offered by traditional ladies' seminaries of the kind satirized in *Middlemarch*, *Vanity Fair*, and Jane Austen's *Emma*, which provided social rather than intellectual training. These schools did not typically offer tuition in the classical languages; they gave their pupils a genteel degree of familiarity with ancient history and mythology from textbooks like Richmal Mangnall's *Historical and Miscellaneous Questions, for the Use of Young People*, written by a woman and so extensively used in the education of girls that it might be seen as the feminine equivalent of the *Eton Latin Grammar*. In Gaskell's *Wives and Daughters* (1866), Mrs Gibson's superficial allusion to Greek mythology, based solely on this work, is a reminder of the shallow mental accomplishments she brought to her career as a schoolmistress, and suggestive of the kind of teaching available in small seminaries: 'There was one of the heathen deities in Mangnall's Questions whose office it was to bring news.'[61] Gaskell is not the only novelist to invoke this textbook as a satirical shorthand for the kind of superficial learning offered by private seminaries: in *Vanity Fair*, the narrator mocks the 'dear moralists' who think 'a pair of

---

[60] Linda Hunt Beckman, *Amy Levy: Her Life and Letters* (Athens, Ohio: Ohio UP, 2000), 81–2.

[61] Elizabeth Gaskell, *Wives and Daughters* (1866), ed. Pam Mason (Harmondsworth: Penguin, 1996), 647.

pink cheeks and blue eyes' inferior to 'the gifts of genius, the accomplishments of the mind, the mastery of *Mangnall's Questions*, and a ladylike knowledge of botany and geology' (131). However, the book is treated with less scorn in *Middlemarch* (1871–2), being associated not with Rosamond, the perfectly ladylike product of Mrs Lemon's seminary, but with Mrs Garth, a former teacher who successfully educates her own children.

Ancient history was considered an appropriate subject for girls even in the fairly unintellectual seminaries so frequently satirized by novelists. In fact, although there is little depth, the historical sections of *Mangnall's Questions* do equip the student with elementary information on a wide range of topics, including the siege of Troy, Homer, the Olympic games, ostracism, the battle of Thermopylae, funeral ceremonies, the Persian and Peloponnesian Wars, Herodotus, Lysander, Socrates, and so on. The questions and answers are written in paragraphs which were to be learnt by heart and recited in lessons, a process which demanded only an accurate memory. Nevertheless, some teachers created more challenging lessons from the text: Charlotte Brontë's copy contains manuscript additions of names, dates, and other information, which suggest a less mechanical approach to the subject than the choice of textbook might indicate.[62] Mangnall frequently takes the opportunity to offer moralizing judgements as well as information: a question about the character of the Athenians is followed by this answer: 'Glory, liberty, and interest, were their darling passions; but their liberty frequently degenerated into licentiousness: they were capricious and ambitious; excelled in the art of navigation; and were the general patrons of the liberal arts.'[63] This is an extract from a typical lesson: 'Name the great events in the first century. The foundation of London, by the Romans; the persecution of the druids, in Britain; Rome burnt in the reign of Nero, and the christians persecuted by him; Jerusalem destroyed by Titus; and the New Testament written' (12).

The popularity of *Mangnall's Questions* as a school text for girls cannot be doubted: it went through numerous editions in the

---

[62] Barker, *Brontës*, 174.
[63] Richmal Mangnall, *Historical and Miscellaneous Questions, for the Use of Young People*, 3rd edn. (London: Thomas Hurst, 1803), 22.

nineteenth century. In 1869 Francis Young issued a revised and extended edition because 'the work still retains its position as a standard school book, although numerous manuals of a similar scope and character have been introduced'.[64] One of these can be found on a list of books used in the education of Queen Victoria, Mrs Trimmer's *New and Comprehensive Lessons: Containing a General Outline of the Roman History*.[65] Trimmer offers basic historical information ultimately derived from the early books of Livy's history of Rome, with the addition of moralizing comment and a condescending attitude to all pre-Christian religious believers as 'Heathens': for example, 'Romulus required his people to practise such ridiculous ceremonies as children would now laugh at'.[66] Occasionally the book's didactic tone descends into bathos as it attempts to combine moral admonitions to its young readers with the description of crimes far beyond their experience. Having related how Tullia drove her chariot over her father's body after he had been killed by her second husband (the brother of her first husband, whom she disposed of herself), Trimmer comments: 'This account of Tullia should be a warning to children not to give way to passion and pride in their early years; since they cannot tell what monsters they may become in time, if they do so' (38).

There were some interesting exceptions to the poor quality of girls' education in the early nineteenth century, such as an expensive finishing school in Bath, where the six pupils were taught by visiting masters because 'women in those days were not sufficiently learned for the task'. The girls learnt French by speaking it all day, but 'Latin was taught more seriously' and there was 'an astonishing amount of stiff reading'; this was regarded as necessary not so much for the girls' own intellectual development as to prepare them to be the wives and mothers of educated men.[67] A more unusual solution was found for

[64] Francis Young, *Mangnall's Historical and Miscellaneous Questions, Revised and Extended* (London: T. J. Allman, 1869), p. v.

[65] Tim Reid, 'Victoria, Princess in a Class of her own' and 'Bookish Girl Nourished on a Diet of History and Grammar', *The Times* (28 Apr. 2001). The list also includes Dryden's *Aeneid*, Pope's *Iliad*, Goldsmith's histories of Greece and Rome, *Mangnall's Questions*, the *Eton Latin Grammar*, and Latin poets—Ovid, Virgil, and Horace.

[66] Mrs Trimmer, *New and Comprehensive Lessons: Containing a General Outline of the Roman History* (London: John Harris, 1835), 19–20.

[67] M. V. Hughes, *Vivians: A Family in Victorian Cornwall* (1935; Oxford: OUP, 1980), 8.

Harriet Martineau (1802–76) and her sister, who attended Isaac
Perry's school in Norwich at the point when he became 'a girls'
schoolmaster' after losing most (but not all) of his male pupils on
his conversion to Unitarianism. Recalling her 'delectable schooling',
she claimed that the presence of boys (in a separate part of the classroom) stimulated the girls to emulate the 'thorough way in which the
boys did their lessons' so that they 'worked as heartily as if we had
worked together'. There is no suggestion in Martineau's account of
the dullness of learning Latin by rote, although she comments
obliquely on the shortcomings of the *Eton Latin Grammar*:

We learned Latin from the old Eton grammar, which I therefore, and against
all reason, cling to,—remembering the repetition-days (Saturdays) when we
recited all that Latin, prose and verse, which occupied us four hours. Two
other girls, besides Rachel and myself, formed the class; and we certainly
attained a capability of enjoying some of the classics, even before the two
years were over. Cicero, Virgil, and a little of Horace were our main reading
then: and afterwards I took great delight in Tacitus. I believe it was a genuine
understanding and pleasure, because I got into the habit of thinking in
Latin, and had something of the same pleasure in sending myself to sleep
with Latin as with English poetry. Moreover, we stood the test of verse-
making, in which I do not remember that we ever got any disgrace, while we
certainly obtained, now and then, considerable praise.[68]

While other nineteenth-century women might have envied
Martineau's experience of masculine schooling, it was only ever a
temporary solution (two years in her case, from 11 to 13) as propriety
would not allow teenage girls to remain in a mixed classroom. The
clear distinction between the licence allowed in childhood and
the restrictions imposed in adolescence still operated in the early
years of the twentieth century: as the only girl at the Dragon School
in Oxford, Naomi Mitchison (1897–1999) received the same classical
education as her brother until she was forced by her mother to leave
the school at the onset of puberty. She was then educated at home by a
governess with four other girls before becoming a Home Student at
Oxford.[69]

---

[68] Sanders (ed.), *Records of Girlhood*, 138–9.
[69] Elizabeth Maslen, 'Mitchison, Naomi Mary Margaret, Lady Mitchison
(1897–1999)', *Oxford Dictionary of National Biography* (Oxford: OUP, 2004),
<http://www.oxforddnb.com/view/article/50052>, accessed 3 June 2005. Mitchison

The novelist Mrs Humphry Ward (Mary Arnold, 1851–1920) commented in 1918 on an 'astonishing rise in the intellectual standards of women, which has taken place in the last half century'.[70] There was a major shift in middle-class women's education, as girls' public schools and colleges for women came to offer more formal environments for learning than the home, in which application to books was not seen as selfish or unfeminine: 'studiousness meant diligence and was even rewarded'.[71] Although Ward had shared the frustrating experience of seeing a brother of a similar age receive an education far more solid than her own, she was so close to fundamental developments in women's education that her sister Julia (born in 1862) could attend the newly established Oxford High School and become one of the first students at Somerville.[72] Ward's commentary on her deficient schooling in the 1850s and 1860s, her persistence in educating herself, and her involvement in the development of women's education at Oxford (as one of the founders of Somerville College) make her a fascinating representative of women's relationship to classical literature in the late Victorian period and early twentieth century. She is an incisive critic of the aimless education offered to girls of her own and earlier generations:

As far as intellectual training was concerned, my nine years from seven to seventeen were practically wasted. I learned nothing thoroughly or accurately, and the German, French and Latin which I soon discovered after my marriage to be essential to the kind of literary work I wanted to do, all had to be relearned before they could be of any real use to me; nor was it ever possible for me—who married at twenty—to get that firm hold on the structure and literary history of any language, ancient or modern, which

wrote novels set in ancient Greece and Rome: see Ruth Hoberman, *Gendering Classicism: The Ancient World in Twentieth-Century Women's Historical Fiction* (Albany, NY: SUNY Press, 1997), 25–6.

[70] Ward, *Recollections*, 96. As the granddaughter of Thomas Arnold of Rugby School, and niece of Matthew Arnold and W. E. Forster (whose Education Act laid the foundations for a state system of elementary schools), Ward felt a personal involvement in debates about education, and believed that women should influence educational policy.

[71] Carol Dyhouse, *Girls Growing up in Late Victorian and Edwardian England* (London: Routledge & Kegan Paul, 1981), 173.

[72] John Sutherland, *Mrs Humphry Ward: Eminent Victorian, Pre-Eminent Edwardian* (Oxford: Clarendon, 1990), 166.

my brother William, only fifteen months my junior, got from his six years at Rugby and his training there in Latin and Greek. (96–7)

At first she attended a fairly good example of the small private school run by Anne Jemima Clough (later the first Principal of Newnham College, Cambridge), who wrote an individual curriculum for each of the pupils, and taught unusual subjects: 7-year-old pupils read Greek history from a book which Arthur Hugh Clough lent to his sister. Later on she was sent to an old-fashioned boarding school, where lessons were taken from *Mangnall's Questions*.[73] After her haphazard formal education, she joined her family in Oxford and began to study by herself, helped by her family connections and acquaintance with prominent scholars, which enabled her to gain access to the Bodleian Library.[74] The process of self-education in adulthood that Ward describes is old-fashioned and prolonged, very much like that of autodidacts such as George Eliot, who also began serious study after completing a more conventional schooling. These women experienced an intense pleasure in finally making sense of classical texts, after years of arduous and solitary study. The reading of a once-forbidden text long contemplated, studied in hours snatched from domestic tasks, and scrutinized for significant meaning, was a crucial event:

I shall never forget the first time when, in middle life, I read in the Greek, so as to understand and enjoy, the 'Agamemnon' of Aeschylus. The feeling of sheer amazement at the range and power of human thought—and at such a date in history—which a leisurely and careful reading of that play awakened in me, left deep marks behind. (344)

Academic standards for girls were gradually raised by the influence of the girls' schools which were first established in the 1840s and 1850s, although they catered for relatively small numbers. Even

---

[73] Ibid. 27–8.

[74] Having been advised by Mark Pattison, the Rector of Lincoln College, to choose a subject and learn everything about it, she came to feel that she 'ought to have been told to take a history examination and learn Latin properly' (*Recollections*, 106). She began by researching early Spanish, and later decided to learn Latin and Greek. When she became engaged to T. Humphry Ward, he gave her Latin lessons, and in the 1880s, she and her children studied Greek with Eugénie Sellers, who, after reading classics at Girton, became a private teacher of Latin and Greek and a student of archaeology at the British Museum.

pioneering high schools such as the North London Collegiate evolved from small family ventures, in which male relatives initially helped with the teaching of subjects like mathematics, Latin, and divinity.[75] In the early years they focused on educating the next generation in order to reduce the shortage of competent teachers for girls. By the end of the nineteenth century, there were three kinds of reputable secondary schools for girls: high schools, Ladies' Colleges, and public schools. Day schools modelled on the North London Collegiate preserved home ties and permitted parents to control friendships; Ladies' Colleges were socially selective in admissions and cultivated ladylike deportment but were also academically demanding; boarding schools such as Roedean and Wycombe Abbey were modelled on boys' public schools, with games, uniform, and prefects.[76] The women who set up such schools sought to conceal their radical aims by stressing that girls would not become unfeminine, and concerns about propriety were paramount. When Netta Syrett took Lemprière's *Classical Dictionary* to school with her, it was confiscated: 'Up to that moment in perfect innocence (if anyone had been so unwise as to set it) I could have passed an examination in the stories of the gods and goddesses, sexual vagaries and all, for I looked on these as part of the general incomprehensibility of grown-up people. But when the book was removed I never rested till I knew, at least dimly, why I was not allowed to keep it in my possession.'[77]

Latin was a marker of intellectual seriousness in these schools; Greek remained a luxury associated with college entrance and was offered, if at all, only to the ablest pupils—at the North London Collegiate those who were destined for Girton studied the language by themselves in the school library. Girls began Latin significantly later than boys, usually at 12 rather than 7, but Sara Burstall, the

[75] Gillian Avery, *The Best Type of Girl: A History of Girls' Independent Schools* (London: Deutsch, 1991), 6. Frances Buss founded the North London Collegiate School in 1850 with just thirty-five pupils. She wanted to give girls some training which would enable them to support themselves if they did not marry.

[76] Dyhouse, *Girls*, 56; Sally Mitchell, *The New Girl: Girls' Culture in England, 1880–1915* (New York: Columbia UP, 1995), 76. See also Joan N. Burstyn, *Victorian Education and the Ideal of Womanhood* (London: Croom Helm, 1980); Felicity Hunt (ed.), *Lessons for Life: The Schooling of Girls and Women 1850–1950* (Oxford: Blackwell, 1987); Barbara Stephen, *Emily Davies and Girton College* (1927; Westport, Conn.: Hyperion, 1976).

[77] Netta Syrett, *The Sheltering Tree* (London: G. Bles, 1939), 20.

headmistress of Manchester High School for Girls, remarked that 'where one can eliminate the advantage boys have through spending a longer time on the subject, the girls do as well', and indeed 'with careful teaching and the elimination of the unfit, the forms make progress at a rate which surprises the master in a boys' school'.[78] Perhaps a more typical experience is that of M. V. Hughes (whose four brothers were educated at public schools), who went to the North London Collegiate at 17 to prepare for a career as a teacher. She found the academic standard lower than she had anticipated, especially in Latin: 'In the Upper Fifth the teacher had kept a crib on her lap even for the syntax sentences, and we were not allowed any variety of rendering. A fair copy placed boldly on the desk would have been respectable, but a crib on the lap, hidden (supposedly) by the desk, was quite another thing.' In the sixth form, however, there was a very different atmosphere with 'a Classic mistress who was a mental aristocrat' and 'might have stepped straight out of a public school or a tutor's room at the university'.[79] Hughes's disappointing experience of learning Latin at school shaped her contribution to an innovative Latin textbook with stories of everyday life in ancient Rome instead of the disconnected sentences traditionally used in grammar practice, 'so that learners should not think of the Romans as consisting entirely of soldiers marching about Gaul, demanding hostages'. Her co-author, a school inspector, wrote the grammar and vocabulary sections of the textbook, which was intended for private students, evening classes, and schools which had not previously offered Latin. The book focused on the 'humane aspects' of classical study instead of the traditional 'gerund-grinding' approach.[80]

[78] S. A. Burstall, *English High Schools for Girls: Their Aims, Organisation and Management* (London: Longmans, Green, 1907), 13, 110.

[79] M. V. Hughes, *A London Girl of the 1880s* (1936; Oxford: OUP, 1978), 57. M. V. Hughes could not afford to study at Newnham or Girton (only one of her four brothers went to Cambridge, on a scholarship). After leaving school she attended a new teacher training college in Cambridge (established in 1885 and later named Hughes Hall after its first Principal, Miss E. P. Hughes). She worked as a teacher and head of the teacher training department at Bedford College before her marriage, and became a school inspector and examiner after her husband's death: see M. V. Hughes, *A London Home in the 1890s* (1937; Oxford: OUP, 1978).

[80] M. V. Hughes, *A London Family between the Wars* (1940; Oxford: OUP, 1979), 27–8; Walter Ripman and M.V. Hughes, *A Rapid Latin Course* (London: J.M. Dent, 1923), p. vi.

Oxford and Cambridge created Junior and Senior Local examinations in the 1850s for boys who would not go to university but
whose employers wanted to know what they had learnt at school.[81]
One of the first preoccupations of the Ladies' Educational Associations founded in the 1860s and 1870s (such as the North of England
Council for Promoting the Higher Education of Women, 1867) was
to get these examinations opened to girls.[82] A. M. A. H. Rogers came
top in the Oxford Senior Local in 1873 and was awarded scholarships
at two Oxford colleges; the offers were withdrawn when it became
clear that the successful candidate was a girl. In *Schools for Girls and
Colleges for Women* (1879) Charles Eyre Pascoe gives examples of
questions: the Oxford Junior Local papers (to be taken at 16) include
passages for translation (Caesar and Virgil for Latin, Xenophon and
Homer for Greek) which Pascoe describes as 'easy', and he finds the
Cambridge translation exercises 'no more difficult'.[83] He also discusses the examiners' reports, which are generally favourable to girls,
and comments 'I am little short of astonished at the degree of
excellence to which the teaching at Cheltenham Ladies' College has
attained.' In the 1879 Senior Local, Oxford's set books were Cicero,
De Amicitia and book 1 of Virgil's *Aeneid*, or book 5 of Herodotus
and Aeschylus' *Prometheus Bound*, and 'no one will obtain a place
among the first twenty in either language unless she satisfies the
Examiners in unprepared work as well as in the books here spe-
cified'.[84] When Vera Brittain took the Oxford Senior Local in 1914
(her place at Somerville College depended on the result) she found
the Latin prose composition paper the most difficult: 'my Latin Prose

---

[81] Burstyn, *Victorian Education*, 24–5.

[82] Carol Dyhouse, *No Distinction of Sex? Women in British Universities, 1870–1939*
(London: UCL Press, 1995), 13.

[83] There is also a selection of brief sentences to be translated into the chosen
language (Pascoe, *Schools*, 29–31). 'Translate into Latin: (a) Your father and I are here.
(b) He lived ten years. (c) He is worthy to die. (d) If I had known I would have told
you. (e) Tell me if you have been at Rome.'

[84] Pascoe, *Schools*, 37, 91. The examiners' report on the Cambridge Senior Local of
1878 says that the set texts were Cicero's orations *pro Archia* and *pro Balbo*, and book
6 of Ovid's *Fasti*; Greek passages were taken from Isocrates, Panegyricus, and Aeschylus. There was also an unseen passage 'for translation into English, with questions
on the historical and geographical allusions and on grammar. Without a fair knowledge of Accidence a candidate could not pass' (94).

was distinctly bad, but as the Unseen & Vergil papers were practically correct, perhaps they had mercy on me, or perhaps the actual copy of Prose I sent up was not so bad as the rough copy'.[85] Some schools prepared pupils to take the Matriculation examinations of the newer universities, which was an important contribution to the acceptance of women as students. The University of London Matriculation Examination was taken by eleven women in 1879; Latin and two other languages were required (Greek was optional). Latin set texts were taken from the following list: Virgil, one book of *Georgics*, one of *Aeneid*; Horace, two books of *Odes*; Sallust, *Conspiracy*; Caesar, two books of *Gallic War*; Livy, one book; Cicero *De Senectute* or *De Amicitia* and one oration; Ovid one book of *Metamorphoses*, one book of *Heroides*. The paper included passages for translation into English, with questions in history or geography arising from them, short and easy passages for translation from other books, grammar questions, and 'simple and easy sentences of English to be translated into Latin'.[86]

Women writers born in the 1850s and 1860s, such as May Sinclair and Amy Levy, were among the first to be affected by the changes in women's education, and to undertake serious study at school or college for at least a year or two; larger numbers of aspiring writers passed through girls' schools in the twentieth century.[87] May Sinclair

---

[85] V.B. to Roland Leighton, 27 Aug. 1914. *Letters from a Lost Generation: The First World War Letters of Vera Brittain and Four Friends, Roland Leighton, Edward Brittain, Victor Richardson, Geoffrey Thurlow*, ed. Alan Bishop and Mark Bostridge (London: Abacus, 1999), 28.

[86] Pascoe, *Schools*, 97–8.

[87] The poet Stevie Smith and the novelist Stella Gibbons were classmates at the North London Collegiate from 1917. Gibbons did not learn Latin or Greek at school; Smith studied Latin and also acted in school productions of the *Bacchae* (which influenced her *Novel on Yellow Paper*) and *Alcestis*. Her poems allude to her study of Greek myth and tragedy, and Latin poetry such as the *Aeneid* and Catullus' lyrics as well as classically derived literature like Racine's *Phèdre*. She writes dramatic monologues spoken by female characters such as Persephone, Helen of Troy, Dido, and Antigone. See Jack Barbera and William McBrien, *Stevie: A Biography of Stevie Smith* (London: Heinemann, 1985); Frances Spalding, *Stevie Smith: A Biography* (Stroud: Sutton, 2002). In the 20th-cent. novel, girls' grammar schools enable social mobility by offering Latin and Greek, so that girls from poor or uneducated families can become teachers or get degrees. In *South Riding*, Latin and Greek could help to free Lydia Holly from relentless domestic labour for a large and poor family and equip her for a college education and teaching career; Ursula Brangwen, who 'trembled like a

(1863–1946) studied Latin and Greek at Cheltenham Ladies' College and enjoyed the discipline of formal education for a short period, but her experience of learning still reflects that of earlier women writers, with a lot of solitary and self-motivated study. As an only girl with five brothers, she had access to classical textbooks although she did not share the Latin lessons which prepared her brothers for public school. Nevertheless, she taught herself German, Greek, and French, and read Plutarch, Homer, Aeschylus, Sophocles, Aristophanes, Euripides, and Plato.[88] Dorothea Beale encouraged her pupils to continue 'self-culture' when they left school: she 'demanded an extraordinary amount of effort and self-discipline from the girls under her care even after they had left the school'.[89] For Sinclair, this meant studying philosophy, reading Greek tragedy in the original, and writing poetry, novels, and philosophical essays. Her autobiographical novel *Mary Olivier: A Life* (1919) represents an interesting combination of traditional home education, modern schooling, and solitary and intensive study of the classics. Sinclair began her writing career by contributing to *The Cheltenham Ladies' College Magazine*, which Dorothea Beale established in 1880 to create a link between past and present pupils.

The first Jewish woman at Newnham College, and the second at Cambridge, Amy Levy (1861–89) attended Brighton and Hove High School for Girls, 'one of the new secondary schools established to provide girls with an education based on solid academic achievement', where the subjects taught included classics. She 'defined herself as a woman with a university education' but 'grew increasingly critical of the academic mind'.[90] She was remarkably well educated for a woman of her background because of her family's liberal and secular inclinations (she wrote periodical articles which criticize the conservatism of Jewish society). She felt isolated by the anti-Semitism she encountered at Cambridge, and stayed for less than two

postulant when she wrote the Greek alphabet for the first time', continues to teach herself Latin while working as a teacher, in order to get a degree. Winifred Holtby, *South Riding: An English Landscape* (1936; London: Virago, 1988), 149; D. H. Lawrence, *The Rainbow* (1915), ed. Kate Flint (Oxford: OUP, 1998), 267, 408.

[88] Suzanne Raitt, *May Sinclair: A Modern Victorian* (Oxford: Clarendon, 2000), 24.
[89] Ibid. 27.
[90] Beckman, *Amy Levy*, 8.

years. Grant Allen used her suicide as an example of the psychological disorders suffered by over-educated women: 'A few hundred pallid little Amy Levys sacrificed on the way are as nothing before the face of our fashionable juggernaut. Newnham has slain its thousands and Girton its tens of thousands.'[91]

COLLEGES AND UNIVERSITIES

The kind of teaching offered by the new kind of academic girls' schools did not necessarily appeal to parents from upper-class, clerical, or university backgrounds—the traditional providers of classical education for girls—who continued to educate their daughters mainly at home. These daughters were more likely to go to university, especially Oxford or Cambridge, where their fathers and brothers were educated: the first College for Women (later Girton) was established in 1869. Women's colleges occupied a prominent place in the public imagination, as places where talents were fostered instead of being obliterated by domestic duties, or, to more conservative onlookers, subversive institutions which dangerously empowered rebellious women by taking them away from home and giving them a sense of collective power. Girls with literary ambitions had directed their academic aspirations at the universities even before women's colleges existed, but the existence of women's colleges made it possible to replace the image of the solitary female intellectual like Elizabeth Barrett or George Eliot with representations of groups of women—Princess Ida's maidens and Girton Girls—stereotypes which strengthen the association between educated women and the classics, especially Greek. The first readers of Tennyson's *The Princess* (1847) received the idea of a women's university as a fantasy— Elizabeth Barrett described the poem as a fairy tale and questioned its relevance in the age of steam—but although the associations it created were 'sublime, sentimental, absurd—anything rather than practical', Tennyson's poem created a discursive space for exploring

---

[91] Grant Allen, 'The Girl of the Future', *Universal Review*, 7 (1890), 56.

the idea of a women's university, providing phrases such as 'sweet girl-graduates', which stood for proper and ladylike figures whose intellectual achievements were unthreatening.[92]

Although women's colleges at Oxford and Cambridge were more than twenty years in the future when *The Princess* was published, concern about low standards in girls' education in the late 1840s did result in the founding of colleges for women. If the education of middle-class girls was to be systematically improved as that of boys had already been, the first step was to ensure that governesses and schoolmistresses were well educated. In London, Queen's College was established by tutors from King's College, including Tennyson's friend F. D. Maurice, and funded by the Governesses' Benevolent Institution; amongst the first students were Dorothea Beale and Frances Mary Buss, later famous as the pioneering headmistresses of Cheltenham Ladies' College and the North London Collegiate. Elizabeth Reid (a Unitarian) founded Bedford College (in Bedford Square, London) as a non-Anglican alternative in 1849. Prominently associated with these two colleges were writers such as Jean Ingelow, Anne Adelaide Procter, and Dinah Mulock Craik, as well as those who would take the lead in establishing women at Cambridge, Anne Jemima Clough and Emily Davies.[93] Early students at Bedford College who were instrumental in founding women's colleges at Oxford and Cambridge included Barbara Leigh Smith (later Madame Bodichon), who was Florence Nightingale's cousin and a friend of George Eliot, and Anna Swanwick, the translator of Aeschylus, who attended mathematics and Greek classes.

Women in London, therefore, were comparatively well provided for from 1849 onwards, especially after the University of London (free of the residence requirements and centuries of tradition which contributed to the slowness of change at Oxford and Cambridge) was the first to make women completely equal and admitted them to full membership in 1878, a move which was quickly followed by provincial and Scottish universities. Even before the formal opening of universities to women students, some were able to join classes: A. Mary F. Robinson (1857–1944) read classics at University College

[92] Stephen, *Emily Davies*, 148.
[93] Bremner, *Education*, 128.

from 1875 to 1878 (she was said to be the only woman who took the advanced Greek course) and later published a translation from Euripides in *The Crowned Hippolytus* (1881).[94] Women could also go to the Ladies' Department of King's College, where most students were 'living at home, desirous of working up certain subjects in which they feel an interest'.[95] Virginia Woolf (1882–1941) attended Greek classes at King's College before being taught at home by Dr George Warr, Clara Pater, and Janet Case. 'Michael Field'—Katherine Bradley (1846–1914, who was for a short time one of the first students at Newnham College, Cambridge) and Edith Cooper (1862–1913)— studied at University College, Bristol, which offered day and evening classes including Greek and Latin. Changes were slowly taking place within more traditional institutions, as Charles Eyre Pascoe's overview of the situation in 1879 suggests: women could attend many of the public, intercollegiate lectures at Cambridge (for example, those of classics professors B. H. Kennedy and J. E. B. Mayor), or lectures for women by Jebb (English), Henry Sidgwick (Latin), and R. D. Archer-Hind (Greek).[96] What was lacking for these women was the uninterrupted time for study and the camaraderie that college residence offered male undergraduates; it was rare for women writers born before the 1880s to live in college and pursue full-time degree courses for three years.

In *Jude the Obscure*, Hardy famously critiques the snobbery of 'Christminster' and the established Church which demands classical learning of its ministers; he suggests that in some ways it is easier for a woman to circumvent the system which officially excludes her by means of a personal relationship with a member of the university. Sue Bridehead, as an unmarried woman living with an undergraduate, does not gain access to libraries, attend lectures, or learn classical languages, yet by reading in translation she acquires a wider knowledge of the classics than Jude, whose labours over the Greek grammar prove futile.[97] This is an important point, since unofficial access

[94] Sylvaine Marandon, 'Duclaux, (Agnes) Mary Frances (1857–1944)', *Oxford Dictionary of National Biography* (Oxford: OUP, 2004), <http://www.oxforddnb.com/view/article/59577>, accessed 3 June 2005.

[95] Bremner, *Education*, 140–3.

[96] Pascoe, *Schools*, 153, 163–4.

[97] Rossen, *University*, 28.

to academic resources was what enabled the sisters, wives, and daughters of scholars to educate themselves and prove that their privileges should be extended to other women. The women who set up girls' schools and women's colleges had undoubtedly been excluded by their gender from membership of public schools, Oxbridge, and the ministry, which were all strongly associated with the classics, yet many of the most remarkable figures came from families involved in these institutions, who considered their daughters no less deserving of a thorough liberal education than their sons. Educational reformers often came from clerical families where education was a priority (Emily Davies, Elizabeth Wordsworth), or from high-achieving families that produced writers (Anne Jemima Clough, Clara Pater), so they had much in common with women writers, who tended to support campaigns for women's higher education.

Women felt passionately about success in traditionally masculine subjects like Greek and mathematics, since for those with brothers of a similar age, awareness and resentment of the gender inequalities in education began early in life. George Eliot's friend Barbara Leigh Smith Bodichon proposed the plan for a college (Girton) at which women would receive the same education as men, fulfilling an intention she had formed in 1848 when her brother went to Jesus College, Cambridge.[98] Emily Davies argued for the establishment of a women's college 'to meet the wants of the two thousand sisters of the two thousand undergraduates of Cambridge.'[99] The issue of sibling rivalries in education was prominent in literary culture because of the compelling representation of sisters attempting to keep up with their brothers in fictions like *The Daisy Chain* and *The Mill on the Floss*, which still reflected girls' lives more than half a century after the publication, and a century after the setting, of Eliot's novel. These reformers drew on their own experiences of intellectual frustration based on gender to improve the education offered to younger women. Augusta Webster deprecated the idea of women of her own

[98] Pam Hirsch, *Barbara Leigh Smith Bodichon 1827–1891: Feminist, Artist and Rebel* (London: Chatto & Windus, 1998), 31. Bodichon's protégée Hertha Marks, the model for Mirah in *Daniel Deronda*, studied Greek and Latin at Girton (278).
[99] Stephen, *Emily Davies*, 175.

generation going to the new women's colleges, claiming that they would be like 'Atalanta stopping and groping for a golden apple instead of spending her strength on the race she is running ... they will always be the weaker for the want of training in due time, but it would be worse than futile to track back for it too late'.[100] Webster was concerned to see women's higher education achieved on equal terms with that of men. She wrote articles pointing out the anomalous position of women students at Cambridge in the 1870s and warning the supporters of women's education that no kind of equality could be achieved while an examination 'comes as a polite attention on the part of the examiners and on their part a voluntary heroism: to undergo it is in itself a distinction'.[101]

The 'Girton Pioneers' were at the forefront of the movement for women's education, preceding Oxford by a decade (although Cambridge did not admit women to full membership until 1948). 'As the first university-based college for women, Girton occupied a particularly strong emblematic space', comments Sally Mitchell.[102] Girton receives more attention than any of the other Oxbridge women's colleges in periodicals like *Lady's World*, a shilling monthly which, concerned with fashion and the leisure occupations of 'High Society', also had a regular section recording women's achievements in education, art, science, and literature and another on 'The Lives of Lady Students, Lady Lecturers, &c', designed to familiarize readers with the college setting and to correct misconceptions about women's motives in going to university. In November 1886, M. F. Donaldson writes about a visit to Girton and contradicts the view that studying makes women unhealthy: 'they looked well and happy, with neither the frivolous, giddy look of the ordinary school-girl ... or the objectionable, self-conscious "blue-stocking" '.[103]

Greek is the key intellectual achievement of the Girton Girl in the popular imagination. Andrew Lang's 'Ballade of the Girton Girl' describes the typical Girton student as 'learned in Latin and Greek' (2) although he patronizingly rehearses the old jibe 'In her accents,

---

[100] Augusta Webster, *A Housewife's Opinions* (London: Macmillan, 1879), 103–4.
[101] Ibid. 92.
[102] Mitchell, *New Girl*, 52.
[103] M. F. Donaldson, 'A Day at Girton College', *Lady's World* (Nov. 1886), 143.

perhaps, she is weak | (Ladies *are*, one observes with a sigh)' (5–6).[104]
She publicly demonstrated the classical learning which earlier women
had kept in a domestic context, and this is one of the characteristics
which attracted the most mockery. Although there is no Girton
Girl figure in *She* (1887), Lang's friend H. Rider Haggard seems to
express male anxieties about losing control of this valuable cultural
territory to women, and fears that it might not prove to have intrinsic
value at all. The narrator is an eminent classical scholar at Cambridge, but his laboriously acquired Greek cannot match Ayesha's
experience of speaking Greek and Latin as living languages: that she
can cap every learned allusion to ancient history from her own
memory is merely a tiny part of her power, and one she does not
particularly prize. Women quickly learnt to fight the Girton Girl
image, or claim that it was outdated. In the very popular *Ships that
Pass in the Night* (1893), Beatrice Harraden (who studied classics and
mathematics at Bedford College) has her heroine remark that the
type is now redundant, although she is still recognized as a pioneer.
Again, the signifier of her intellectual achievement is Greek: ' "The
Girton girl of ten years ago," said Bernadine, "was a sombre, spec-
tacled person, carelessly and dowdily dressed, who gave herself up to
wisdom, and despised everyone who did not know the Agamemnon
by heart ... She fought for women's right to education, and I cannot
bear to hear her slighted." '[105]

The Girton Girl often resembles a George Eliot heroine who has
been given the access to education which her women characters
tragically lack. Sally Ledger comments that Eliot's heroines could be
'construed as embryonic New Women', and Chris Willis notes that an
education at Girton is 'the stock attribute of the intellectual New
Woman of popular fiction'.[106] This association is strengthened by
Eliot's links with the college, to which she donated money and books.

[104] *The Poetical Works of Andrew Lang* (London: Longmans Green, 1923),
i. 189–90.
[105] Beatrice Harraden, *Ships that Pass in the Night* (London, 1893), 168–9.
[106] Sally Ledger, *The New Woman: Fiction and Feminism at the Fin de Siècle*
(Manchester: Manchester UP, 1997), 2. Chris Willis, ' "Heaven Defend me from
Political or Highly-Educated Women!": Packaging the New Woman for Mass Consumption', in Angelique Richardson and Chris Willis (eds.), *The New Woman in
Fiction and in Fact: Fin-de-Siècle Feminisms* (Basingstoke: Palgrave, 2001), 55.

Yet the connection was not always beneficial: the atmosphere of sexual impropriety attached to Eliot and (later) to the New Woman gave anti-feminists the opportunity to condemn higher education for women on moral grounds. In Grant Allen's *The Woman who Did* (1895), when Herminia Barton (educated at Girton) refuses to marry her lover, she gives Mary Shelley and Eliot as examples of women who have lived in free unions. She is described as a tragic heroine who risks everything for a man who is not worthy of her. In New Woman fiction as in Eliot's novels, Greek, and especially tragedy, stands for (often disastrous) intellectual aspirations: Herminia is a serious and unpopular novelist and the author of an edition of *Antigone* used at Girton and Somerville. Her principles ultimately lead to her suicide, an act of 'Iphigenia-like ... self-imposed sacrifice' which enables her aggressively conventional daughter to marry. Achieving the tragic self-destruction which heroines like Dorothea Brooke narrowly avoid, on her deathbed she looks like a 'saint of the middle ages', a martyr from whose grave 'shall spring glorious the church of the future'.[107]

The continuing centrality of the classics at Oxford and Cambridge raised issues about assimilation and the appropriateness of training women to excel in a traditionally masculine classical curriculum that was already under threat from reformers. The two women's colleges at Cambridge initially exemplified different approaches to the problem of claiming a place for women in universities.[108] Newnham was more closely allied to a wider project of university reform, and promoted the new courses in modern languages, philosophy,

---

[107] Grant Allen, *The Woman who Did* (London: John Lane, 1895), 26, 240. In Victoria Crosse's riposte, *The Woman Who Didn't* (London: John Lane, 1895), a key to the heroine's character is given by her choice of books: 'Latin authors of the irreproachable order, Martial and his school being missing; Greek seemed represented by Sophocles and only one innocent volume of seductive and reprehensible Plato' (121). It is not ignorance which maintains this woman's 'reposeful innocence', but a careful selection of reading in which the emotional influence of Greek literature is balanced by the rationality of Latin.

[108] See Gillian Sutherland, ' "Girton for Ladies, Newnham for Governesses" ', in Jonathan Smith and Christopher Stray (eds.), *Teaching and Learning in Nineteenth-Century Cambridge* (History of the University of Cambridge, Texts and Studies, 4; Woodbridge: Boydell Press in association with Cambridge University Library, 2001), 139–49.

economics, and history. The authorities at Newnham encouraged women students to do work which would be of use to them as teachers, not to take the Previous Examination (or 'Little-Go', the examination which involved compulsory Greek), necessary for the degrees which women could not officially receive. Emily Davies wanted Girton students to take the Tripos within three years and one term, just like male undergraduates. Girton's policy involved great risks—no woman student had received the kind of training in classics and mathematics on which university examinations were based: they were at a disadvantage which would not be taken into account if they failed, and 'might confirm beliefs about women's intellectual inferiority'.[109] While these pragmatic aims remained dominant, it is perhaps not surprising that the colleges produced only a few notable women writers, yet their impact on literary culture in the late nineteenth century cannot be disputed: there are numerous representations of college girls in fiction and journalism, especially in the 1890s.

From 1879 the Cambridge Tripos was divided into two parts, the first of which concentrated on the traditional elements of classical study, including translation and composition. It was impossible to excel in Part I without doing well in these papers, but to learn verse composition from scratch was too time-consuming for all but the most exceptional candidates, so women's results in Part I were consistently lower than men's until 1887, when Agnata Ramsay was the only candidate to be placed in the first division of the first class. This achievement reached a wider public in a *Punch* cartoon by George du Maurier which depicted her entering a railway carriage marked 'First Class—For Ladies only'. Part II of the course was not required for a degree, and was 'taken by few students, male or female', but contributed to women's successes in the Tripos examinations as they 'were less hampered by their lack of linguistic training and found more scope to excel.'[110] First-class honours and other notable achievements

---

[109] Martha Vicinus, *Independent Women: Work and Community for Single Women 1850–1920* (London: Virago, 1985), 125.

[110] Claire Breay, 'Women and the Classical Tripos 1869–1914', in Christopher Stray (ed.), *Classics in 19th- and 20th-Century Cambridge: Curriculum, Culture and Community* (Cambridge: Cambridge Philological Society, 1999), 48–70.

by women students were described in magazines like L. T. Meade's monthly *Atalanta*, which promoted the cause of women's education by showing its readers the opportunities available to them, with articles on prominent female novelists, artists, and philanthropists, and on girls' schools and women's colleges. The magazine's cover depicted the Greek heroine Atalanta winning a race, an image of success which was well chosen to inspire ambitious girls for whom 'both athletics and classics were key signifiers of their brothers' masculine world'.[111]

JANE ELLEN HARRISON

Educated first by governesses (one of whom learnt German, Latin, and Greek at the same time as her pupil), then at Cheltenham Ladies' College (before Greek was taught there), and finally as one of the first women students at Cambridge, Jane Ellen Harrison (1850–1928) lacked the intensive classical training of her male peers. Although she 'caught up sufficiently to be able to read Greek and Latin fluently and with ease ... she never felt confident when it came to philology'.[112] This contributed to her second class in the Tripos (although she got first-class marks in philosophy) and her decision to concentrate on archaeology, which she studied and lectured on for the next twenty years at the British Museum. Like other women writers, she realized that attempting to catch up in the narrowly linguistic version of classical studies was pointless, and developed a new approach to the subject, informed by 'a rare kind of imaginative flair that has been denied to many persons with a firmer grasp of Greek grammar and of systematic thinking'.[113] Her knowledge of Greek could be supplemented through friendship and collaboration with male scholars who were sympathetic to her feminism and her radical ideas about

---

[111] Mitchell, *New Girl*, 12.

[112] Robinson, *Life*, 38.

[113] Hugh Lloyd-Jones, 'Jane Ellen Harrison, 1850–1928', in Edward Shils and Carmen Blacker (eds.), *Cambridge Women: Twelve Portraits* (Cambridge: CUP, 1996), 32.

ritualism, such as Gilbert Murray, whose translations and interpret-ations of Euripides she quotes in her work.[114] Although she was able to study and lecture in London, Harrison's undergraduate studies at Newnham in 1874–9 (the college was founded in 1871) and her position as the college's first Research Fellow from 1898 emphasize how much her career depended on a very recent institution. This is underlined by one of the most notable incidents in what Mary Beard describes as the 'Harrison mythology': her meeting with George Eliot at Newnham.[115] It is possible to imagine Eliot, had she been born thirty or forty years later, in Harrison's place as a student whose energies would be directed into classical scholarship rather than journalism and then fiction.

A New Woman who contributed to the continuing importance of Greek as a symbol for women's achievement of intellectual equality with men, Harrison was 'the first English woman to make a name in classical scholarship ... not only a scholar and a pioneer in scholar-ship, but something of a literary artist'.[116] She showed that it was not only in poetry and fiction that women could make use of their distance from the traditional methods of classical learning. By applying the increasingly fashionable methods of archaeology, an-thropology, and psychology to what had formerly been an almost purely literary discipline, she influenced the study of Greek religion, although her opinions attracted ridicule from some male scholars and have remained controversial.[117] In books such as *Myths of the Odyssey in Art and Literature* (1882) and *Prolegomena to the Study of Greek Religion* (1903), she discussed anthropological evidence which could explain mythology in terms of primitive religious ritual, not poetic imagination. She focused on a matriarchal culture preceding the worship of the Olympian gods and delighted feminists with her 'descriptions of Zeus and the Olympians as a version of the Victorian patriarchal family', an institution she hoped would be superseded by communities on the collegiate model.[118] Harrison believed that a

---

[114] Prins, 'Maenads', 69–70.

[115] Beard, *Invention*, 8–9.

[116] Lloyd-Jones, 'Jane Ellen Harrison', 29.

[117] See Shelley Arlen, ' "For Love of an Idea": Jane Ellen Harrison, Heretic and Humanist', *Women's History Review*, 5 (1996), 165–90.

[118] Jane Marcus, 'Critical Response, I: Quentin's Bogey', *Critical Inquiry*, 11 (1985), 488.

female community fostered artists and scholars: in the magazine *Woman's World* (previously *Lady's World*, renamed under Oscar Wilde's editorship), she discussed the role of collegiate life in reviving the social instincts which had allowed Sappho to flourish in 'a woman's world'—the reference to the magazine's title suggests that the female readership forms a kind of intellectual community.[119] *Woman's World* strikingly accommodates the apparently disparate groups of socialites and scholars by combining gossip, fashion, and fiction with more serious material on women's lives in various countries and periods of history, including ancient Greece, Rome, and Pompeii.

Harrison's impact on a wider literary culture has mainly been examined in relation to Virginia Woolf, who published Harrison's *Reminiscences of a Student's Life* (1925) and portrayed her as an inspirational figure for women in *A Room of One's Own*. Linking Harrison with Ariadne, an important mythical figure for Woolf (and one who was erased from James Joyce's version of the Daedalus myth), Carolyn Heilbrun observes 'she provided the thread through the labyrinth of Greek myth to her fellow scholars, Frazer, Murray, Cornford and others'.[120] It is worth considering her in the context of earlier Victorian women writers, since contemporary attacks on her scholarship are reminiscent of the 'lady's Greek' label which had been used to denigrate Elizabeth Barrett Browning. A fervent admirer of Eliot, Harrison humorously claimed that beneath her 'bland cosmopolitan courtesy and culture' lay the provincial conservatism and prejudice of Aunt Glegg from *The Mill on the Floss*.[121] Kate Flint observes that this 'implicitly cautions one against assuming all Eliot's woman readers would automatically identify with Maggie's independent wilfulness', yet in Harrison's anecdote about an aunt who found her reading a Greek grammar and asked her what use Greek would be when she had a home and family of her own, she represents her childhood self as closer to Maggie than to the aunts in Eliot's

---

[119] Jane Harrison, 'The Pictures of Sappho', *Woman's World* (Apr. 1888), 275.

[120] Carolyn G. Heilbrun, *Hamlet's Mother and Other Women* (New York: Columbia UP, 1990), 66.

[121] Jane Ellen Harrison, *Reminiscences of a Student's Life* (London: Hogarth Press, 1925), 11–12.

novel.[122] As a scholar in her own right, Harrison offered younger women a more positive (although still conflicted) alternative to Eliot's influential narratives about intellectual women. In the context of women writers, the most distinctive feature of her career is her freedom from family and domestic anxieties—as a professional classicist, she did not have to decide between Greek and sewing. She commented on the 'miracle' of escaping marriage, which 'for a woman at least, hampers the two things that made life to me glorious—friendship and learning ... Family life has never attracted me. At its best it seems to me rather narrow and selfish; at its worst a private hell.'[123] This last sentence could easily have come from Florence Nightingale's *Cassandra*; the opportunity to live in a community of learned women, where learning and teaching Greek was not only acceptable but a duty to the college, saved Harrison some of the bitterness and guilt which rebellious Victorian daughters suffered.

GREEK TRAGEDY IN THE UNIVERSITIES

The 1880s saw a remarkable number of performances of Greek drama, particularly in universities. Between the Balliol *Agamemnon* of 1880 (which inspired George Eliot to begin rereading Greek tragedy with her husband J. W. Cross, a project interrupted by her death) and the OUDS *Alcestis* in 1887, productions included Sophocles' *Ajax* (1882) and *Electra* (1883), Aristophanes' *Birds*, and Aeschylus' *Eumenides* (some of which were performed in English). Women were initially active in the production of classical drama, and the planned performance of Sophocles' *Electra* at Newnham in 1877 would have been the first of the university Greek plays if Anne Clough had not cancelled it because she feared alienating the Cambridge ladies, who might be scandalized by 'the bare flesh that was to be on view, not to mention the dubious morality of young ladies playing male parts'.[124] This was typical of the caution which

---

[122] Flint, *Woman Reader*, 229.
[123] Harrison, *Reminiscences*, 88.
[124] Beard, *Invention*, 47.

was repeatedly manifested by the authorities at women's colleges. They were aware that any hint of impropriety would not only reflect badly on the college but damage the reputation of educated women. However, after the first Cambridge Greek Play by men (*Ajax*, 1882), Girton responded the following year with *Electra*, an 'alternative, female appropriation of Sophocles' with three main female characters and a chorus of women.[125] The choice of a Sophoclean play with strong heroines seems particularly appropriate considering Girton's connections with George Eliot.

Woman's World responded to the popularizing of Hellenism in the 1880s with reviews such as 'Greek Plays at the Universities' in January 1888, which claimed that the representation of Greek plays in England had become 'so common that one naturally seeks some justification for it'.[126] There were also new entertainments with ancient Greek settings, such as *The Tale of Troy* (1883) a selection of scenes and tableaux from Homer with costumes and scenery designed by eminent artists—Leighton, Poynter, Alma-Tadema, Burne-Jones, and Millais. These tableaux connected Hellenism with the higher education of women, since they raised funds for a permanent site for the Ladies' Department of King's College, London. There were four performances, two in English and two in Greek: Jane Harrison played Penelope in the Greek version.[127] In Oxford, Jowett would not permit male undergraduates to represent female characters, so Harrison played Alcestis in 1887.[128] However, scruples about displaying flesh or cross-dressing did not prevent the development of the Greek Play in Cambridge when performed by an all-male cast (after Janet Case as Athena in the *Eumenides* in 1885, there were no women until 1948).

Women students were allowed to attend performances, and often brought texts so that they could follow the Greek. Having seen Sophocles' *Electra* and Aeschylus' *Eumenides* in Cambridge, the

[125] Edith Hall, 'Sophocles' *Electra* in Britain', *Sophocles Revisited: Essays Presented to Sir Hugh Lloyd-Jones*, ed. Jasper Griffin (Oxford: OUP, 1999), 291. Janet Case, who played Electra, later taught Greek to Virginia Woolf.
[126] A Graduate of Girton, 'Greek Plays at the Universities', *Woman's World* (Jan. 1888), 121.
[127] For *The Tale of Troy*, see Beard, *Invention*, 37–44.
[128] Ibid. 48–50.

Woman's World reviewer concludes that the Sophoclean play 'has a better chance of awakening the interests of a modern audience' because it is 'intensely human'. Although (like George Eliot in her article on Antigone) she concedes that it is difficult for the nineteenth-century audience to sympathize with Greek religious ideas, she claims not only that the plays of Sophocles retain their appeal for a modern audience, but that the qualities of tenderness and pathos are actually enhanced by the 'modern imitative method of acting'. The *Eumenides* certainly seems to have been more difficult to appreciate: M. V. Hughes emphasizes the cultural appeal of the Greek Play, the financial sacrifice, and the disappointment involved for those who could not follow the Greek. Although well educated, she and her fellow students were not equipped to understand the play: 'Throughout the performance disappointment, anger, and boredom seized me in turn. That anything Greek could be so dull was my first surprise; then as it got still duller, anger at the loss of mother's good ten shillings took the field; then boredom overcame all other feelings, at last became unbearable, and I fell asleep.'[129] One woman counted the Furies and found that there were fourteen, the same number as the students at their college, so they adopted this name for themselves (113). This identification with a group of female characters is interesting, as the shift from single heroines such as Medea or Antigone suggests that collegiate life encouraged women to see themselves as deriving power from the group, rather than the individual. As Yopie Prins has observed, the Bacchae or Maenads were important symbols for women students, figures who appeared 'to subvert the social order but also sustained it'.[130]

OXFORD AND THE DECLINE OF CLASSICS

For women born in the first half of the nineteenth century who could only study the classics privately at home, there was no more potent symbol of the classical culture from which they were officially

---

[129] Hughes, *A London Girl*, 112.
[130] Prins, 'Maenads', 49.

excluded than an Oxford degree. Once women began to encounter classical literature in more formal educational settings, to sit in classrooms and lectures, to analyse grammatical structures, and to write prose and verse compositions, Greek and Latin lost some of the allure they had possessed for the ambitious Victorian girl. The gradual broadening of the Oxford curriculum did not succeed in displacing the classics from their position of dominance in the education of the privileged male, but a decline in the prestige of the classics in the early years of the twentieth century led Vera Brittain to observe that classical study could safely be left to women during the First World War because it had become unimportant. As early as 1922, two female Oxford graduates were describing classical education as an irrelevance in the modern world: 'The classical point of view is one of those "lost causes" for which Oxford has become a byword.'[131]

Oxford was never in the forefront of the movement for women's higher education (the first colleges for women were established ten years later than Girton) and developed in a pattern of gradual and comparatively smooth integration.[132] One of the most important developments in women's education was the creation of residences for women from outside Oxford; women students were treated as daughters subject to the strictest rules of Victorian propriety, a model which imposed constraints on women students well into the next century. The women's colleges at Oxford, like those at Cambridge, developed in two directions. The Girton approach, to prove that women were entitled to degrees by demonstrating that they could succeed in the established curriculum, was followed in Oxford by Somerville. The more ladylike reputation of Newnham was shared by Lady Margaret Hall (LMH), where it was felt that 'higher education should never supersede the claims of domestic life'.[133] St Hugh's was designed as a cheaper version of LMH, which would produce church

---

[131] Muriel St Clare Byrne and Catherine Hope Mansfield, *Somerville College 1879–1921* (London: OUP, 1922), 83.

[132] See Janet Howarth, ' "In Oxford But ... Not of Oxford": The Women's Colleges', *The History of the University of Oxford*, vii. *Nineteenth-Century Oxford, Part 2*, ed. M. G. Brock and M. C. Curthoys (Oxford: OUP, 2000), 237–307.

[133] Vera Brittain, *The Women at Oxford: A Fragment of History* (London: Harrap, 1960), 36.

workers and schoolmistresses, just as Keble produced parsons and schoolmasters, and the students were largely daughters of parsons, doctors, solicitors, and schoolmasters.[134]

Lectures for women were first organized by a committee of academics and new wives in 1873, the year after the statute which permitted Oxford dons to marry; the Latin and Greek lectures were given by Henry Nettleship. There was a separate women's examination in which Greek and Latin were optional and papers in English literature and modern languages could be taken (neither of these was yet a degree subject for men). However, women found that their separate qualifications were not taken seriously by employers, and they campaigned for the right to sit the official degree examinations.[135] The relevant exams were gradually opened to women during the 1890s, but no degrees were awarded to women until 1920. As with the women's suffrage movement, progress in the campaign for women's degrees would probably have been slower without the increasing freedom and responsibilities experienced by women during the First World War. At the beginning of the Michaelmas Term of 1914, writes Vera Brittain, 'two months of World War had altered Oxford more drastically than six centuries of change': the majority of male undergraduates had joined up and the university was overwhelmingly female.[136] Somerville's buildings became a hospital for officers, and many of the women students were rehoused in Oriel College. This relocation and the newly prominent position of women within the university gave them an opportunity to experience what

---

[134] Penny Griffin, *St. Hugh's: One Hundred Years of Women's Education in Oxford* (Basingstoke: Macmillan, 1986), 8, 20.

[135] Caroline Winterer notes that whereas in Oxford separate classical examinations were set for women students, by 1885 'Greek and Latin language requirements to Harvard and Bryn Mawr were identical (translations of Caesar's *Gallic War*, Virgil's *Aeneid*, and Xenophon's *Anabasis*)'. The process of achieving 'classical equity' between men and women appears to begin later and conclude earlier in America than in Britain, yet there is a similar fall in the value of the classics in both countries: women achieved 'classical equity' in America 'just as classicism's importance in the political, intellectual and cultural life of America was declining'. Caroline Winterer, 'Victorian Antigone: Classicism and Women's Education in America, 1840–1900', *American Quarterly*, 53 (2001), 85–7. See also Caroline Winterer, *The Culture of Classicism: Ancient Greece and Rome in American Intellectual Life, 1780–1910* (London: Johns Hopkins UP, 2002).

[136] Brittain, *Women*, 136.

Oxford was like for men. The college authorities, however, made sure that they continued to observe strict rules, so that no accusations of impropriety could damage their cause. After the war, the issue of degrees for women, who had kept the university going both financially and academically, as tutors and students, was far less controversial than it had been.

Few women took the full set of examinations required for an Oxford classical degree, although most were required by their colleges to pass the preliminary exams: Responsions (nicknamed 'Smalls') in the second term, which tested Latin and Greek grammar, Latin prose composition, Latin unseens, and mathematics; Moderations ('Mods') in the fifth term (including Divinity Mods—passages for translation from the Greek Gospels), for which prose composition and reading a minimum of one Greek and one Latin author were required—verse composition was optional, and few students attempted this part of the exam.[137] Somerville, where a scholarly atmosphere was cultivated, achieved notable success: in 1888 Elizabeth Hodge's First in Mods led to women being admitted to the Honour School of Literae Humaniores, in which she obtained a Second in 1890. Emily Penrose (later Principal of Somerville) came to Oxford at the age of 31 with no Latin and a little modern Greek, 'prepared for the Final School unimpeded by preliminaries, and in 1892 became the first woman to win a First in "Greats".[138] One student from LMH became the subject of a limerick which indicates her success in verse composition:

> I go every day to the crammer,
> And he marks all my verses with 'gamma';
> While that girl over there
> With the flaming red hair,
> Gets 'alpha plus' easily,—her![139]

---

[137] Robert Currie, 'The Arts and Social Studies, 1914–1939', *The History of the University of Oxford*, viii. *The Twentieth Century*, ed. Brian Harrison (Oxford: OUP, 1994), 110. Richard Jenkyns, 'The Beginnings of Greats, 1800–1872: Classical Studies', *The History of the University of Oxford*, vi. *Nineteenth-Century Oxford, Part 1*, ed. M. G. Brock and M. C. Curthoys (Oxford; OUP, 1997), 513–20.

[138] Brittain, *Women*, 85.

[139] Gemma Bailey, *Lady Margaret Hall: A Short History* (London: OUP, 1923), 54.

Despite these successes, it was a struggle for most women to achieve the required standards in grammar, prose composition, and textual study (all of which their male contemporaries had been practising for years at school) and they had to be coached by their colleges. Dorothy L. Sayers's description of the work for Responsions gives an impression of rapidity and violent efforts to accomplish a task so nearly impossible that the Somerville students almost become the heroes of the ancient literature they read: she describes her tutor as

the indefatigable seagull, forever winging his way through the clashing rocks of Latin Prose and Greek Unseens with a fleet of dismal and inexperienced Argonauts thrashing the seas at his tail ... In two terms he accomplished what my school-teachers had not ventured to undertake in four years. We pounded our way through the Hecuba and the Alcestis; we coped with the Aorist; we mowed down under our feet that weedy growth of repulsive particles with which the Greek language is infested.[140]

Although the majority of women students were not studying classics, they were interested in classical topics. At LMH a literary society was established to 'mitigate' the 'evil' of people only discussing their own subjects.[141] At Somerville there were several classically influenced entertainments, such as the 1904 masque *Demeter*, written by Robert Bridges, and the Second Year Plays of 1908 and 1912: 'Horace at Athens' and Gilbert Murray's translation of Aristophanes' *Frogs*. Murray himself gave lectures to the college's Literary and Historical Society, such as 'English Imitations of Greek Poetry' in 1909, and Emily Penrose lectured on Greek and Roman architecture as well as directing an 'Athenian Trial' in 1910.[142] Hostility to the higher education of women was expressed in periodicals such as the *Oxford Magazine* through gibes at the industry and unattractiveness of women students. Prevented from responding publicly, they gained satisfaction by composing ripostes which could be shared by the readers of journals such as *The Daisy*, an LMH magazine. One example is 'The Eminent Professor and the Diligent Student'

[140] Dorothy L. Sayers, *The Poetry of Search and the Poetry of Statement* (London: Gollancz, 1963), 183.

[141] 'Literary Society', *The Daisy*, 9 (1891), 2–3.

[142] Pauline Adams, *Somerville for Women: An Oxford College, 1879–1993* (Oxford: OUP, 1996), 118.

(1890), which highlights the reputation of male undergraduates for idleness, suggesting that they relied on cribs to understand 'the mysterious and awful tongue of the Romans'.[143] Another issue of this magazine contains an article purporting to be a translation of part of a poem by Homer, in which travellers seek the 'temple, sacred to grey-eyed Athene, wherein the maidens of this land are wont to learn all manner of wisdom and knowledge'—Lady Margaret Hall. The travellers enquire of an 'aged handmaiden' (the goddess in disguise) about the maidens' lives and the wisdom they acquire in the temple.[144] This 'translation' demonstrates that the stereotypes which are found in twentieth-century novels about women's colleges were already fixed by the early 1890s—in novels such as Vera Brittain's *The Dark Tide* and Rosamond Lehmann's *Dusty Answer*, the candidate who overworks before finals is punished with failure and a nervous breakdown, while the heroine achieves a First by balancing work and leisure.

Literary responses to the classics by Oxford women in the late nineteenth and early twentieth centuries are mediated by their chosen subjects and clearly influenced by their awareness of their position within a masculine institution. Those who intended to pursue careers in literature usually chose to read English or Modern History rather than Literae Humaniores, but they still had to study Latin and Greek for preliminary examinations.[145] Since aspiring writers such as Rose Macaulay, Vera Brittain, and Dorothy L. Sayers had to study classical texts like the *Iliad* and the *Aeneid* in the original languages, intensively acquiring the literary background which their masculine contemporaries had absorbed more slowly at school, this policy had a discernible influence on twentieth-century women's

[143] U.T., 'The Eminent Professor and the Diligent Student', *The Daisy*, 3 (1890), 6.

[144] A.M.S., 'Fragment of a lost MS', *The Daisy*, 7 (1891), 3–4.

[145] Few women writers read classics—those who did include Ivy Compton-Burnett (1884–1969) and Richmal Crompton (1890–1969), both at Royal Holloway College. See Heather Ingman, *Women's Fiction between the Wars: Mothers, Daughters and Writing* (Edinburgh: Edinburgh UP, 1998), 6; Patrick Lyons, 'Burnett, Dame Ivy Compton- (1884–1969)', *Oxford Dictionary of National Biography* (Oxford: OUP, 2004), <http://www.oxforddnb.com/view/article/32524>, accessed 3 June 2005; Mary Cadogan, 'Lamburn, Richmal Crompton (1890–1969)', *Oxford Dictionary of National Biography* (Oxford: OUP, 2004), <http://www.oxforddnb.com/view/article/34386>, accessed 3 June 2005.

literary culture. There was a notable decline in poetry which makes
use of classical figures and idioms in women's magazines like *The
Fritillary*, an inter-collegiate women's magazine, in the early years of
the twentieth century, the result of prevailing literary fashions as
much as of the small number of female classicists. Introducing the
1910–13 volume of *Oxford Poetry*, Gilbert Murray noted 'a few
touches of classicism, but that is almost more out of fashion at the
Universities than elsewhere'.[146] As the First World War progressed,
the classical literature which influenced poets in the trenches also
drew Oxford poets back towards classicism, before a decisive post-
war rejection of epic models of heroism.

[146] Gilbert Murray, introduction to G. D. H. Cole, G. P. Dennis, and W. S. Vines
(eds.), *Oxford Poetry, 1910–1913* (Oxford: Blackwell, 1913), p. xiv.

3

'Unscrupulously Epic'

Elizabeth Barrett Browning has been described as 'the most scholarly woman poet of the nineteenth century'.[1] It is important to note that her own aspirations were consistently focused on a poetical rather than a scholarly career: she later claimed that her wish to learn Greek had been 'a child's fancy', and that she studied the language 'for Homer's sake ... that is for poetry's generally'.[2] The image of Barrett as a scholarly female poet and classicist was self-consciously created by R. H. Horne in *A New Spirit of the Age* (1844). Horne commented on her literary productions and flatteringly linked her to the tradition of aristocratic female scholars rather than the figure of the 'bluestocking': 'Letters and notes, and exquisite English lyrics, and perhaps a few elegant Latin verses, and spirited translations from Æschylus ... frank correspondence with scholars, such as Lady Jane Grey might have written to Roger Ascham'.[3] Barrett complained of inaccuracies in Horne's representation, and denied his report of her proficiency in Latin verses, which confirms that even the most 'scholarly' of women writers had little experience of and possibly little inclination for this traditional method of forming a gentlemanly literary taste. Horne finds it necessary to defend Barrett against the charge of 'ungenial pedantry' by pointing out that her reading of the classics is balanced by more typically feminine reading matter: 'there is probably not a single good romance of the most romantic kind

[1] Wallace, 'E.B.B.', 329.

[2] *The Letters of Elizabeth Barrett Browning to Mary Russell Mitford, 1836–1854*, ed. Meredith B. Raymond and Mary Rose Sullivan (Waco, Tex.: Armstrong Browning Library of Baylor University, 1983), i. 340.

[3] R. H. Horne, *A New Spirit of the Age* (1844) (New York: Garland, 1986), ii. 133.

in whose marvellous and impossible scenes she has not delighted' (ii. 135). This combination is significant, and it points towards Barrett Browning's most successful poetry, which draws on ancient epic and modern romances; her epic aspirations culminate in *Aurora Leigh*, a verse *Bildungsroman* about a woman poet which claims such diverse texts as *Jane Eyre* and the *Iliad* as predecessors and models.

Barrett's considerable achievements in the classics belong to the poetic tradition of Romantic Hellenism (she had little interest in Latin), and it is not surprising that she was interested in Prometheus, 'an often invoked self-image among the Romantic poets', who features in poems by Goethe, Shelley, and Barrett's childhood hero, Byron.[4] Her best-known scholarly works are her two translations of *Prometheus Bound* (the first in 1833, and the second completed in 1845 and published in 1850).[5] Alice Falk describes Barrett's first attempt at translating *Prometheus Bound* (written in a fortnight) as a 'reasonably accurate, readable, almost line-for-line verse translation of the least easily translated Greek tragedian'.[6] The few contemporary responses were almost entirely negative, and patronized the translator by declaring that it was not her fault if a woman could not resolve problems which baffled male scholars. However, it was a different kind of failure that preoccupied Barrett, and she wrote to Mary Russell Mitford: 'It is not *scholastically* that I am so ashamed of it ... but poetically. It is correct enough as far as the letter goes'. She felt that the translation was 'unfaithful to the genius if servile to the letter of the great poet'.[7] Barrett withdrew the first translation from circulation, and later attempted a less literal and more poetic version

---

[4] Anne K. Mellor, *Mary Shelley: Her Life, her Fiction, her Monsters* (London: Routledge, 1988), 71.

[5] Her other published translations include poetry by Bion, Anacreon, Sappho, Theocritus, and Homer, most of which were written for a projected 'Classical Album', which was to be 'modelled on the popular keepsakes of the day' and therefore 'faintly amatory and attractive to women'. This mode of publication is more usually associated with poets like Hemans or L.E.L., who needed the financial support provided by such ventures. See Wallace, 'E.B.B.', 333–4.

[6] Alice Falk, 'Elizabeth Barrett Browning and her Prometheuses: Self-Will and a Woman Poet', *TSWL* 7 (1988), 72.

[7] *E.B.B. to M.R.M.*, i. 338–9; *BC* v. 297 n. 4. Mitford appears to have been largely self-educated through voracious reading after leaving school at 15. Apart from her most famous work, the sketches of country life collected in *Our Village* (1824–32),

which emphasized the hero's Christ-like self-sacrifice and suffering. This second translation of the play, Robert Browning's response to it, and the continuing discussion in their subsequent correspondence are crucial to both poets' ideas about translation and originality, as Yopie Prins demonstrates. For Elizabeth Barrett and Robert Browning, as for Percy and Mary Shelley, Greek is 'their special language of desire', and *Prometheus Bound* a key text: 'they increasingly translate Aeschylus' text into the context of their courtship' and ultimately 'invoke Aeschylus' drama of rebellion to justify eloping together'.[8] Lorna Hardwick observes that the poets' figuring of Barrett as Prometheus, with her father as the tyrannical Zeus, 'suggests that Elizabeth Barrett saw her translation work and its reception by critics as emblematic of the restriction she suffered in her personal life'.[9] This identification with a rebel against tyranny is much closer to the image Barrett projects in her early writing than her later persona as the Andromeda of Wimpole Street, rescued from her tyrannical father by means of a secret marriage with Browning in 1846. Neither of her translations of the *Prometheus* was regarded as definitive, but her choice of a play which 'dramatises issues of obligation, community, freedom, tyranny and the oppression of women'[10] may

she was a tragedian whose plays were performed at Covent Garden and Drury Lane with actors such as Kemble and Macready in the title roles. Her plays were influenced by ancient drama—in 1821 she reviewed a production of Euripides' *Orestes*, performed in Greek by pupils at Reading School: Edith Hall, 'Greek Plays in Georgian Reading', *Greece & Rome*, 44 (1997), 59, 70–2. She exchanged opinions on Greek tragedy with Barrett, concentrating on the content of the play rather than the linguistic elements. One of the texts they wrote about was Sophocles' *Philoctetes*, an unconventional tragedy with a hero who is stranded on an island and immobilized by a wound. Barrett could not agree with Mitford's elevation of the play to the status of tragic masterpiece: 'The defect of that play is that it is founded upon physical suffering, and its glory is that from the physical suffering is deduced so much moral pathos and purifying energy' (*BC* iv. 18). However, the combination of confinement, enforced passivity, and hidden power recalls Barrett's interest in Prometheus, and has obvious resonances for Victorian women who sought to transcend their physical and spatial limitations by writing.

[8] Yopie Prins, 'Elizabeth Barrett, Robert Browning and the *Différance* of Translation', *VP* 29 (1991), 435–7.

[9] Hardwick, *Translating Words*, 32.

[10] Hardwick, 'Women', 183. Adrienne Munich comments that some male writers (such as Keats and Robert Browning) replaced Prometheus with Andromeda as a figure for poetry or the poet: Adrienne Munich, *Andromeda's Chains: Gender and Interpretation in Victorian Literature and Art* (New York: Columbia UP, 1989), 10.

have influenced later women writers: despite the difficulty of translating Aeschylus' language, Augusta Webster and Anna Swanwick
produced versions of *Prometheus Bound*.[11]

CLASSICAL EDUCATION

Barrett's classical reading compares with that of Percy Shelley, who
also did most of his Greek reading outside school and university.[12]
Her diaries and letters refer to many authors, including Euripides,
Sophocles, Virgil, Callimachus, Epictetus, Isocrates, Meleager, and
Moschus. Her translations include authors who were not usually
studied in the nineteenth century, such as Theocritus and Nonnus,
and in her essay on the Greek Christian poets (1842) she deliberately
moves away from the classical canon to discuss Hellenistic and
Byzantine literature. The dominance of Greek authors reflects her
Romantic distaste for the secondariness of Latin literature, and
especially of the poetry of the Augustan period. Interestingly, Norman
Vance demonstrates that an earlier Roman poet, Lucretius, 'both

---

[11] Webster's attempt to give her learning a feminine touch is strongly marked in
her husband's preface: 'The reason why the title-page of this book bears the name of
an Editor as well as that of a Translator is, that my wife wished for some better
guarantee of accuracy than a lady's name could give.' To reassure readers who might
believe that her diffidence was likely to be justified, he continued: 'I have most
carefully compared this translation, line by line, with the original, and am not afraid
to vouch for its conscientious adherence to the letter of the text.' It is interesting that
Webster's translation should be prefaced with an implied doubt that a woman could
translate the play accurately; for all the intellectual humility described in the preface,
the translation was clearly an attempt to surpass Barrett by producing an English
version of the tragedy which could be compared with the Greek 'line by line'. Thomas
Webster, 'Editor's Preface', in Augusta Webster, *The Prometheus Bound of Æschylus:
Literally Translated into English Verse*, ed. Thomas Webster (London: Macmillan,
1866). 'Late Fellow of Trinity College Cambridge', the editor lends academic credibility to his wife's translation.

[12] Critical assessments of Barrett's classical studies include Mary Jane Lupton,
'A Little Hemming and More Greek', in Sandra Donaldson (ed.), *Critical Essays
on Elizabeth Barrett Browning* (New York: G. K. Hall, 1999), 32–7; Dorothy
Mermin, *Elizabeth Barrett Browning: The Origins of a New Poetry* (London: University
of Chicago Press, 1989), 19–21; Marjorie Stone, *Elizabeth Barrett Browning* (Basingstoke: Macmillan, 1995), 19–20.

worried and impressed' Barrett, and influenced 'A Vision of Poets' and 'A Sea-Side Meditation'.[13] As a nature poet, Lucretius could be assimilated to Barrett's Romantic aesthetic more easily than the Virgil of the *Aeneid* (although Barrett, like Mary Shelley and Sara Coleridge, seems to have enjoyed the *Georgics*).

The variety of references to the ancient world in *Aurora Leigh* reflects the poet's extensive self-education in the classics. The writers mentioned include Theophrastus (also a favourite with George Eliot), Plato, Pindar, Aeschylus, Horace, and uncanonical authors such as Longus, Plotinus, Aelian, and Proclus. It would be misleading to suggest that *Aurora Leigh* simply represents Barrett Browning's recollections of studying the classics, but the poem offers an insight into what a woman with poetic ambitions might feel about her relationship to the masculine literary tradition. The heroine is first initiated into the mysteries of Latin and Greek by her father. After his death, she receives a conventional feminine education at the hands of her aunt, until she rediscovers her father's books and begins to reacquaint herself with ancient authors because of their sentimental connections:

> I read much. What my father taught before
> From many a volume, Love re-emphasised
> Upon the self-same pages: Theophrast
> Grew tender with the memory of his eyes,
> And Aelian made mine wet ...

$$(1.\ 710–14)^{14}$$

Aurora's intensely emotional reaction to Greek texts, which is not a response to the content of the books but the memories that they evoke, resembles Barrett's own descriptions of learning Greek with her brother Edward ('Bro'). As a child, she received much encouragement to write and study, and a letter from her mother suggests that she took an active interest in her children's studies, questioned the purpose and the methods of the accepted system of classical education, and oversaw at least the routine grammatical part of their Latin lessons: 'I am surprised to find that Sams Latin exercise consists of merely *Copying* from the grammar ... Stormy is making

---

[13] Vance, *Rome*, 98–9.
[14] Elizabeth Barrett Browning, *Aurora Leigh*, ed. Margaret Reynolds (Athens, Ohio: Ohio UP, 1992).

[progress] in the most advanced stage of exercises on the united noun adjective & verb, which he writes very correctly.'[15] When Bro had a tutor who taught him Latin and Greek as a preparation for public school, Barrett (aged about 12) shared his lessons. Bro's departure for Charterhouse interrupted her brief experience of a boy's classical education, presented sentimentally in an autobiographical essay in which Barrett completely erases the gender difference between the two scholars:

Together we have conversed, read, studied—together we have fagged at the grammar, wept over the torn dictionary—triumphed over classical difficulties & reaped the glorious reward of perseverance—success! If there be any ties stronger than these, I know not of it! Let the cold reasoner scoff but let those who have perused together the Roman & Greek Classics, and who have together resisted difficulties of style & language decide whether or not our attachment be founded on folly—![16]

Although this idyllic relationship was over, they continued to share information on classical topics through their letters and Barrett continued her studies at home, although without a tutor. Apparently more sympathetic towards his sister's desire for knowledge than others like Hartley Coleridge, Bro explained details of school routines and the principles of composition in hexameters, and was willing to pass on his learning so that she could continue to compete with him, even though she would inevitably fall behind in the compositional tasks which were a daily routine for schoolboys. Instead of attempting to keep pace with her brother, Barrett found a new interest in the work of Sir Uvedale Price, 'a classical scholar of European renown', who admired her *Essay on Mind* and asked her to criticize his book, *An Essay on the Modern Pronunciation of the Greek and Latin Languages*.[17] Their correspondence is full of learned allusions and detailed notes on metre. Her next mentor was a blind scholar-poet, Hugh Stuart Boyd, in relation to whom she has been characterized as 'a living amalgamation of Dorothea Brooke and Milton's daughters'.[18] However, unlike these women, Barrett could

[15] Mary Moulton-Barrett to E.B.B., [Dec. 1821], *BC* i. 139.
[16] 'My Character and Bro's Compared', *BC* i. 358.
[17] Barbara Dennis, *Elizabeth Barrett Browning: The Hope End Years* (Bridgend: Seren, 1996), 79.
[18] Ibid. 80–1.

understand and discuss the Greek texts she read aloud, which included Homer, Aeschylus, and the Greek Christian poets. The strongly emotional tone of her writing about studying the classics with Bro is found again in her accounts of Boyd.

Barrett later found that her approach to Greek had not been systematic enough to enable her to teach schoolboys what they needed to know. In 1831, she writes of reading Aeschylus for her own interest and at the same time learning basic verbs in order to teach: 'It certainly was disgraceful that I who can read Greek with some degree of fluency should [have] been such and so long an ignoramus about the verbs. And besides, I have done what *Mr. Boyd wished*.'[19] Barrett associated Greek grammar with male scholars and did not think it an essential requirement for the understanding of Greek texts, which was her primary use of the language. As the comment about learning verbs to please Boyd suggests, he led her to take a 'more orthodox approach to classical texts, trying to conform through attention to grammar and linguistic detail'.[20] This is the most 'scholarly' period in her study of the classics, and Boyd tried to stimulate her in the direction of more traditional scholarship by nicknaming her 'Porsonia', after Richard Porson, the textual critic and editor of Euripides. She did some work on Greek accents, but emphasized that her motivation for learning Greek was more connected with literature than with scholarship: 'With regard to your questions,—I intend to give up *Greek*, when I give up *poetry*; &, as Porson said on a case equally decided,—"*not till then*". Tho' I never become a critical scholar, I may continue to enjoy the divine poetical literature, for whose sake I encountered her language'.[21]

Barrett's remark that critical scholarship is not the only worthy use of Greek studies, and the conflict between her aims in learning Greek and those of the men she studied with, recalls the allusion in *Aurora Leigh* to 'lady's Greek | Without the accents' (2. 76–7).[22] Whatever

---

[19] *Diary by E.B.B.: The Unpublished Diary of Elizabeth Barrett Barrett, 1831–1832*, ed. Philip Kelley and Ronald Hudson (Athens, Ohio: Ohio University Press, 1969), 23–4.

[20] Wallace, 'E.B.B.', 338–9.

[21] E.B.B. to Hugh Stuart Boyd, 23 Apr. 1827. *BC* ii. 56.

[22] 'The letters of Shelley, Peacock, and Robert Browning reveal that men were equally content to drop accents when quoting Greek out of school.' Falk, 'Lady's Greek', 91.

Aurora's shortcomings in Greek composition, her understanding of and responses to classical literature clearly place her in a different tradition from the scholastic one Romney is trying to uphold, and the poetic tradition is implicitly seen as superior. Barrett wrote to Mary Russell Mitford: 'It puts me out of all patience to see people glorying, evidently however silently, in the multitudes of grammars, when the glorious rich literature of our own beloved England lies by their side without a look.'[23] She became increasingly concerned about the usefulness of conventional classical scholarship, based on grammar and largely ignoring content, as a training in literary appreciation. She believed that women should learn to think actively and to love literature by reading the Elizabethan poets, and only study the classics for reasons connected with poetry, writing to Anne Thomson in 1845: 'Perhaps I do not (also) partake your "divine fury" for converting our sex into Greek scholarship, and I do not, I confess, think it as desirable as you do.'[24] Barrett felt that she had spent too much time trying to become a linguist in her youth, and moved away from the classics as she became interested in writing poetry which would engage with contemporary issues such as the mistreatment of child workers in factories and the Risorgimento in Italy. Aurora Leigh undergoes a similar change, and sells most of her father's classical texts (retaining those with the most sentimental associations) to finance her journey to Italy. Classical allusions gradually decrease in Barrett Browning's poems after the mid-1840s, with a strong resurgence in *Aurora Leigh* (1856) and a final treatment of the Pan myth in 'A Musical Instrument' (1860). However, the most significant effect of Barrett's immersion in classical studies is to be found in her revisions of the epic tradition, from *The Battle of Marathon* (1820) to *Aurora Leigh.*

GENDER AND GENRE

Barrett's early strategy of identifying herself with the male tradition in poetry by imitating poets such as Pope and Milton was partly inspired

---

[23] *E.B.B. to M.R.M.*, i. 340.
[24] E.B.B. to Miss Thomson, *The Letters of Elizabeth Barrett Browning*, ed. Frederic G. Kenyon, 2nd edn. (London: Smith Elder, 1897), i. 260.

by her wish to be received as a 'poet' and not a 'poetess': in terms of the classical tradition, she aspired to the universality of Homer rather than the lyric pre-eminence of Sappho. She produced close imitations of the masterpieces of the masculine canon: 'in composing epics, verse-dramas, and long philosophical-didactic poems, the poet was deliberately violating the existing norms governing the relationship between gender and genre'.[25] However, Aurora Leigh's dismissal of her 'lifeless imitations of live verse' as 'effete results | From virile efforts!' (1. 974, 984–5) probably represents Barrett Browning's assessment of these early poems as less subversive in terms of gender than they were intended to be. The status of Sappho's poetry, both as an example of the acceptably feminine genre of love lyric, and as a fragmentary text, had made it a less intimidating model for women writers than epic. Barrett initially rejected this model of poetry because the melodramatic emphasis on suffering, abandonment, suicide, infanticide, and release through death had been mocked by Byron.[26] Christina Rossetti identifies with the Sapphic tradition of Hemans and L.E.L., as well as satirizing it in 'What Sappho Would Have Said Had Her Leap Cured Instead of Killing Her' (1848). In response to her brother's description of her treatment of Homeric themes in 'The Lowest Room' (1856) as 'falsetto muscularity', she differentiates herself from Barrett Browning by claiming an 'inability' to write 'a classic epic'.[27] Interestingly, Rossetti's sister Maria (who had taught herself Greek from her brothers' textbooks) was closer to Elizabeth Barrett in reading Euripides and in having a passion for 'all things Homeric': her grandfather Gaetano Polidori read the Greek legends with her in Italian and connected his family's name with Polydorus, the son of Priam.[28]

---

[25] Deborah Byrd, 'Combating an Alien Tyranny: Elizabeth Barrett Browning's Evolution as a Feminist Poet', in Donaldson (ed.), Critical Essays , 206.

[26] See Susan J. Wolfson (ed.), Felicia Hemans: Selected Poems, Letters, Reception Materials (Oxford: Princeton UP, 2000), esp. pp. xiii–xxiv.

[27] Christina Rossetti, The Complete Poems, ed. R. W. Crump and Betty S. Flowers (London: Penguin, 2001), 934. C.R. to Dante Gabriel Rossetti, 10 [Feb. 1865], The Letters of Christina Rossetti, ed. Antony H. Harrison (London: UP of Virginia, 1997), i. 226.

[28] Jan Marsh, Christina Rossetti: A Literary Biography (London: Pimlico, 1995), 29.

Recent critics of Barrett Browning's poetry have constructed a narrative of poetic development starting from her youthful imitation of canonical male poets, moving towards a self-consciously female poetics which is influenced by nineteenth-century women novelists and deals with modern life, and finally combining the two tendencies in *Aurora Leigh*, authoritatively rewriting the masculine genre of epic from a woman poet's point of view. In placing Barrett Browning in relation to male poets, and particularly the major Romantics, Marjorie Stone adapts both Bloom's concept of the 'anxiety of influence' and feminist revisions which see a women poet as suffering from 'anxiety of authorship'. Stone observes that from 1820 to 1844, Barrett is like the male 'strong poets' described by Bloom, struggling with predecessors like Milton and displaying a remarkable 'audacity of authorship' which she never entirely lost.[29] There is some disagreement as to the decisive moment in Barrett Browning's shift to female identification. Deborah Byrd perceives Barrett's emulation of women poets such as Hemans and L.E.L. in the late 1830s as the 'first step towards transforming herself into a woman-identified poet', by composing poems in which female characters act assertively and independently.[30] The 1844 volume participates in both male and female traditions, but ends with an apparent rejection of the classical tradition in poetry. The final poem in this collection, deliberately placed in that position for emphasis, 'The Dead Pan' (inspired by John Kenyon's translation of Schiller's *Die Götter Griechenlands*) shows the 'gods of Hellas' losing their powers after the death of Pan (which is identified with the death of Christ on the cross) and being replaced by the Christian God. The refrain 'Pan is dead' shifts from a lament by the classical gods to the joyful proclamation of the Christian poet.[31] Alice Falk notes that although 'The Dead Pan' apparently signals a determination to leave behind classical themes and concentrate on modern life, Barrett Browning's second translation of *Prometheus Bound* followed it; in Falk's opinion *Sonnets from the Portuguese* is the 'crucial' poem in 'Barrett

---

[29] Stone, *E.B.B.*, 55.
[30] Byrd, 'Combating', 203.
[31] Margaret M. Morlier, 'The Death of Pan: Elizabeth Barrett Browning and the Romantic Ego', in Donaldson (ed.), *Critical Essays*, 258.

Browning's development of her voice as a female subject'.[32] Dorothy Mermin points out that the overall shape of Barrett Browning's career is remarkably similar to that of Tennyson: both began by writing 'dreamy, self-enclosed verse and mediaevalizing and apparently escapist narratives', both published long confessional lyric sequences in 1850, wrote controversial political poetry, and dealt with contemporary issues in new kinds of epics.[33] In terms of gender, Tennyson's development might be seen as the mirror image of Barrett Browning's: from his early lyrics (influenced by Sappho) with their 'feminine' preoccupation with deserted heroines, through public, political, and military themes, to the combination of both in *The Princess* (1847) and *Idylls of the King* (1859–85).[34] Poets of both sexes had an uneasy, yet potentially liberating, relationship to dominant gender ideologies in the Victorian period; poetry seemed inimical to the rigid structures of bourgeois masculine culture.

Rather than attempting to identify a shift from male to female identification, it is interesting to note Barrett's playful approach to the intersections of gender and genre, most particularly in the traditionally masculine genre of epic. It is significant that the male poets Barrett chose as models had in some way overcome obstacles (physical or social) to their achievement of poetic fame. Homer and Milton, whose poems inspired *The Battle of Marathon* and *A Drama of Exile*, were both blind; Barrett later claimed that in her seclusion from real life she too had been a blind poet. Pope's physical weakness enforced a domestic existence and he was labelled 'effeminate'; he (as a Catholic) was debarred from a university education on the grounds of religious affiliation (as was Robert Browning, a Nonconformist).[35] Their examples might offer encouragement to

[32] Falk, 'Lady's Greek', 85.

[33] Mermin, *E.B.B.* 2.

[34] Catherine Maxwell reads *The Princess* as 'an allegory of male poetic development, where in order to achieve his goals the Prince has to impersonate a woman and to enter the specifically female space of Ida's University': *The Female Sublime from Milton to Swinburne: Bearing Blindness* (Manchester: Manchester UP, 2001), 108.

[35] Pope's *Iliad*, intended as a guide to manliness, may have been intended to save Pope from the charge of effeminacy by creating a place for him in the 'transmission of classical literature [which] enacts the patriarchal elitism it teaches'. Carolyn D. Williams, *Pope, Homer, and Manliness: Some Aspects of Eighteenth-Century Classical Learning* (London: Routledge, 1993), 60.

a young poet who wanted to overcome the restrictions imposed on her by her gender.

A valuable insight into the ideas behind Barrett's 'audacity of authorship' and the fluid notions of gender that inform her poetry throughout her career is provided by her autobiographical essays. In 'Glimpses into My Own Life and Literary Character', Barrett outlines the beginning of her poetic career and gives some information about her childhood reading: 'at 8 I perused the History of Greece and it was at this age that I first found real delight in poetry... Popes "Illiad" [sic] some parts of the "Odyssey" passages from "Paradise lost" selected by my dearest Mama'.[36] This essay, mainly written when Barrett was 14 and later expanded to include her fifteenth birthday, is crucial to an understanding of her relationship to the classical tradition, since she comments on the writing techniques she developed in childhood, which were to dominate her work for much of her career. She first enjoys and then rejects literature associated with pleasure, particularly novels by women, and chooses to read and write in genres which are regarded as more serious and prestigious. At 9, Barrett aspires to be a novelist, and finds 'gratification' in 'works of imagination'; by the time of writing the essay, she feels 'conscientious scruples' about 'wasting time in frivolous pleasures'. At 11 she wishes 'to be considered an authoress', casting aside novels in favour of poetry and essays, and having 'the most ardent desire to understand the learned languages—To comprehend even the Greek alphabet was delight inexpressible'. Barrett Browning's successful combination of these two forms of literature in her later (and to some extent autobiographical) poem, *Aurora Leigh*, may thus be seen as the culmination of a negotiation between feminine and masculine literatures which dominates her poetic career.

The essay significantly shows Barrett trying out a number of literary roles, only one of which is scholarly. In her reading, as early poems like *The Battle of Marathon* and *A Drama of Exile* suggest, the emphasis is very much on the epic tradition, with 'Shakespeare & Novels' as her other main interests. Barrett's audacity is visible in her reiterated desire to 'gain the very pinnacle of excellence', to outdo her models (i. 351). With internalized standards of excellence derived

---

[36] *BC* i. 350. Further references are given parenthetically in the text.

from the masculine literary tradition, she feels more than equal to the epic poet's task of rewriting and outdoing the work of predecessors. When writing *The Battle of Marathon*, she comments, she compared a page of her own writing to Pope's *Iliad*, confident that her poem was the superior, but on reading the two she realized her 'immense & mortifying inferiority'. With this release from 'vanity' and 'ridiculous dreams of greatness' came an obsession with Homer (in Pope's translation) which lasted for a year: 'From this period for a twelvemonth I could find no pleasure in any book but Homer. I read & longed to read again and tho I nearly had it by heart I still found new beauties & fresh enchantments—' (i. 351). This concentrated reading of Pope's translation certainly affected Barrett's perception of Homer, although she was reading the *Iliad* and Virgil's *Aeneid* in the original languages by the age of 14.

'THE FEMININE OF HOMER … A LITTLE TALLER THAN HOMER IF ANYTHING'

In an essay about a girl called Beth with poetical ambitions, Barrett declared that she aspired to the status of the first great woman poet: 'As Homer was among men, so w^d she be among women—she w^d be the feminine of Homer' (i. 361). Beth's aspiration is humorously elaborated—she will be 'a little taller than Homer if anything', will either live on a Greek island and teach the islanders ancient Greek or live in a cave on Parnassus and drink from the Helicon. Beth is also to be a warrior, and to have a poet, probably Byron, as her lover. Beth chooses to measure herself against Homer because he is considered the first and best of poets, but she aims at a relative, gendered version of his greatness. The most obvious way to rival Homer was to write an epic, but 'the feminine of Homer' would perhaps wish to highlight the position of women in a society of heroes, to redefine heroism in a way that would allow women to achieve this ideal, and to condemn and perhaps replace stories of war and violence. Barrett Browning uses these approaches in several poems: *The Battle of Marathon*, 'Hector and Andromache', *Casa Guidi Windows*, and *Aurora Leigh*.

It is helpful to think of epic as a 'tradition' rather than a 'genre', an approach which allows for variations in form, to avoid classifying epic writing into 'subgenres' or 'antigenres', since the most striking fact about epic poetry is the poets' constant attempts at innovation.[37] Ancient epic establishes three main elements: the heroic ideal, which is interrogated by the poet from Homer's *Iliad* onwards; the creation or rebuilding of a myth of national identity; and the formal features such as the twelve-book structure, hexameter verse, epic formulae, the narrative set pieces such as the visit to the underworld, and extended similes. The idea of a tradition embraces mock-epic uses of these elements and their reworking within other literary forms. Among the long poems of the nineteenth century, Words-worth's *Prelude* (published posthumously in 1850), Tennyson's *Idylls of the King* (1859–85), Barrett Browning's *Aurora Leigh* (1856), and Browning's *The Ring and the Book* (1868–9) were envisioned in relation to the epic tradition. While it is unproductive to claim that these poems are epics like those of Homer, Virgil, or Milton, it is profitable to read them as part of a continuing tradition of epic influence that includes ancient epyllion, modern mock-epic, and the novel.

Epic is an obviously gendered literary form: the political content of epic and its focus on the father–son relationship are not character-istic of women's writing. Ancient epic was 'composed by men, consumed largely by men, and centrally concerned with men'.[38] There is no poem by a woman writer that can be claimed as an epic in the same way as the *Iliad* or the *Aeneid*, and critics have generally agreed that a woman's epic, if such a thing could exist, would involve radical changes to the heroic ethos of the genre. Mary Ann Stodart wrote that women could not 'pourtray with the vivid power of Homeric song, the horrid din of war' but could 'follow one solitary soldier' and his thoughts of home and family.[39] This kind of concen-tration on an individual's suffering was already a feature of the *Iliad*,

---

[37] See Brian Wilkie, *Romantic Poets and Epic Tradition* (Madison: University of Wisconsin Press, 1965), 3–29. J. B. Hainsworth, *The Idea of Epic* (Oxford: University of California Press, 1991), 5; Alastair Fowler, *Kinds of Literature: An Introduction to the Theory of Genres and Modes* (Oxford: Clarendon, 1982), 175.

[38] A. M. Keith, *Engendering Rome: Women in Latin Epic* (Cambridge: CUP, 2000), 1.

[39] Stodart, *Female Writers*, 86.

occurring in episodes such as Hector's farewell to Andromache (which Barrett Browning translated), a scene which women found one of the most striking in the poem. Another way for women to approach epic was suggested by Samuel Butler, who thought that a woman could have a male hero but 'minimise him' and 'maximise his wife and daughters'.[40] In fact, the women of Troy (as Barrett Browning would have been aware) were not ignored by ancient poets but were central figures in tragedies such as Euripides' *Trojan Women*, *Hecuba*, and *Helen*. A woman's epic, then, might draw on the tragic tradition as George Eliot did and as Virgil had done when he represented the emotional costs imposed by the masculine warrior code in the *Aeneid*. Aeneas saves his father and son from the burning city of Troy, as he must in order to fulfil his destiny, but loses his wife—a loss that is mirrored with a more deeply tragic colouring in the fate of Dido.

In distancing the *Iliad* from the masculine literary tradition in which it was embedded, Barrett drew on the translation of the poem which had obsessed her as a child. Pope was not an inhibiting predecessor, since his example suggested that imperfect classical scholarship might produce a poem which would become a classic in its own right. He was clearly indebted to the work of a woman: Anne Dacier, a Greek scholar to whom he pays tribute in the Postscript to the translation. He relied on the collaboration of university-educated men, particularly in composing the critical apparatus surrounding the text, but also in the translation: he 'had

---

[40] Samuel Butler, *The Authoress of the 'Odyssey': Where and When She Wrote, Who She Was, The Use She Made of the 'Iliad', And How the Poem Grew Under Her Hands* (London: A. C. Fifield, 1897), 114. Butler identified the 'authoress' with Nausicaa because he felt that her character and the court of Alcinous had been depicted with the greatest affection and enthusiasm. When he lectured the Fabian Society on the topic 'Was the *Odyssey* written by a woman?', George Bernard Shaw agreed that female authorship was evident within the first hundred lines of the poem: Peter Raby, *Samuel Butler: A Biography* (London: Hogarth, 1991), 244–5. Recent feminist criticism emphasizes that the female narrators within the poem (the Sirens, Helen, Penelope) retard the forward movement of the poem and pose a threat to the narrative's focus on Odysseus; their stories 'are contained within larger narrative frameworks that do not allow them the last word'. Lilian E. Doherty, 'The Snares of the Odyssey: A Feminine Narratological Reading', in S. J. Harrison (ed.), *Texts Ideas, and the Classics: Scholarship, Theory, and Classical Literature* (Oxford: OUP, 2001), 130.

to take the finer textual and grammatical points on trust'.[41] His version of the *Iliad* inspired a notoriously condescending remark from the classical scholar Richard Bentley, later caricatured in Pope's *Dunciad*: 'it is a pretty poem, Mr Pope; but you must not call it *Homer*'.[42] In producing the translation Pope was threatening the aristocratic male's monopoly on classical knowledge, much as the bluestockings did. Helen Deutsch comments that Pope was participating in a 'mass-marketing of culture' which made high culture, and particularly classical literature, 'accessible to women and other middle-class readers'.[43] The translation was very popular with women readers, and was greatly admired by Lady Mary Wortley Montagu (who recommended that girls learn Latin and Greek because they had so much time to fill, but cautioned her granddaughter to conceal her learning as solicitously as she might hide a physical handicap).[44]

In her first epic endeavour, *The Battle of Marathon*, written in the style of Pope's *Iliad*, (published when she was 14) Barrett adopted a masculine persona and attempted to mimic Pope very closely. Her youthful erudition was helpful, in that it enabled her to make this move before she was old enough to be labelled a 'woman poet'. *The Battle of Marathon*, although the poem's title-page showed that the author was not only female but a young child, was confidently introduced as an epic, addressed by a masculine poet to a male audience and identifying hero and poet: 'He who writes an epic poem must transport himself to the scene of action; he must imagine himself possessed of the same opinion, manners, prejudices and belief; he must suppose himself to be the hero he delineates'.[45] Barrett's 'act of homage to male values and culture' promotes the

[41] Anne Dacier produced French prose translations of the *Iliad* (1711) and *Odyssey* (1716). She occupied a prominent position in the 18th cent., having edited and translated several Greek and Latin texts; her comprehension of Homer's Greek was unprecedented. See Williams, *Pope*, 68–70, 147–9.

[42] Samuel Johnson, *Lives of the English Poets*, ed. George Birkbeck Hill (Oxford: Clarendon, 1905), iii. 213 n. 2.

[43] Helen Deutsch, *Resemblance and Disgrace: Alexander Pope and the Deformation of Culture* (London: Harvard UP, 1996), 66.

[44] Williams, *Pope*, 167.

[45] Elizabeth Barrett Browning, *The Battle of Marathon: A Poem* (1820), ed. H. Buxton Forman (London: 1891), p. xiii.

ideal of a young man willing to die for his country, and presents few challenges to epic convention.[46] However, there are heroic females in the poem, notably Delopeia, whose speech to the Greek commander combines pathos and patriotism, as she begs him to resist for the sake of Athens and for the children who will grow up to be heroes like him. In this speech, Barrett negotiates between the desire for victory and the emotion of the mother who dedicates her sons to a cause in which they may die: 'Thus thro' her griefs, the love of glory broke, | The mother wept, but 'twas the Patriot spoke' (2. 755–6). This is a remarkable anticipation of a theme which dominates Barrett Browning's poetry about the Italian Risorgimento, especially the second part of Casa Guidi Windows and 'Mother and Poet'.

Although there is no obvious source for Delopeia's speech in the Iliad, Barrett's emphasis on the consequences of war for women and children is enabled by Homer. Apart from the extended similes, which famously incorporate the peacetime world into the Iliad, there are scenes which emphasize the domestic life that war denies, such as Hector's poignant farewell to his wife and baby son, whose future is endangered by the certain death to which the heroic code is to lead Hector. This scene appears to have had a greater resonance for women writers than any other in the Iliad.[47] The Trojan princess Andromache meets Hector at the city gates and begs him not to go and fight outside the walls but to remain and defend the most vulnerable part of the city. She foretells Hector's death, recounts the losses she has already sustained at the hands of Achilles and reminds him that he is all the family she has left. Hector replies that he could not behave like a coward, although he already believes Troy to be doomed and knows that Andromache will become a slave to one of the Greek heroes. The baby Astyanax is frightened by his father's plumed helmet, so the parents laugh at him and Hector takes it off, before praying to Zeus that his son will be an even greater hero

[46] Mermin, E.B.B., 24.
[47] e.g. Anna Jameson wrote that 'The Iliad ... wearied me, except the parting of Hector and Andromache, in which the child, scared by its father's dazzling helm and nodding crest, remains a vivid image in my mind': Sanders (ed.), Records of Girlhood, 85. For Vera Brittain's response to this scene, see Ch. 6.

than his father. After the prayer, he sends his wife back to the women's quarters and returns to the conflict in which he will eventually be killed. Mihoko Suzuki reads this farewell scene and Hector's subsequent death as condemnation both of the heroic ideology of personal glory (which is often achievable only by death), and the 'separate spheres' principle which polarizes human activity into men fighting and women weaving.[48] For a Victorian poet, the inadequacy of an ideal of heroism based on conflict and the challenging of a rigid division of work along gender lines have obvious contemporary resonance; Barrett Browning's treatment of these themes in *Casa Guidi Windows* and *Aurora Leigh* will be examined later. Barrett's blank verse is more literal than Pope's balanced and stately couplets but uses equally self-consciously literary diction:

> Achilles the divine,
> *He* slew my father, sacked his lofty Thebes,
> Cilicia's populous city, and slew its king,
> Eëtion—father!—did not spoil the corse,
> Because the Greek revered him in his soul,
> But burnt the body with its dædal arms,
> And poured the dust out gently.
>
> (20–6)

When Andromache returns to the women's quarters, she is described as looking backwards, with tears falling from her 'reverted face' (116–17). The word 'reverted' suggests a connection with one of the few scenes in Latin literature which seem to have made an impression on Barrett. In the *Aeneid*, when Aeneas encounters Dido in the underworld among those who have committed suicide, he protests that he could not help leaving her because he was fated to do so. Dido averts her gaze and stares at the ground while he speaks, *illa solo fixos oculos aversa tenebat* (6. 469), and then walks away without replying. Barrett thought that this much-praised episode actually demonstrated Virgil's lack of judgement, since she could not imagine a woman remaining silent in Dido's circumstances.[49]

---

[48] Mihoko Suzuki, *Metamorphoses of Helen: Authority, Difference, and the Epic* (Ithaca: Cornell UP, 1989), 4.

[49] E.B.B. to Hugh Stuart Boyd, 3 Mar. 1828, *BC* ii. 107–8.

'MOTHER AND POET'

There was an obvious counterpart to Dido's story in the narrative of the Risorgimento, the death of Anita Garibaldi, which is described with great pathos in Harriet Hamilton King's *The Disciples* (1873), and even more strikingly in *Casa Guidi Windows* (1848–51), where the unborn child's instinctive revulsion from the violence of the world draws the mother towards death. In the arrival of the hero from far away, the sudden, intense passion, and the tragic sacrifice of the heroine to the hero's high destiny, which is the founding (or refounding) of Rome and Italy, the story of Garibaldi and Anita resembled that of Aeneas and Dido. Yet if Anita's death appeared initially to fit the Dido pattern, if she was sacrificed to the Italian cause, a woman poet did not have to accept that the death of a mother was a marginal event in the story of the Risorgimento. In *Casa Guidi Windows*, a poem in which mothers and children are poets and prophets of liberty, the simply narrated death of a mother and child is as disturbing as the death of a hero in epic. It may seem that there is little resemblance between ancient epic and Barrett Browning's valorization of women who do not fight, but her poetry reflects women's readings of classical epic and writings of war.

The events she describes appeared to invite an epic treatment, yet the impossibility of reproducing the long-outmoded classical form in a contemporary situation, however fraught with epic possibility, demanded ingenuity. Italy's 'narrative of national resurgence and redemption'[50] was easier to celebrate in heroic terms than Britain's industrial dominance. The Risorgimento made a significant impact on intellectual life in England through the work of writers from Byron and Shelley to Swinburne and Meredith. 'Epic' is a recurrent adjective in accounts of Italy's part in the revolutions which swept across Europe in 1848–9, particularly in relation to the events in Florence and Rome. Battles with foreign invaders, the siege of a great city, a homecoming from exile, a hero who had travelled and fought in strange lands, and the founding of a new state, all

---

[50] David Quint, *Epic and Empire: Politics and Generic Form from Virgil to Milton* (Princeton: Princeton UP, 1993), 360.

contribute to an epic reading. Poetic discourses on the status of Rome, the creation of a national consciousness for a united Italy, and the construction of a new kind of hero to lead the state, inevitably challenged comparison with ancient epic, and particularly with Virgil's *Aeneid*.

The uprisings in major Italian cities were observed and documented by English writers—Barrett Browning, watching a demonstration from Casa Guidi, her home in Florence, and Arthur Hugh Clough, like the protagonist of his poem *Amours de Voyage* (1858), a tourist caught up in the revolution in Rome. Aware that there was little accurate information available to their correspondents in England, they found themselves writing historical records of the events, which were later to feed into poems. As a forerunner of the revolutions which swept Europe in 1848, the Brownings witnessed a demonstration in Florence on 12 September 1847, a celebration of political concessions made by the Austrian monarch of Tuscany. Inspired by this demonstration, Elizabeth Barrett Browning, already a celebrated poet, exploited and endangered her public position for the sake of Italy as her hero Byron had for Greece, and was attacked in Britain for the poem's unfeminine subject matter.[51] Barrett Browning was meditating a new development in the epic tradition: the woman's epic or verse novel. If this was an epic moment in European history, she might be expected to exploit her unique proximity to it. Yet, despite the epic situation, *Casa Guidi Windows* does not employ what, even using the term loosely, could be considered epic form. Like Clough in *Amours de Voyage*, Barrett Browning invokes ancient epic only to demonstrate how out of place the heroic code, based on the values of an aristocratic warrior society, would be in the modern world, and to provide a context for the examination of other forms of heroism. Barrett Browning and Clough realized that they were competing with the popularity of the novel, and responded by adapting a subdued epic impulse into new forms. Barrett's definition of epic in the preface to *The Battle of Marathon* had suggested that the poet must identify with 'his' hero, must be at the scene of action and share the thoughts of those present. Looking down from her window, she does not identify with a hero, because she cannot find one.

<hr />

[51] Mermin, *E.B.B.*, 163.

The leader she wants for Italy is not a Homeric warrior but a Carlylean hero. He is an imaginary construct rather than someone she expects to see from her window. In the first part of the poem (1848), the liberal Pope is a possible hero, but the second part of the poem (1851) is disillusioned and replaces all hope of a genuine hero with visionary rhetoric.

Barrett Browning emphasizes the traditionally hidden life of women in war, showing them in the roles of mother, nurse, and singer. If the Risorgimento seems uniquely appropriate as a site of epic endeavour in the mid-nineteenth century, it also represents an opportunity for female heroism in the context of war. For a foreign woman living in Italy, the most obvious ways to participate in the Italian struggle were by nursing the wounded, or by writing both private letters and public poetry or articles to draw English readers' attention to the oppression of Italy by foreign forces. Barrett Browning points out that physical bravery is not enough to ensure liberty, and that it is artists and mothers who are the real heroes. Images of children represent hope in *Casa Guidi Windows*, which opens with the poet being inspired by a child singing of liberty, and ends with the Anglo-Florentine mother and son standing in the sunlight. Sandra M. Gilbert suggests that Italy is 'ultimately redeemed by the voices and visions of mothers and children'.[52]

Casa Guidi Windows replaces the father and son relationship of epic with a maternalist point of view that promotes peace, not war. Elizabeth Barrett Browning's 'feminine' war poetry refuses epic's glorying in violence by valorizing qualities associated with peace and regeneration, which are explicitly linked to motherhood. The strong mother figure at the end of the poem contrasts with the weak woman in need of rescue at the beginning (that is, the personified Italia). The mother-poet is herself a hero, the poet who is greater than Homer, because she teaches children—her own son and the people of Florence—how to live in peace. She looks forward to a time when there will be no more fighting. In this ideal moment, she will no longer wish to be the feminine of Homer, because Homer will be not merely equalled, but surpassed:

---

[52] Sandra M. Gilbert, 'From *Patria* to *Matria*: Elizabeth Barrett Browning's Risorgimento', *PMLA* 99 (1984), 200.

> The poet shall look grander in the face
> Than even of old, (when he of Greece began
> To sing 'that Achillean wrath which slew
> So many heroes,')

(1. 731–4)[53]

Barrett Browning does not completely repudiate the ancient world in this poem about contemporary events, but the references are generally brief and simple, not excluding a less educated audience. Opening up the classics to a wider audience, she associates them with childhood enjoyment, not male power and war, by concentrating on mythology:

> Who loved Rome's wolf, with demi-gods at suck,
> Or ere we loved truth's own divinity,—
> Who loved, in brief, the classic hill and brook,
> And Ovid's dreaming tales...

(1. 1193–6)

In *Casa Guidi Windows*, the classics, like the epic actions of the Risorgimento, are domesticated by the woman who stands at the window, safely observing the public world whilst remaining separate from it. This epic moment in Italian history enables the woman poet to assimilate some of the prestige that attaches to epic but looks forward to a new kind of poetry which will be both morally and aesthetically superior to Homeric epic.

'ACHILLES IN PETTICOATS'

Having placed woman, as mother and poet, at the centre of a poem about politics and combat, and made the impossibility of epic heroism not a subject for lament but a hope for a future in which martial prowess will no longer qualify as heroism, Barrett Browning had prepared to write an entirely new kind of epic which incorporated the strengths of the novel and replaced male warrior

---

[53] Elizabeth Barrett Browning, *Casa Guidi Windows*, ed. Julia Markus (New York: Browning Institute, 1977).

with woman poet. This long-meditated poem of modern life, centred around a heroine, was *Aurora Leigh*, which redefines epic by making it more like the novel, the pre-eminent genre for Victorian women writers, and one in which Barrett Browning took a greater interest than male poets like Robert Browning and Matthew Arnold. Like many Victorian novels, the poem is preoccupied with love and the institution of marriage, although the shift in emphasis from the heroine's romantic fortunes to the hero's also allows for a wider range of commentary on women in the nineteenth century, with representatives of different classes being tried out as potential wives. The male protagonist relinquishes his traditionally active character and gains feminine qualities which complement the heroine's masculine attributes: this is the relationship Barrett Browning depicts in *Sonnets from the Portuguese* and at the end of *Aurora Leigh*. A woman poet who has performed many different masculine and feminine voices in a variety of poetic modes, Barrett Browning blurs gender boundaries in her ideal of complementarity, unlike Tennyson, who 'unsettles conventional genre and gender distinctions in *The Princess* only to uncover or reconstitute those he sees as fundamental'.[54]

Following the success of 'Lady Geraldine's Courtship', Elizabeth Barrett planned to write 'a sort of novel-poem' as early as 1844, although *Aurora Leigh* would have been very different if it had been written then: the narrative is clearly indebted to novels such as *Jane Eyre* (1847) and *Ruth* (1853). Barrett Browning claimed that the infliction of blindness on Romney, following the destruction of his house by fire, was not a conscious allusion to Brontë's novel, yet Romney Leigh unmistakably reflects both Rochester and St John Rivers. *Aurora Leigh* also shares the pervasive fire imagery of *Jane Eyre*, including suttee as a symbol of the kind of devotion which Jane rejects as a betrayal of her integrity. Aurora sees Marian's feeling for Romney as a religious adoration which is so different from middle-class views of marriage as a contract implying equality that it can be characterized as self-immolation: 'And certain brides of Europe duly ask | To mount the pile as Indian widows do' (4. 195–6).

[54] Marjorie Stone, 'Genre Subversion and Gender Inversion: *The Princess* and *Aurora Leigh*', VP 25 (1987), 115.

Although Barrett Browning explicitly alludes to the Indian practice of suttee, the image of a woman dying on a funeral pyre may have reminded some readers of Dido. Despite Barrett Browning's dislike of Virgil, she continued to find Dido an interesting figure. Lady Waldemar compares herself to Dido when she tells Aurora how she travelled to Paris to forget Romney, returning from the Champs Elysées (Elysian fields) as a 'ghost, and sighing like Dido's' (3. 473). The allusion casts Romney as Aeneas, a parallel also suggested by his narrative of the fire at Leigh Hall, which resembles Aeneas telling Dido about the burning of Troy, and by his vision of the founding of a new city. At the same time, it is Aurora who journeys by way of the Parisian underworld to Italy and founds a new community there, emulating on a smaller, more human scale the hero's actions in the second half of the *Aeneid*. As in *Casa Guidi Windows*, Barrett Browning's conception of heroism is influenced by Carlyle, this time by his idea of the modern hero as a poet. Although neither Aurora nor Romney is a traditional epic hero, these resonances suggest that their lives are on a grander scale than those usually depicted in modern fiction. Herbert F. Tucker observes that Barrett Browning uses epic conventions to loosen the realist novel's grip on Victorian narrative as a shaper of women's lives.[55] Since its first publication critics have found that *Aurora Leigh* invites the term 'epic' (either as noun or adjective) or that it may be meaningfully compared with the poetry of Homer, Virgil, and Milton. Peter Bayne described it as a 'modern epic', singing not of arms and the man, 'but social problems and the woman'.[56] Comparisons with epic are not always positive: the *Athenaeum* reviewer praised the 'greatest English poetess of any time' for her attempt to 'blend the epic with the didactic novel', but complained that 'we have no experience of such a mingling of what is precious with what is mean … as we find in these nine books of blank verse. Milton's organ is put by Mrs. Browning to play polkas on May-Fair drawing-rooms.'[57]

[55] Herbert F. Tucker, '*Aurora Leigh*: Epic Solutions to Novel Ends', in Alison Booth (ed.), *Famous Last Words: Changes in Gender and Narrative Closure* (London: UP of Virginia, 1993), 62.

[56] Peter Bayne, *Two Great Englishwomen, Mrs Browning and Charlotte Brontë* (London: James Clarke, 1881), 107.

[57] H. F. Chorley, '*Aurora Leigh*', *Athenaeum*, 1517 (22 Nov. 1856), 1425.

Aurora's comments on her attempts at epic and the artistic manifesto she lays out in book 5 invite consideration of Barrett Browning's aims. Epic is a self-reflexive genre: commentary on the role of the poet and the functions of poetry are traditional from the time of Homer. The poet-heroine 'envisions a new epic poetry whose vitality comes from its contemporary focus and realism'.[58]

> Nay, if there's room for poets in this world
> A little overgrown, (I think there is)
> Their sole work is to represent the age,
> Their age, not Charlemagne's—this live, throbbing age,
> That brawls, cheats, maddens, calculates, aspires,
> And spends more passion, more heroic heat,
> Betwixt the mirrors of its drawing-rooms,
> Than Roland with his knights at Roncesvalles...
>
>   Never flinch,
> But still, unscrupulously epic, catch,
> Upon the burning lava of a song
> The full-veined, heaving, double-breasted Age
>
> (5. 200–7, 213–16)

Aurora refuses to believe those pessimists who state that epic has died out along with the myths of ancient Greece, and urges poets to seek out the heroic features of life in 'drawing-rooms' and 'Fleet Street'. Looking back over her poetic career, which includes some of the traditional preparations for epic, such as bucolic poetry, Aurora concludes that poetic greatness will elude her unless she undertakes an epic of modern life. However, she does not commit herself to producing a poem which resembles the conventional form of epic, claiming that the spirit should not be constrained by the form:

> What form is best for poems? Let me think
> Of forms less, and the external. Trust the spirit,
> As sovran nature does, to make the form;
> For otherwise we only imprison spirit
> And not embody.
>
> (5. 223–7)

Since Barrett Browning self-consciously situates the poem in the epic tradition by means of Aurora's observations, the violation of

[58] Susan Stanford Friedman, 'Gender and Genre Anxiety: Elizabeth Barrett Browning and H.D. as Epic Poets', *TSWL* 5 (1986), 210.

epic decorum deprecated by readers like H. F. Chorley must be a deliberate challenge to the reader's expectations of what constitutes an epic. In translating the *Iliad*'s most poignant critique of the culture which valorized personal glory over the preservation of the family, Barrett Browning had rejected the poem's dominant values. If *Aurora Leigh*'s divergence from the *Iliad* is obvious, the poem's closer connections with romantic epic and mock epic are worth exploring. The 'feminine of Homer' seems to have decided to explore those qualities of the *Odyssey* which have led readers to see the poem's resemblance to domestic fiction.[59] The *Odyssey* initiates the substitution of a feminized ethic of domestic virtue for the epic's masculine warrior code, which influences the romance tradition and then the novel. A hero who has escaped death in battle and whose greatest desire is to return home was problematic for those readers who saw the short lives and violent deaths of Hector and Achilles as a glorious example of masculine heroism. Prominent female characters (some of them, like Penelope and the Sirens, artists and figures for the poet) and many domestic scenes 'led to the opinion that much of the *Odyssey* was too low for epic'.[60] Pope's translation often alters descriptions of domestic life and household management to elevate them to an appropriate level for heroic poetry. Samuel Butler described the action of the poem in a way which made it sound like a novel, as if the genre which was to take over many of the functions of the epic in the nineteenth century was already present in one of the earliest epics.

The mock-heroic poetry in which Pope and Byron employ the traditional paraphernalia of epic to a parodic end is also an important influence on *Aurora Leigh*. Their ludic versions of epic conventions suggest that a serious epic may no longer be possible, but they still engage with the tradition and in doing so, they become an important part of it. As a fervent admirer of both poets in her childhood, Barrett Browning inherited a view of the epic tradition which allowed for a critique of the traditional heroic ethos and suggested how it might be translated into modern terms.

---

[59] For a discussion of the novelistic qualities of the *Odyssey*, see John Purkis, 'Reading Homer Today', in C. Emlyn-Jones, Lorna Hardwick, and J. Purkis (eds.), *Homer: Readings and Images* (London: Duckworth, 1992), 11–13.

[60] Williams, *Pope*, 121.

Holly A. Laird suggests that in *Aurora Leigh* epic battles become verbal debates 'in the social arena of women's drawing rooms and in the bookshops of Fleet Street'.[61] If ballrooms and Grub Street are substituted for the Victorian settings, it becomes clear that *The Rape of the Lock* and *The Dunciad* are important predecessors for Barrett Browning's nineteenth-century epic. *The Rape of the Lock* contains epic convention in a poem of a thousand lines, with a card game representing a battle, the loss of a lock of hair instead of a hero's death, and the 'machinery' of sprites instead of the Olympian gods. Although the poem was written before Pope's translation of Homer, critics have noted similarities in the texts. For example, Belinda's dressing for the ball has been compared to Hera's preparations before the seduction of Zeus in *Iliad* 14.[62] Belinda's unsurpassed beauty is equivalent to the supreme valour of Achilles, and her withdrawal from society is comparable to Achilles' refusal to fight. Pope reduces to mock-epic size features such as similes, dream visions, and the journey to the underworld. Such reductions are not always favourable towards the heroine: Christa Knellwolf argues that the Umbriel passage in Canto IV represents women's anger (the wrath of Achilles being the archetypal subject of epic) as 'ridiculous, wrong and unnatural' by rendering it in mock-heroic style.[63] Although Barrett Browning does not use gender reversals and alterations in scale for comic purposes, she seems to have been influenced by 'Pope's transformational tricks', which 'almost always resolve around and figure themselves through gender'.[64] The same could be said of the treatment of Greek myth in *Aurora Leigh*, as when Romney is represented as 'a male Iphigenia' (2. 779), who is to be sacrificed at the marital altar to secure Aurora's share of the family property. Epic conventions are similarly 'revised by gender reversals', such as the catalogue of ships or warriors which is replaced by a 'satiric catalogue of the "accomplishments" taught to young ladies'.[65]

[61] Holly Laird, 'Aurora Leigh: An Epical Ars Poetica', in Sandra Donaldson (ed.), *Critical Essays on Elizabeth Barrett Browning* (New York: G. K. Hall, 1999), 281.

[62] See Alexander Pope, *Iliad I–IX*, ed. Maynard Mack (London: Methuen, 1967), p. ccxliv.

[63] Christa Knellwolf, *A Contradiction Still: Representations of Women in the Poetry of Alexander Pope* (Manchester: Manchester UP, 1998), 143.

[64] Deutsch, *Resemblance*, 77.

[65] Stone, 'Genre Subversion', 126.

Byron's 'Epic Satire' *Don Juan*, 'an infamously impure poem' in terms of genre and gender, characterized by 'social and linguistic cross-dressings', is an important intertext for *Aurora Leigh*.[66] Elizabeth Barrett had pictured herself dressing as a boy and running away to become Byron's page, enticed by 'the prospect of a transvestite emancipation from the restricting dress of femininity'.[67] A more complex gender subversion is invoked when Aurora Leigh compares herself, in learning Greek and Latin, to Achilles, disguised as a girl so that he would not have to fight at Troy:

> And thus, as did the women formerly
> By young Achilles, when they pinned a veil
> Across the boy's audacious front, and swept
> With tuneful laughs the silver-fretted rocks,
> He wrapt his little daughter in his large
> Man's doublet, careless did it fit or no.

> (1. 723–8)

Both Achilles and Aurora are children dressed by their parents in clothes which do not fit them (it was Achilles' mother Thetis who hid him among the women on the island of Scyros). For Aurora, the 'doublet' of a classical education 'covers up and attempts to deny her natural body while at the same time offering her access to an otherwise forbidden world'.[68] The allusion strips Achilles of his bravery and heroic destiny, and associates him with the maternal love and avoidance of war that are central to Barrett Browning's version of epic. Simply by referring to this non-Homeric episode, Barrett Browning makes the comparison between the ancient epic hero and the modern heroine less incongruous than it might otherwise have seemed.

In revising epic tradition, Barrett Browning first employs the obvious strategy of highlighting female characters and pointing out the plight of women in a society which values heroic death in single combat above all other achievements and leaves women and children

---

[66] Susan J. Wolfson, ' "Their She Condition": Cross-Dressing and the Politics of Gender in *Don Juan*', *ELH* 54 (1987), 591–3.

[67] Angela Leighton, *Victorian Women Poets: Writing Against the Heart* (Hemel Hempstead: Harvester Wheatsheaf, 1992), 82.

[68] Wallace, 'E.B.B.' 341.

as the property of the victor. By selecting an episode from the *Iliad* which highlights the pathos of this situation, she begins to interrogate the values of a martial society as expressed in a poem which was one of the central texts of the masculine classical education. By examining these values in a contemporary context, she shows how inadequate they are in the present, and how unsuited to her vision of a future without conflict, in which the feminine imperatives of life-giving and survival will dominate. Finally, in her most consistently epic poem, she uses the techniques of an alternative (more feminine) epic tradition, starting with the *Odyssey*, to suggest that modern heroism lies in domestic life and in building up a new society by means of art, not arms.

4

Classics and the Family in the Victorian Novel

Maggie Tulliver's attempt to follow her brother into the unfamiliar world of classical education is perhaps the most memorable fictional representation of the gender separation performed by Victorian education, and the brother–sister rivalries it produced, but it is by no means the only story that nineteenth-century novelists chose to tell about women's encounters with the classics. Eliot's essay 'Silly Novels by Lady Novelists' (1856) satirizes a conflicting fictional convention which is no longer familiar to novel readers. Heroines in what Eliot calls the '*mind-and-millinery* species' of novel include among their accomplishments apt quotations from classical texts: 'Greek and Hebrew are mere play to a heroine ... she can talk with perfect correctness in any language except English ... In "Laura Gay" ... the heroine seems less at home in Greek and Hebrew, but she makes up for the deficiency by a quite playful familiarity with the Latin classics.'[1] As well as representing a site of competition between siblings in *The Mill on the Floss* and Yonge's *The Daisy Chain*, classical study figures prominently in Victorian fiction as a tie between affec- tionate fathers and compliant daughters, a relationship controlled by the father-tutor whose patriarchal authority is often strengthened by his position as a minister of the Church. Entering into intertextual dialogue with Trollope's *Last Chronicle of Barset* and Anne Brontë's *Agnes Grey*, Elizabeth Gaskell revises this pattern in *Cousin Phillis* by putting it into the context of Dissent. As the previous chapters have

---

[1] George Eliot, *Selected Critical Writings*, ed. Rosemary Ashton (Oxford: OUP, 1992), 299–300.

demonstrated, the support of male relatives was a crucial factor in the provision of classical texts and tuition for those whose education was based in the home, but these novels question the motives of men who teach their daughters to read Greek. Clergy fathers cling to their academic achievements as proof that they are gentlemen in spite of their poverty, a class marker they strive to pass on to their sons and daughters through education. Milton trained his daughters to read to him in languages they did not understand: Eliot reworks their story to fit the situation of a young woman disastrously entering into a marriage with an older scholar to gain access to sources of masculine knowledge such as Greek and Hebrew. What the novelists make clear is that there was a price for being allowed to learn Latin and Greek: the daughter must compensate for her desire to study masculine subjects by giving equal attention to her mother's domestic instruction; she studies only those texts her father chooses to teach her; she will probably be required to use her learning in the service of the family, either by teaching a younger brother or by working as a governess. The conventional opposition of learning and domestic duty is complicated by heroines who see Latin and Greek in pragmatic ways, as part of their duty to maintain the family's status and to increase its income.

BROTHERS AND SISTERS

In Charlotte M. Yonge's *The Daisy Chain* (1856), Ethel May tries to emulate her brother's classical learning, but is compelled to give it up because of her father's fears that her health and femininity are endangered by her ambitions. The novel's full title, *The Daisy Chain, or, Aspirations: A Family Chronicle*, suggests that what is at stake in this narrative is the conflict between selfish 'aspirations' and the needs of the family. Although Ethel is eventually compensated for sacrificing her Greek by notable successes as substitute mother to her younger siblings, teacher and patroness to a working-class community, and founder of a new church, the novel also works to provoke the reader's indignation that an intelligent girl whose chief transgression is a private attempt to equal her brother in learning should be consistently thwarted by her family. Yonge's role in per-petuating the ideology which represented the perfect lady as entirely ignorant of the classics should not be underestimated, but (like *Aurora Leigh*, published in the same year) *The Daisy Chain* also irritated readers who did not see why intelligent girls should spend all their time on French and embroidery, or learning fragments of Latin grammar to help their slower brothers.

Yonge's fiction, enormously popular with her contemporaries, displays 'an almost obsessional concern about what it is to be femi-nine, about what behaviour, language, and concerns are appropriate for women and what are not'.[2] John Keble advised her that the women in her novels should not lay claim to classical knowledge: 'It had occurred to me whether, when the ladies quote Greek, they had not better say that they have heard their fathers and brothers say things.'[3] Ethel is conscious that Greek is not an accomplishment for which a woman would receive praise, and which she ought to con-ceal: she 'would not, for the world, that anyone should guess at her classical studies—she scarcely liked to believe that even her father knew of them'.[4] Ethel's 'aspirations' are associated with domestic negligence even when she tries to combine learning with sewing. Her father repeatedly threatens her with an end to her studies when she fails to take proper care of younger siblings, or to nurse her sister Margaret with sufficient gentleness. The narrator's opinion seems equally negative:

Ethel lighted on a work-basket in rare disorder, pulled off her frock, threw on a shawl, and sat down cross-legged on her bed, stitching vigorously, while meantime she spouted with great emphasis an ode of Horace, which

---

[2] June Sturrock, *'Heaven and Home': Charlotte M. Yonge's Domestic Fiction and the Victorian Debate over Women* (Victoria, BC: University of Victoria Press, 1995), 15.

[3] Charlotte M. Yonge, *Musings Over 'The Christian Year' and 'Lyra Innocentium'; Together with a Few Gleanings of Recollections of the Rev. John Keble* (Oxford: J. Parker, 1871), pp. xxvi–xxvii.

[4] Charlotte M. Yonge, *The Daisy Chain, or, Aspirations: A Family Chronicle* (1856; London: Virago, 1988), 7. Further references are given parenthetically in the text. Yonge's autobiographical writing shows that she had internalized the precept that female erudition should be hidden—she records a conversation with the Warden of Winchester College about the story of Clytemnestra, writing that she felt 'preternat-urally virtuous' for concealing that she knew it already. Coleridge, *Charlotte Mary Yonge*, 102.

Norman having learnt, by heart, she had followed his example; it being her great desire to be even with him in all his studies, and though eleven months younger, she had never yet fallen behind him. On Saturday, he showed her what were his tasks for the week, and as soon as her rent was repaired, she swung herself down-stairs in search of him for this purpose.   (7)

The narrator implies that Ethel's short-sightedness, presumably a result of her devotion to reading, is as disgraceful as the 'work-basket in rare disorder'. The virtue of sewing is counteracted by the masculine adverb 'vigorously' as well as the recitation of Latin poetry, described by the uncomplimentary word 'spouted'. Her combination of a girl's work and a boy's is made to seem ridiculous and presumptuous, and signifies dangerously divided attention.

Ethel vicariously experiences Norman's classical schooling (this cannot be justified as a necessary aid to his progress, since he is an exemplary scholar) when she attempts to teach herself exactly what he learns at his grammar school; she is irked by the gender distinctions which make Norman's industry creditable whereas hers is culpable. Of all the fictional women who learn Greek at home she receives the closest approximation to a masculine classical education: like a schoolboy, she spends a great deal of time in composing verses in Latin and Greek on set subjects, a feat which few women could match.[5] Norman's faint praise of her verses is a variation on the familiar critical complaint about learned women's mistakes in Greek accents: 'Yes, you have made a capital beginning. If you won't break down somewhere, as you always do, with some frightful false quantity, that you would get an imposition for, if you were a boy. I wish you were' (21). Ethel's fallibility has a useful function later on, when a dishonest boy finds her verses and pretends that they are his but does not benefit from his cheating:

'He showed them up, and would have got some noted good mark, but that, by great good luck, Ethel had made two of her pentameters too short, which

---

[5] Another heroine who practises verse composition is Swinburne's 'poetess and pagan' Lesbia Brandon, whose father boasts: 'Lesbia could do your verses for you when you go to Eton; she can manage elegiacs ... If my daughter had been a boy she'd have been still at Eton, and I'd have told her to look after you; she's half male as it is I think sometimes ... she can do Sapphics fit for a sixth-form.' Algernon Charles Swinburne, *Lesbia Brandon*, ed. Randolph Hughes (London: Falcon, 1952), 53.

he hadn't the wit to find out ... So he has shown up a girl's verses—isn't that rare?' cried Harry, dancing in his chair with triumph.
'I hope no one knows they were hers?'
'Bless you, no!' said Harry, who regarded Ethel's attainments as something contraband.   (91)

Harry's hilarity at the thought of Ethel's strange talents suggests that her 'attainments' are a family joke, but her relationship with her elder brother Richard, who takes over Tom's lessons from Margaret, is more troubling. Ethel listens to the lesson, which makes Richard 'nervous and uneasy':

He had a great dislike to spectators of Latin lessons; he had never forgotten an unlucky occasion, some years back, when his father was examining him in the Georgics, and he ... had gone on rendering word for word—*enim* for, *seges* a crop, *lini* of mud, *urit* burns, *campum* the field, *avenæ* a crop of pipe, *urit* burns it, when Norman and Ethel had first warned him of the beauty of his translation by an explosion of laughing ...   (155)[6]

Unlike Harry and Richard, Norman is the kind of brother who is happy to share his learning with a sister, and they maintain their alliance for much of the novel. Criticism of her domestic shortcomings from other members of the family, especially her father, does not convince Ethel to abandon her classical studies; Margaret exerts a more subtle pressure by discouraging her attempt to keep pace with Norman. Ethel's resistance is couched in emotional terms, since she sees their parallel endeavours as creating a bond between herself and Norman which would be compromised by intellectual inequality:

'Oh! Margaret! Margaret!' and her eyes filled with tears. 'We have hardly missed doing the same every day since the first Latin grammar was put into his hands!'
'I know it would be very hard,' said Margaret, but Ethel continued, in a piteous tone, a little sentimental: 'From *hic hæc hoc* up to Alcaics and *beta* Thukididou we have gone on together, and I can't bear to give it up'.   (181)

Margaret, well trained in feminine self-abnegation, represents Ethel as an impediment to Norman's academic progress, destroying Ethel's conviction that it is a mutually beneficial partnership. Ethel, claims

---

[6] Virgil, *Georgics* 1. 77, *urit enim lini campum seges, urit avenae* (for a crop of flax parches the field, a crop of oats parches it).

her sister, is falling behind because of a natural feminine inferiority: 'we all know that men have more power than women, and I suppose the time has come for Norman to pass beyond you. He would not be cleverer than any one, if he could not do more than a girl at home' (181). Margaret emphasizes that the separation of brother and sister is inevitable. Ethel may continue to keep pace with Norman in learning, but she will never receive the public acknowledgement due to his scholarship, an Oxford degree. Margaret does not suggest that Ethel should entirely abandon Greek, but that she should not work as if the acquisition of the skills required for university examinations were important to her. In telling Ethel 'to give up the verse-making, and the trying to do as much as Norman, and fix some time in the day—half-an-hour, perhaps, for your Greek' (182), Margaret attempts to transform Ethel's studies into a ladylike, if somewhat unorthodox, accomplishment, a more exotic form of the commonplace French or Italian. At this point, Norman agrees that Ethel should give up her masculine studies, or she will 'get into a regular learned lady, and be good for nothing', although he later argues that Ethel has a superior mind and should not have had to give up her Greek. Having internalized the negative connotations of her classical learning, Ethel questions 'whether her eagerness for classical learning was a wrong sort of ambition, to know what other girls did not, and whether it was right to crave for more knowledge than was thought advisable for her' (182–3).

Yonge's emphasis on the danger to feminine propriety represented by the study of Greek is complicated by questions about the absolute value of a classical education. She suggests that classical study suits the immature personality and must be superseded by religious pre-occupations. The competitive ethos of grammar school and university does not provide the boys with adequate resources for moral or financial difficulties, which are always solved by the application of precepts learnt at home. Norman's success at school is achieved at a cost to his health, and his father forbids him to read Latin and Greek during the holidays, saying, 'I had rather see you a healthy, vigorous, useful man, than a poor puling nervous wretch of a scholar, if you were to get all the prizes in the University' (118). This is part of a general Tractarian questioning of established educational institutions: the grammar school and Oxford are represented as 'fostering unhappiness, loss of religious faith and a decline in moral standards'.[7] Norman's resentment of the family's enthusiasm for the school plan which replaces Ethel's intellectual ambitions makes it clear that he values academic achievement more than good works. He too must eventually give up the classics for a Christian mission, and after a successful career at Oxford he rejects college life and goes to New Zealand. Nevertheless, despite Yonge's overt moralizing about competitiveness and ambition, she allows Ethel a vicarious success when Norman wins the prestigious Newdigate Prize (for English poetry) with a poem which draws on Ethel's old verses, and Ethel visits Oxford to see him receive the prize (386).

Yonge's harsh treatment of Ethel is modified in a later novel which deals with the May family, *The Trial* (1864), in which her Latin and Greek are of use to the family (although by this time medicine is seen as a more important discipline than classics). Ethel's classical knowledge becomes acceptable once she is teaching a younger brother rather than competing with one nearer her own age. This aligns her with Yonge's own experience of learning Latin, and with more conventional heroines like Florence in *Dombey and Son* (1846–8), who has 'a naturally quick and sound capacity' and is 'taught by that most wonderful of masters, love': she helps Paul with his Latin but has no desire to learn on her own behalf.[8] Significantly, this kind of assistance is usually associated with hearing lessons from the *Eton Latin Grammar* (which could be done without any real knowledge of the language), rather than the more difficult and prestigious study of Greek. In *The Daisy Chain*, the virtuous and long-suffering Margaret undertakes this task, listening patiently as Tom repeatedly attempts to recite 'the same unhappy bit of *As in Præsenti*, each time in a worse whine' (113). In *The Trial*, Ethel teaches her younger brother Aubrey, and is so effective as a tutor that he is far better prepared for Cambridge than his contemporaries. Once her intellectual talents

---

[7] Sturrock, *Heaven*, 43.

[8] Charles Dickens, *Dombey and Son* (1846–8), ed. Alan Horsman (Oxford: Clarendon, 1974), 164. This novel also contains a daughter whose classical studies are undertaken for the benefit of her father—the grotesque Cornelia Blimber, who is 'dry and sandy with working in the graves of deceased languages. None of your live languages for Miss Blimber. They must be dead—stone dead—and Miss Blimber dug them up like a Ghoule' (143).

are directed towards this practical end, a closer relationship with Aubrey consoles her for Norman's absence and the end of her own studies. Aubrey credits Tom rather than Ethel as his tutor, 'to spare Ethel publicity', so clearly the family's obsession with hiding her learning still has force.[9]

With her firm belief in the inferiority of woman (physical weakness and subordination imposed as a punishment for Eve's sin) and her advocacy of self-sacrifice to the point of masochism, it is easy to represent Yonge as an extreme anti-feminist, yet 'all Victorian women novelists, whether we now label them radical or conservative, were fundamentally conflicted in their beliefs about women's proper role'. In *The Clever Woman of the Family* (1865), the adult heroine's concentration on cultivating her intellect is seen as selfish and arrogant, causing discord within her family and leading to a debilitating illness for herself, but 'a substantial part of the book is devoted to exploring Rachel's aspirations in a sympathetic way'.[10] Ethel May learns to undertake suitably feminine duties and obtains the paternal approval which her classical studies denied her, choosing power in the domestic sphere rather than personal fulfilment. When her aspirations are properly redirected towards religion and family welfare, her energies are no longer regarded as negative, and the novel ends with Ethel standing in the church she has founded, where her brother Richard is the vicar. Yonge was aware of the tension between women's willing subordination to the welfare of the family and the pathos of wasted abilities: sympathy for her clever heroines leads her to credit Ethel and Rachel as superior versions of the Christian gentlewoman because of their strong-mindedness. She recognized that home education was not always stimulating enough for clever girls, and (encouraged by her cousin Mary Coleridge) started an essay society in 1859 for 'daughters of rural clergymen and landowners [who] led isolated and monotonous lives' while their brothers went away to school and university. The members of the Gosling

---

[9] Charlotte M. Yonge, *The Trial: More Links of the Daisy Chain* (1864; London: Macmillan, 1891), 226.

[10] Nicola Diane Thompson, 'Responding to the Woman Questions: Rereading Noncanonical Victorian Women Novelists', in Nicola Diane Thompson (ed.), *Victorian Women Writers and the Woman Question* (Cambridge: CUP, 1999), 3, 5.

Society (including Mary Arnold and Sara Coleridge's niece Christabel) wrote two essays a month on subjects which included classical literature, ancient history, and comparative mythology, such as 'What parallel stories does folklore in different countries present to the adventures of Ulysses in the Odyssey?'[11]

Yonge's novels overtly warn girls against intellectual ambition, yet Sally Mitchell comments that readers could ignore such didactic messages if 'the right emotional cues' are present in the text.[12] The idea that women who were cushioned by scholarly and supportive families took from *The Daisy Chain* was not that their femininity was compromised by their learning, but that girls like Ethel May should be given an education as good as their brothers'. Several of the founders of women's colleges, including Annie Moberly and Elizabeth Wordsworth, counted Yonge as a friend and mentor; far from accepting the reasoning that women should not undertake serious study because they could not get degrees, they were active in the campaign for women's higher education. Elizabeth Wordsworth, by offering women students at Lady Margaret Hall an educational establishment outside the home but structured like a family, and requiring from them both scholarship and a scrupulous adherence to feminine codes of propriety, both challenged and endorsed Yonge's conservative ideals.[13] Despite her reservations about institutions which took girls away from their families, Yonge gradually came to accept that girls' schools and women's colleges might be a worthy alternative to home education when they were conducted on religious principles and did not encourage intellectual vanity.

[11] Charlotte Mitchell, '*The Gosling Society, 1859–1877*', Charlotte Mary Yonge Fellowship website, 'http://www.dur.ac.uk/c.e.schultze/context/goslings.html', 7 June 2005.

[12] Mitchell, *New Girl*, 5.

[13] In *The Long Vacation* (1895), Yonge allows two of her heroines a year or two at LMH (but only once their brothers' education is provided for). One of the heroines of this novel plans to 'enter a ladies' college' and 'qualify herself for lecturing' before marrying; her fiancé dies at the end of the novel, so she might even end as a career woman rather than a wife. Charlotte M. Yonge, *The Long Vacation* (London: Macmillan, 1895), 223.

MILTON'S DAUGHTERS

The transmission of learning from fathers to daughters suggests a more hierarchical, authoritarian approach to the classics than the exchange of knowledge between brothers and sisters: when George Eliot did allow a heroine a fraction of the classical learning she herself possessed, in *Romola* (1862–3), she exposed selfish fathers who only teach girls Latin and Greek when they need assistance in their own scholarship. In *Middlemarch* Eliot again confronts this important paradigm of nineteenth-century women's classical education in her allusion to the story of Milton's daughters, who were forced to read to their father in Latin, Greek, and Hebrew without understanding what they read. This situation became a symbol of a particular approach to women's education in the nineteenth century, a powerful image of female oppression based on complete subordination to the needs of others. Samuel Johnson's 1779 essay quotes from the biography by Milton's nephew Edward Phillips to reiterate the image of the blind poet's daughters reading aloud from books in languages they could not understand: 'condemned to the performance of reading and exactly pronouncing all the languages of whatever book he should at one time or other think fit to peruse, viz. the Hebrew (and I think the Syriac), the Greek, the Latin, the Italian, the Spanish and French'. Johnson sees that 'this mode of intellectual labour' might be a source of 'misery' to the daughters, yet his chief concern seems to be the inadequacy of such a method, since it limits the father's 'pleasure' and probably hinders the 'meaning' conveyed to him: 'it is hard to determine whether the daughters or the father are most to be lamented. A language not understood can never be read so as to give pleasure, and very seldom as to convey meaning.'[14] A small number of new biographies of Milton were produced in the nineteenth century, as well as Edward Bulwer-Lytton's poem 'Milton' (1831) and novels about Milton's first wife Mary Powell and his daughter Deborah.[15] The *People's Journal* condemns Milton for

[14] Johnson, *Lives of the English Poets*, i. 145.
[15] Anna Nardo, '*Romola* and Milton: A Cultural History of Rewriting', *Nineteenth-Century Literature*, 53 (1998), 337.

reducing his 'automaton daughters' to 'mere reading machines': 'it is
difficult to say which is the stronger feeling—compassion for them,
or indignation towards him'.[16] Others were indignant about the
treatment Milton received from his family: David Masson's introduction to Milton's poems (1890) describes the daughters as rebellious and even 'monstrous', although this harsh judgement does not
seem to include Deborah, who 'was visited in her later years by
Addison and others, ... whom she surprised by repeating stray
lines she remembered from Homer, Euripides, and Ovid'.[17]

Dorothea Brooke's proposal that she should be to her husband
what Milton's daughters were to their father is undeniably ominous.
Dorothea hopes to acquire learning from Casaubon because—ironically, given the turn of events—she thinks that 'The really delightful
marriage must be that where your husband was a sort of father, and
could teach you even Hebrew, if you wished it' (10). Jennifer Wallace
observes that such relationships between passionate young women
and older male scholars whose virility is questionable 'are represented frequently in the nineteenth century and intimate the perceived perversity of Victorian female attraction towards the
classics'.[18] Eliot exploits the distance between idealized images of
Milton's daughters and the accounts which registered the underlying
tensions: the model of feminine self-sacrifice she has chosen is
one which even Casaubon declares to be 'wearisome', leading to
'rebellion':

'Could I not be preparing myself now to be more useful?' said Dorothea to
him, one morning, early in the time of courtship; 'could I not learn to read
Latin and Greek aloud to you, as Milton's daughters did to their father,
without understanding what they read?'
'I fear that would be wearisome to you,' said Mr Casaubon, smiling; ' ... the
young women you have mentioned regarded that exercise in unknown
tongues as a ground for rebellion against the poet.'   (62–3)

[16] Mrs Leman Gillies, 'Milton and His Daughters', *People's Journal*, 5 (1848), 227,
quoted in James G. Nelson, *The Sublime Puritan: Milton and the Victorians* (Madison:
University of Wisconsin Press, 1963), 175–6.
[17] *The Poetical Works of John Milton*, ed. David Masson, 2nd edn. (London:
Macmillan, 1890), i. 55–6, 63.
[18] Wallace, 'E.B.B.', 336. See also A. D. Nuttall, *Dead from the Waist Down: Scholars
and Scholarship in Literature and the Popular Imagination* (London: Yale UP, 2003);
Dinah Birch, 'The Scholar Husband', *Essays in Criticism*, 54 (2004), 205–15.

Dorothea's reply reveals her own ambitions: she says that Milton's daughters 'might have studied privately and taught themselves to understand what they read, and then it would have been interesting'. When she offers to learn to copy the Greek alphabet, her ultimate aim is to learn to read the language: 'it was not entirely out of devotion to her future husband that she wished to know Latin and Greek. Those provinces of masculine knowledge seemed to her a standing-ground from which all truth could be seen more truly.' Eliot ironizes Dorothea's idealization of the classics by pointing out that the superior morality she attributes to classical scholars is clearly lacking in Casaubon and his like, but we should not assume that Eliot thought women like Dorothea should not have the opportunity to study the texts she herself devoted so much time to understanding.

Given the importance of the classics in nineteenth-century fiction as a source of enlightenment from which women are excluded, it is tempting to assume that women bitterly resented their ignorance of Latin and Greek, yet some novelists responded to the self-conse- quence of male classicists with an affectionate mockery which under- mines their importance. Rhoda Broughton (1840–1920) parodies Dorothea Brooke's marital ambitions in *Belinda* (1883), which chronicles the young heroine's marriage to an Oxbridge don, Profes- sor Forth.[19] Initially Belinda and her sister Sarah appear like Doro- thea and Celia Brooke, but Broughton twists the situation so that it is the worldly Sarah who is initially engaged to the prominent scholar, having vanquished rivals such as an adoring Girton student. Sarah is interested only in social prestige—'I can assure you that he is con- sidered a great luminary at Oxbridge ... it seems he has written a book upon the Digamma!'[20]—and becomes bored with Forth once he is outside the Oxbridge environment. After a failed affair with

[19] A clergyman's daughter, educated at home, Broughton studied English litera- ture, Greek, Latin, French, German, and Italian. Her novels are 'liberally besprinkled with quotations and classical allusions, often to the detriment of her style': Marilyn Wood, *Rhoda Broughton (1840–1920): Profile of a Novelist* (Stamford: Paul Watkins, 1993), 9. A typical example is a heroine's pretentious comment on her first ball: 'I dated from it as the Greeks did from the first Olympiad, or the Romans, *ab urbe condita.*' Rhoda Broughton, *Cometh Up as a Flower* (London: Richard Bentley, 1867), i. 24.
[20] Rhoda Broughton, *Belinda* (London: Richard Bentley, 1883), i. 4. Further references are given parenthetically in the text.

David Rivers, the Ladislaw figure who returns later in the novel, it is Belinda who marries the professor. She takes over the secretarial duties which Sarah refused to perform and regrets her inability to read and write Greek. Broughton parodies Dorothea's earnestness by making it clear that Belinda's obsession with the classics is a substitute for love:

Belinda's fervour for learning rages with a feverish heat that might make a thoughtful looker-on inclined to question its solidity or its continuance ... Mostly she remains downstairs, writing Latin Exercises, learning Irregular Greek Verbs; working, working on until late into the night. She would like never to stop; to leave no single chink or cranny by which memory may enter.   (ii. 4–5)

The reader is left in no doubt that Belinda's worldlier relations are correct in seeing her studies as evidence of her perversity, and in opposing her 'marriage of the mind'. The incongruity of marrying a pretty young girl to an infirm classical scholar is emphasized by a comic portrayal of the best man at the wedding, 'staring in gaping wonder at the beautiful broken-hearted-looking girl' who is to marry his colleague and 'ruefully reflecting' on the end of forty years of 'discussions on the Enclitic de, and such-like light subjects' (ii. 99). Despite her parodic intentions, Broughton allows her heroine greater success in her task than is granted to Eliot's Dorothea: she learns Greek well enough to allow her to suggest emendations to the text her husband is editing. His work, although only of interest to a ludicrously limited audience, does get finished and published: 'The "Fragments of Menander" have been given to the world; and as certainly not less than three people have read them, they may be said to have been a success' (iii. 149). Belinda agrees to run away with Rivers but then goes back to her husband, only to find him dead. Again it is a comic version of a climactic moment in *Middlemarch*, and the obstacle to Belinda's happiness is cheerfully dismissed in the novel's final sentence: 'As for him, he has for ever vindicated his character from the imputation of being a malade imaginaire, and the Professorship of Etruscan in the University of Oxbridge is vacant!' (iii. 289).

THE RECTOR'S DAUGHTERS

The story of Milton's daughters contributed to the association of classical studies and rebellion against authority for women, but novels like Anne Brontë's *Agnes Grey* (1847) represent a harmonious familial relationship based on study and religion. The rector's daughter became a prominent type of the female student of the classics in Victorian fiction.[21] Like other clergy daughters, Charlotte, Emily, and Anne Brontë learnt Latin from their father, and their ability to teach the subject is suggested by the advertisement for the school which they proposed to establish in 1844: Latin, French, and German, as well as music and drawing, were offered as extras which would cost a guinea each per quarter. Agnes Grey's father instructs his daughters in Latin (the only subject his wife is unable to teach), which is seen initially in terms of preserving the family's social status, and later as an acquirement Agnes must advertise in order to earn money as a governess: 'Music, Singing, Drawing, French, Latin, and German ... are no mean assemblage'.[22] When Agnes attempts to prepare her employer's sons for school—'to get the greatest possible quantity of Latin grammar and Valpy's Delectus into their heads ... *without* trouble to themselves' (64)—Brontë is drawing on her own experience: her copy of the Latin textbook *Delectus Sententiarum et*

[21] Novelists continued to be fascinated by clerical families and the classics in the 20th cent. In *The Three Sisters* (1914) May Sinclair satirizes a clergyman's attempt to be thought a 'scholarly recluse' by prominently displaying editions of Plato, Sophocles, Homer, and Aeschylus (the presence of modern translations by Jowett, Butcher and Lang, and Robert Browning suggests that standards of classical scholarship were already slipping). Although he 'carried the illusion of scholarship so far as to hide his Aristophanes behind a little curtain, as if it contained for him an iniquitous temptation', the vicar's preferred reading is sensation novels. May Sinclair, *The Three Sisters* (1914; London: Virago, 1982), 17–18. A genuine interest in the classics characterizes the old-fashioned country rector as being mentally stuck in the Victorian era, like Flora Mayor's Canon Jocelyn, who prefers Virgil to all Christian classics and considers his learning 'simply as what was suitable for a scholar and a gentleman ... He kept up his marvellous range of reading till about 1895. Then his mind closed to new ideas.' He is snobbish about the new generation of churchmen who make incorrect classical allusions, and therefore are not gentlemen, but his priorities are no longer relevant. *The Rector's Daughter*, 8.

[22] Anne Brontë, *Agnes Grey* (1847), ed. Hilda Marsden and Robert Inglesfield (Oxford: Clarendon, 1988), 56.

Historiarum is inscribed 'Anne Brontë Thorp Green—November 1843'.[23] Although Thackeray recognized that the author of *Jane Eyre* might have been a woman with a classical education, the Latinisms in *Wuthering Heights* were used as evidence of male authorship by Alice Law, who claimed that Branwell Brontë had written the novel (a theory satirized by Stella Gibbons in *Cold Comfort Farm*).[24]

In the Brontës' novels classical learning is not foregrounded in the way that French is in *Villette* (1853) or *Jane Eyre* (1847), but it is assumed that classical texts are easily available, part of the furniture for the clergy and the gentry, although most of the characters may be unable to read them. In *Jane Eyre*, Miss Temple's obvious intellectual and social superiority to the other Lowood teachers is further accentuated by her interest in Latin literature. 'Miss Temple asked Helen if she sometimes snatched a moment to recall the Latin her father had taught her, and taking a book from a shelf, bade her read and construe a page of Virgil.'[25] The possession of classical texts, even if they remain unread, is an indicator of rank, and their presence encourages intellectual curiosity in unexpected people. In *Wuthering Heights* (1847) Nelly Dean informs Lockwood that she has at least looked into all the books in the library at Thrushcross Grange, and can tell Latin, Greek, and French apart, which is 'as much as you can expect of a poor man's daughter'. Hareton, although illiterate, tries to narrow the gap between himself and Cathy by taking from her 'some Latin and Greek, and some tales and poetry', which she describes as 'old friends'; the survival of these books from the cultured world of the Grange in the hostile atmosphere of Wuthering Heights depends on their symbolic value rather than the texts themselves.[26]

The dominant pattern in Charlotte Brontë's novels is the untaught heroine who substitutes her own imaginative constructions for the

---

[23] Barker, *Brontës*, 862. The *Delectus* was a selection of passages chosen from Greek or Latin authors for language learners, e.g. Richard Valpy, *Delectus Sententiarum Græcarum, Ad Usum Tironum Accommodatus* (London, 1815).

[24] Lucasta Miller, *The Brontë Myth* (London: Vintage, 2002), 237.

[25] Charlotte Brontë, *Jane Eyre* (1847), ed. Jane Jack and Margaret Smith (Oxford: Clarendon, 1969), 85.

[26] Emily Brontë, *Wuthering Heights* (1847), ed. Hilda Marsden and Ian Jack (Oxford: Clarendon, 1976), 78, 364.

texts she has not read (although one of her early heroines, Zenobia
Ellrington, is a bluestocking who reads Greek in the original). She
herself wrote poems 'about the nature of poetic genius . . . and about
the progress of literary history'; through the use of fictional personae
she seeks to 'define herself as a poet and to place herself within a
literary tradition of which she was acutely aware', so that literary
influence does not inhibit, but 'stimulate[s] and nurture[s] her
writing'.[27] Brontë's 'The Violet' (1830) resembles Elizabeth Barrett's
'A Vision of Poets' (1844) in paying tribute to Homer, Sophocles,
Euripides, Aeschylus, and Virgil. The poem is attributed to a Glass-
town character, the marquis of Douro, who is described as 'Treasurer
to the Society for the Spread of Classical Knowledge'. The poem
dwells on Byronic topoi such as ruins and degeneracy; the claim
that the nine Muses have deserted Greece for 'fair Britannia' reiterates
the widespread belief that the virtues of ancient Athens were em-
bodied by the British rather than by modern Greeks. The poet prays
to become one of the 'army of Immortals' but the reply promises a
less exalted poetic career, represented by the 'lowly violet' (184)
instead of a laurel wreath.[28]

Agnes Grey, whose benevolent and affectionate father is alive at the
beginning of the novel, is the only Brontë heroine who does not see
classical learning as potentially offering women an opportunity to
fight against patriarchal tradition. Charlotte and Anne Brontë attack
the use of Greek to bolster misogyny: in their novels 'the classics are
seen as weapons with which men oppress and torment women'.[29]
Passages such as the following, from *Villette*, represent female scholarship as an effective means of subversion which is not available to
the heroine because of her limited education: 'In M. Emanuel's soul
rankled a chronic suspicion that I knew both Greek and Latin. As
monkeys are said to have the power of speech if they would but use it,
and are reported to conceal this faculty in fear of its being turned to
their detriment, so to me was ascribed a fund of knowledge which I

[27] Carol A. Bock, 'Gender and Poetic Tradition: The Shaping of Charlotte Brontë's
Literary Career', *TSWL* 7 (1988), 49–50.
[28] *The Poems of Charlotte Brontë*, ed. Tom Winnifrith (Oxford: Blackwell, 1984),
113–20.
[29] Fowler, 'Greek', 345.

was supposed criminally and craftily to conceal.'[30] Lucy regrets her ignorance only because it allows Emanuel to triumph over her, not because she believes, like Dorothea Brooke, that there are sources of truth and wisdom unavailable to her because she cannot read the texts. On the contrary, in writing a 'devoir', she uses classical materials (in translation) as a stimulus to her own creative endeavours, to produce results which are personal and impressionistic versions of canonical literature:

> The subject was classical. When M. Paul dictated the trait on which the essay was to turn, I heard it for the first time; the matter was new to me, and I had no material for its treatment. But I got books, read up the facts, laboriously constructed a skeleton out of the dry bones of the real, and then clothed them, and tried to breathe into them life, and in this last aim I had pleasure.   (580–1)

Lucy's account of her writing privileges not the acquisition of knowledge about the ancients or the power of constructing a convincing historical narrative, but inspiration, the breathing of life into 'the dry bones of the real'. Her devoir resembles Charlotte Brontë's own 'Athènes sauvée par la Poésie', based on an episode in Plutarch's life of Lysander, which she wrote in 1843. As the Spartans hold a feast to celebrate their victory in the Peloponnesian War, Lysander sends for an Athenian poet to sing the city's elegy. Brontë imparts 'life' to the scene with details of the food and the appearance of the characters, focusing, for example, on the physical contrast between classic Athenian beauty and Spartan sturdiness. The Spartan general orders the poet to sing the fall of Athens in Homeric style: the poet refuses this subject. After praying to Orpheus for inspiration, the poet sings one of the traditional stories of Greek tragedy—Agamemnon's departure for the Trojan War and his return ten years later, when he was murdered by his wife and her lover. Electra, mourning her father, recounts the story of his return with the doomed prophetess Cassandra, and their death. Encouraged by the silence with which his story is greeted, the Athenian poet discovers that the Spartans have fallen asleep, and makes his escape. Athens is 'saved by poetry' because Lysander has forgotten his project of vengeance on the city

---

[30] Charlotte Brontë, *Villette* (1853), ed. Herbert Rosengarten and Margaret Smith (Oxford: Clarendon, 1984), 511.

by the time he awakes. This bathetic ending contrasts with Plutarch's version, in which the Spartans are so impressed by the singing of the first chorus from Euripides' *Electra* that 'all were moved to compassion, and felt it to be a cruel deed to abolish and destroy a city which was so famous, and produced such poets'.[31]

Wuthering Heights is a good example of a creative response to the classics, based on the tragedies of Euripides and Aeschylus, on which Emily Brontë made notes in 1838.[32] There is an evident affinity between the author of *Wuthering Heights* and Aeschylus, seen in the nineteenth century as a 'Gothic or romantic artist'.[33] The Greek dramatist's portrayal of doomed families like the House of Atreus influenced Brontë in her representation of the fates of the Earnshaws and the Lintons.[34] Nelly Dean perhaps owes something to the nurse who is the heroine's confidante in tragedies such as Euripides' *Medea*, probably mediated through Shakespeare, who created similar characters like the nurse in *Romeo and Juliet*. *Medea*, a text which greatly influenced women writers, deals with the theme of revenge and may have influenced Brontë's treatment of Heathcliff. Edward Chitham suggests that Brontë was also influenced by Horace's *Ars Poetica*, which is 'extensively concerned with Drama' (she translated this poem in 1839), and that Nelly resembles Horace's idea of a chorus, maintaining an individual identity and active role in the drama.[35]

The Brontës suggest that any woman who engaged herself in serious study of Greek, whether biblical or classical, would challenge established texts and social customs. It is in learning French that Charlotte Brontë's heroines tend to experience the 'emancipatory function' of a second language, 'an alternative form of speech

[31] Charlotte Brontë and Emily Brontë, *The Belgian Essays*, tr. Sue Lonoff (London: Yale UP, 1996), 334–57. Robert Browning's poem 'Balaustion's Adventure' (1871) is based on a similar episode in Plutarch's life of Nicias.
[32] Barker, *Brontës*, 289.
[33] Jenkyns, *Greece*, 88.
[34] A similar influence is acknowledged in Sue Bridehead's comment on the story of an ancestor, 'It makes me feel as if a tragic doom overhung our family, as it did the house of Atreus.' Thomas Hardy, *Jude the Obscure* (1895), ed. C. H. Sisson (Harmondsworth: Penguin, 1978), 350.
[35] Edward Chitham, *The Birth of Wuthering Heights: Emily Brontë at Work* (Basingstoke: Palgrave, 1998), 29–30. Chitham discusses Emily Brontë's translations of part of Virgil's *Aeneid* and a section of the *Ars Poetica* as influences on *Wuthering Heights*, 17–32.

which can both disrupt the repressions of authoritative discourse and ... shelter themes that have not yet found a voice in the text's primary language'.[36] Having experienced this linguistic potential, they project a more fundamental disruption onto texts in unknown languages which embody 'authoritative discourse', especially the Bible. They exploit the gap between the Greek Testament and the King James Bible to suggest that translators have mistakenly imposed their own assumptions. In debating with a man who uses biblical phrases to bolster his own belief that women should submit in everything to their husbands, Caroline Helstone, a clergyman's niece who is unable to read the Latin and Greek books in her uncle's library, boldly suggests that what he believes to be revealed wisdom might be overturned by an educated woman: 'I dare say, if I could read the original Greek, I should find that many of the words have been wrongly translated, perhaps misapprehended altogether. It would be possible, I doubt not, with a little ingenuity, to give the passage quite a contrary turn.'[37] The interrogation of misogynistic statements based on the Bible may have been influenced by Elizabeth Carter's notorious argument with the archbishop of Canterbury about the translation of St Paul. Carter habitually compared translations of the Bible with the Hebrew or Greek originals, and found an anomaly in the rendering of one verb in St Paul's First Epistle to the Corinthians in the Authorized Version: 'When it was applied to the husband, the translators rendered the verb in an active form, when applied to the woman they rendered it passive. For Carter, this was a sign of their support for the superiority of the husband; it demonstrated that translation was not neutral nor was it gender blind.'[38] In *The Tenant of Wildfell Hall*, Helen Graham uses the possibility that the accepted version of the Bible may rely on mistranslations for a similarly defiant interpretation. She refuses to accept that sinners suffer eternal damnation: 'the only difficulty is in the word which we translate "everlasting" or "eternal." I don't know the Greek, but I

---

[36] Patricia Yaeger, *Honey-Mad Women: Emancipatory Strategies in Women's Writing* (New York: Columbia UP, 1988), 36, 40.

[37] Charlotte Brontë, *Shirley* (1849), ed. Herbert Rosengarten and Margaret Smith (Oxford: Clarendon, 1979), 371.

[38] Clarke, *Dr Johnson's Women*, 52.

believe it strictly means for ages, and might signify either endless or long-enduring.'[39]

Whereas the Brontës challenge the translation of the Bible, Eliza Lynn Linton (another clergyman's daughter) employs classical myth to subversive ends in *The Autobiography of Christopher Kirkland* (1885). By making the protagonist of her autobiographical novel a man, Linton reduces the shock which a reader might feel on encountering a heroine reading Ovid, yet she retains the atmosphere of secrecy and defiance which surrounded her own reading of the *Metamorphoses* by having Christopher Kirkland hide under a hedge to read the book, as she had done: 'If my father had seen it in my hands he would have forbidden it to me; which was why I went where I was not likely to be found even if looked for' (i. 134). According to Linton's account such a prohibition would be justifiable, since Ovid's poem subverts the Christian world view by making Bible stories seem like versions of Greek myth. It is through reading Ovid that Christopher Kirkland discovers how closely the stories resemble each other:

'How dear that little idyl of Philemon and Baucis was to me! Its simplicity and realism made it almost Scriptural; and though I did not dare to bracket it with the visit of those three divine beings to Abraham and Sara, still, I thought the one account as true as the other' (i. 131).

Although many Victorian readers saw the correspondences between classical myth and the Bible as evidence of the superior status given to the Greeks, who lacked only the Christian revelation to make them perfect, Linton's hero begins to question the relative status of the narratives. It is not surprising that the *Metamorphoses* should inspire speculation, since the first book begins with a god who creates heaven, earth, and seas out of chaos, followed by the creation of animals and finally of the more god-like form of man, the master of the animals. Ovid offers two alternative explanations of the creation of man, one of which is the Prometheus myth, and the other of which suggests that the creator of the world made man from divine seed.

---

[39] Anne Brontë, *The Tenant of Wildfell Hall* (1848), ed. Herbert Rosengarten (Oxford: Clarendon, 1992), 178.

After the account of creation, Ovid's narrative becomes more distinctively Greek, although the degeneration represented by the myth of the ages of gold, silver, bronze, and iron could be read as a version of the Fall and its consequences. A closer parallel with Christian scripture is the story of the flood which Jupiter decrees as a punishment for human wickedness, which had been incorporated into English literary tradition as 'the Graeco-Roman account of Noah' by writers such as Milton.[40] The god intends to destroy humanity and create a new race, but allows two virtuous people, Deucalion and Pyrrha, who are saved from the flood when their boat runs aground on Mount Parnassus, to become the ancestors of the new generation.

In describing episodes from the *Metamorphoses* which appear analogous to Bible stories, some of Linton's selections seem designed to provoke the reader, to disturb Victorian propriety, and perhaps to point out that even the most immoral episodes represented in Ovid are equalled in the Bible. The most extreme example is the parallel she draws between the story of Myrrha's incestuous passion for her father, and the daughters of Lot, who trick their father into impregnating them. The sacrifice of Iphigeneia by her father cannot be condemned as pagan ignorance when it is compared to that of Isaac and of the daughter of Jephthah. Linton concentrates on female characters and relationships rather than on large-scale events, and especially on daughters and fathers such as Scylla and Nisus, characters in a story from book 8 of the *Metamorphoses*. Nisus has one purple lock, on which the safety of his kingdom depends; his daughter Scylla falls in love with Minos, an enemy general, and decides to betray the city, entering her father's bedroom at night to cut off the lock. The story of Samson and Delilah is offered as a parallel. However, the subversiveness of pointing out parallels which unsettle the unique authority of scripture is only a preparation for questioning on an explicitly sexual theme: 'the loves of the Sons of God for the daughters of men, and those of the gods of Greece for the girls of Athens and Sparta' (i. 136). The temerity of this association induces a 'terrible faintness' in Linton's hero, since the myth of the Incarnation is 'no longer exceptional and divine—it had become historic and human. Therefore, it fell within the range of criticism and might be judged of according to its merits and the weight of evidence at its back' (i. 139).

SEWING AND GREEK

In *Framley Parsonage* (1860–1) and *The Last Chronicle of Barset* (1867), Anthony Trollope overturns the convention that a woman who learns Greek will rebel against her father like Milton's daughters. The transformation of learning into a form of domestic duty, and the careful touches which reassure the reader that Grace and Jane Crawley remain models of conventional girlhood, reinforce essentially conservative gender roles. Although the Church encompassed a wide range from younger sons of the aristocracy to impoverished perpetual curates, all Anglican clergymen were educated at Oxford or Cambridge, and by maintaining a certain level of classical scholarship and passing it on to his children (girls as well as boys), a clergyman could see himself as a gentleman even in poverty. In *Framley Parsonage*, Trollope shows Mr Crawley teaching his children, seen by a lady visitor whose arrival interrupts the lesson. When Lucy Robarts sees a pile of classical texts, she assumes that they belong to Bob, but is contradicted by Grace, who claims most of the books as her own:

'And are you a great scholar?' asked Lucy, drawing the child to her.
'I don't know,' said Grace with a sheepish face. 'I am in the Greek Delectus and the irregular verbs.'
'Greek Delectus and the irregular verbs!' And Lucy put up her hands with astonishment.
'And she knows an ode of Horace all by heart,' said Bob.
'An ode of Horace!' said Lucy, still holding the young shamefaced female prodigy close to her knees.[41]

That Grace is 'sheepish' and 'shamefaced' at Lucy's questioning betrays her awareness that her learning is somehow unusual, a state of mind which Lucy's exclamations and gestures of astonishment can

[41] Anthony Trollope, *Framley Parsonage* (1860–1), ed. P. D. Edwards (Oxford: OUP, 1980), 259.

only reinforce. It is left to her brother to boast on her behalf that she has memorized one of Horace's *Odes*, demonstrating pride in his sister's learning. Mr Crawley acknowledges Lucy's amazement with an uncharacteristically diffident response: 'A little scholarship is the only fortune that has come in my way, and I endeavour to share that with my children' (259).

When the Crawley family reappears in *The Last Chronicle of Barset*, Grace is no longer a 'shamefaced female prodigy'. At 19, she has become a teacher at a fairly typical school for ladies; it seems unlikely that the school would be making use of her classical learning, although 'Roman history' is taught there.[42] Bob is away at school, and expected to continue at Cambridge, so that Crawley's attention is now concentrated on 'Jane, still at home, who passed her life between her mother's work-table and her father's Greek, mending linen and learning how to scan iambics' (7). For Barrett Browning's Aurora Leigh, sewing is a duty which female relatives impose, which interferes with the self-development which reading offers; for Jane Crawley, reading is not a means of gaining intellectual independence, as the choice of texts and the time spent on studying them is determined by her father. Although Mr Crawley had claimed in the earlier novel that he taught his children Greek and Latin because he had nothing else to give them, it becomes clear that for Jane scanning iambics is as much a service to the family as mending linen. Gilbert and Gubar comment that 'the image of the Miltonic father *being ministered to* hints that ... he has been reduced to a state of dependence'.[43] When Jane reads Greek to her father in *The Last Chronicle of Barset*, he is in a similar position, combining power and helplessness. Jane's education provides him with a pretext for concentrating his attention on the grandiloquence of Greek tragedy rather than the petty problems caused by poverty and a false accusation of theft.

' "Where is Jane? Tell her that I am ready to commence the Seven against Thebes with her." ... Mrs. Crawley from the kitchen would hear him reading out, or rather saying by rote, with sonorous, rolling voice, great passages from some chorus, and she was very thankful

---

[42] Anthony Trollope, *The Last Chronicle of Barset* (1867), ed. Stephen Gill (Oxford: OUP, 1980), 85.

[43] Gilbert and Gubar, *Madwoman*, 215.

... ' (132–3). The relationship between the daughter whose classical learning turns out to have been for her father's benefit, and the practical mother who listens indulgently from the kitchen, seems to involve no resentment at this stage. It becomes more strained when Grace returns and is immediately required to read to her father. As Crawley is unable to articulate his emotions in his own words, the closeness of the bond between father and daughters can only be expressed by their shared participation in reading, and the mother is painfully excluded by her ignorance of the language. The risk of alienation between mother and daughters is an aspect of the tension between learning and womanliness which dominates the representation of Grace and Jane, especially through the comments of other characters.

The sometimes controversial interdependence of classics and Anglicanism was based on the argument that the clergy must be able to read the Bible in Greek, but the teaching of Greek in schools and universities was dominated by classical texts which inevitably conflict with Christian values. Crawley is obsessed with Greek tragedy because he sees himself as a tragic hero, understanding his own suffering in terms of 'the glory and the pathos and the humanity, as also of the awful tragedy, of the story of Oedipus' (175). He frequently remembers that that his classical scholarship was superior to that of his contemporaries who have risen within the Church hierarchy and feels that he deserves higher preferment because of it. The belief that his Greek learning (rather than any theological study or parish work) entitles him to a better living is not as eccentric as it might seem to a modern reader, but rather out of date—in *Barchester Towers* (1857) the 'Greek play bishops' whose promotion was based on their distinction in classical scholarship are seen as belonging to an earlier age.[44] The incompatibility of Crawley's ethos, apparently shaped more by his reading of pagan authors than the Bible, with the middle-class feminine ideal becomes increasingly clear. He encourages competition between his daughters, attempting to make Grace afraid that Jane will 'beat' her:

---

[44] Anthony Trollope, *Barchester Towers* (1857), ed. Michael Sadleir and Frederick Page (Oxford: OUP, 1996), 2. 182.

'I am sure I shall not begrudge her her superiority.'
'Ah, but you should begrudge it her!' Jane was sitting by at the time, and the two sisters were holding each other by the hand. 'Always to be best; always to be in advance of others. That should be your motive.'
'But we can't both be best, papa,' said Jane.   (417)

The Homeric phrase 'αἰὲν ἀριστεύειν καὶ ὑπείροχον ἔμμεναι ἄλλων' ('always to be bravest and excel over others') appears twice in the *Iliad* (6. 208 and 11. 784) as a father's advice to a warrior son, and it suits Crawley's own competitive instincts. Crawley's daughters, however, do not adopt the aggressively unfeminine striving he advocates: 'holding each other by the hand', they refuse to engage in intellectual combat. When he recommends that they compete in learning the *Antigone* by heart, Jane complains that it would take too long: she is also registering her reluctance to perpetuate the family's suffering by playing Antigone to his Oedipus, although she and Grace are like Antigone and Ismene in supporting their stricken father in his isolation. Unlike Crawley, his daughters do not identify themselves with tragic protagonists, and their more pragmatic attitude to their classical reading is one with which the reader can more easily sympathize.

Reflecting the connections between the Church and the universities, for the 1890s version of Jane Crawley or Agnes Grey a parsonage education leads to a women's college in novels like *The Junior Dean* (1891) and *A Proctor's Wooing* (1897) by Alan St Aubyn (Frances Marshall).[45] The women students in these novels are the daughters of impecunious clergymen who go to college to prepare for a teaching career after being educated at home. The heroine of *A Proctor's Wooing*, Theo Lee, is radical only 'in the simple minds of west country rustics' in her father's parish who have never heard of women's colleges.[46] St Aubyn's heroines contradict popular stereotypes of college women as unmarriageable and unattractive, and they endorse the idea that college provides a good training for marriage. This is not the case, St Aubyn suggests, for male students, who go to the races, drink too much, are late for lectures, miss chapel, and

---

[45] Frances Marshall was educated at Cambridge and mainly wrote novels about university life: see John Sutherland, *The Longman Companion to Victorian Fiction* (London: Longman, 1988), 549.
[46] Alan St Aubyn, *A Proctor's Wooing* (London: 1897), 13.

become involved with actresses and girls in flower shops. The men in both novels fall prey to the temptations of college life and must be redeemed by suffering before they are worthy of the modest heroines who do not attain great academic success. However, St Aubyn also celebrates women's achievements and includes more exceptional characters who prove women's intellectual equality with men, such as Geraldine, who takes a First in three different Triposes, gets married, and leads the New Woman movement along with her husband.

Tennyson's *The Princess* is invoked by the title of popular and prolific novelist L. T. Meade's *A Sweet Girl Graduate* (1891). Maggie Oliphant, the star student at a women's college clearly based on Newnham, befriends Priscilla Peel because they both love Latin and Greek better than anything else in the world. As the idealized type of the woman student who may not marry, but still devotes her life to others, Priscilla goes to college so that she can become a teacher and support her younger sisters. She encounters all the stereotypical dilemmas of the female student, such as being distracted from her studies by a friendship with a frivolous student and being expected to give up college to look after a sick relative. Her aunt asks her if she will 'give up that outlandish Greek, and all that babel of foreign tongues, and your grand college, and your hopes of being a famous woman by-and-by?'[47] Yet once she has passed this moral test by agreeing to give up her studies, she is allowed to return to college. Her aunt recognizes that sewing has been replaced by Latin and Greek as a fashionable occupation for young women, although she exhorts Priscilla not to forget her domestic skills.

DISSENTERS AND THE CLASSICS

Influenced by her father, William Stevenson, who had given up his position as a classics tutor at Manchester Academy after writing a pamphlet entitled *Remarks on the Very Inferior Utility of Classical*

---

[47] L. T. Meade, *A Sweet Girl Graduate* (London: Cassell, 1891), 195. Further references are given parenthetically in the text. Meade (Elizabeth Thomasina Meade, 1854–1914) was a clergyman's daughter whose father was horrified by her wish to become a professional writer. She moved to London to live independently and pursue her literary career.

Learning (1796), Elizabeth Gaskell's view of the classics in her novels tends towards the utilitarian.[48] The impracticality of classical study and the alienation produced by a system of education based on class and gender segregation are important in *North and South*. Mr Hale is at first the kind of clergyman who remains a gentleman despite poverty, and who might have taught his daughter the classics had she been educated at home. Gaskell's narrative asks what happens if such a man becomes a Dissenter, loses the backing of the established Church, and has to make his living in an industrial town where social precedence is defined in terms of wealth. Thornton's schooling introduces him to classical literature, which is forgotten during the years of struggling to build up his mill, and to which he returns for pleasure: 'I can turn to all that old narration and thoroughly enjoy it'. He quietly contradicts Mr Hale's view that 'the heroic simplicity of the Homeric life' might be an inspiration to the young industrialist as it was believed to be for upper-class boys, and considers classical study as a recreation made possible by his acquisition of wealth rather than an opportunity to mimic the ways of gentlemen.[49] In the utilitarian atmosphere of Milton, Latin and Greek remain a standard to which the true gentleman is drawn—Thornton's appreciation of Homer distinguishes him from other manufacturers—but they are a luxury, not highly valued by most of the characters. To Mrs Thornton, the significance of learning is the social superiority bestowed by knowledge of the classical languages, and she is offended by her son's apparent endorsement of the traditional class system rather than the hierarchy of Milton, which is based on success and money, and in which Mr Hale is merely a poor employee.

Daughters of Anglican clergymen in Elizabeth Gaskell's fiction, such as Matty and Deborah Jenkyns in *Cranford* (1853), lacking the Unitarian emphasis on education, do not learn Latin and Greek. Yet

[48] Stevenson claimed that an education based on Greek and Latin was deficient from a scientific, utilitarian point of view, and that the mind was weakened by the concentration on memory and attachment to authorities rather than individual judgement. See J. A. V. Chapple, *Elizabeth Gaskell: The Early Years* (Manchester: Manchester UP, 1997), 21, 38–9; Jenny Uglow, *Elizabeth Gaskell: A Habit of Stories* (London: Faber, 1993), 9–10.

[49] Elizabeth Gaskell, *North and South* (1854–5), ed. Angus Easson (Oxford: OUP, 1982), 85. See Hilary M. Schor, *Scheherezade in the Marketplace: Elizabeth Gaskell and the Victorian Novel* (Oxford: OUP, 1992), 138–40.

in this novel about a society of gentle, middle-aged 'Amazons', Gaskell sees the humorous potential of the classics: in Cranford men are the outsiders, and 'women's language and values are the accepted currency'.[50] Men's language is liable to be comically misunderstood, especially since 'the worthy rector ... could hardly write a letter to his wife without dropping into Latin'. In 'a fit of writing classical poetry' he sends a *carmen* (poem) to his wife, who writes on it: 'Hebrew verses sent to me by my honoured husband. I thowt to have had a letter about killing the pig, but must wait.'[51] Despite the incomprehension of the supposed addressee, the poem is properly appreciated when presented to the audience for whom it is ultimately intended—the readership of the *Gentleman's Magazine*.

Gaskell adapted the pattern of a clerical father teaching his daughter Latin at home in her pastoral tale *Cousin Phillis* (1863–4). Her version is unusual because of the social background of her characters: instead of an Oxbridge-educated Church of England vicar, she chooses an Independent minister who farms during the day and reads Latin with his daughter in the evenings. The scholars in this story are capable of undertaking practical tasks in the home and on their farm, but their reading leaves them dangerously unworldly and vulnerable to the forces of modernity. Before the arrival of the engineers who disrupt the tranquillity of the countryside, Phillis and her father read Latin and Greek together without any of the tensions associated with the narrative of Milton and his daughters. As in the works of the Brontës and Trollope, there is an emphasis on the availability of books in the home, but here, rather than being identified as the common property of the family, or the father's old college texts, the books specifically belong to Phillis, the only surviving child of the Reverend Holman, as Paul Manning (the narrator) comments: 'Virgil, Cæsar, a Greek grammar—oh, dear! ah, me! and Phillis Holman's name in each of them! ... I gave my cousin Phillis a wide berth, although she was sitting at her work quietly enough' (235).

---

[50] Rowena Fowler, '*Cranford*: Cow in Grey Flannel or Lion Couchant?', *SEL* 24 (1984), 720.

[51] Elizabeth Gaskell, *Cranford and Cousin Phillis*, ed. Peter Keating (Harmondsworth: Penguin, 1976), 88. Further references are given parenthetically in the text.

Whereas the friendships between men in this story all involve both learning and teaching, so that information about classical literature is exchanged for details of engineering and so on, Phillis is always a pupil.[52] Her father teaches her Greek and Latin, Holdsworth Italian: the texts, dictionaries, lessons, and marginal annotations for her work are all provided by men. In this respect she resembles Jane Crawley or Agnes Grey, and also in there being no brother at home to absorb her father's attention: as 'the only child of a scholar' she has received an education in Latin and Greek which Paul thinks of as making her 'more like a man than a woman' (252). Gaskell, like Trollope, draws attention to the disruptive potential of an intellectual bond between father and daughter when it excludes the mother, who is 'a little jealous of her own child, as a fitter companion for her husband than she was herself' (249). Gaskell solves this difficulty by having the minister, at difficult moments, tactfully reintroduce the practical subjects on which she is 'an authority' (271). Phillis remains oblivious to this source of discomfort, which reinforces Paul's perception that her absorption in learning alienates her from a feminine preoccupation with emotional matters. Despite her jealousy, the mother's unselfishness is revealed at the end of the story by her attempt to re-establish the old relationship between father and daughter as a means to restore Phillis: 'I saw her mother bring her the Latin and Italian books that she had been so fond of before her illness—or, rather, before Holdsworth had gone away' (316).

Although she is an enthusiastic and ambitious scholar, Phillis successfully combines learning and domestic duties, and it is the men who think of her as a potential wife who cannot reconcile her two roles. Paul quickly casts himself as a brother to Phillis when he realizes that she finds her classical studies 'of far more interest than any mere personal subjects; that was the last day on which I ever thought of my dear cousin Phillis as the possible mistress of my heart' (244). His father agrees that Latin and Greek are unsuitable accomplishments for a wife, but argues that 'She'd forget 'em, if she'd a houseful of children' (252). Holdsworth, whose relationship with Phillis is not troubled by fears of his own inferiority, as Paul's is,

[52] Philip Rogers, 'The Education of Cousin Phillis', *Nineteenth-Century Literature*, 50 (1995), 28–9.

finds his first sight of her perplexing: 'That quiet girl, full of household work, is the wonderful scholar, then, that put you to rout with
her questions when you first began to come here' (262). Phillis's
ability to be 'a scholar' yet 'full of household work' is glimpsed by
the reader when Paul finds her in the kitchen, 'peeling apples with
quick dexterity of finger, but with repeated turnings of her head
towards some book' (242). Philip Rogers considers her reading 'an
awkward distraction from a more pressing responsibility',[53] but the
phrase 'quick dexterity' argues that she is completing her task skilfully. It seems likely that Gaskell intended to suggest that an interest
in books did not harm women's domestic capabilities. Her own
letters reveal that her successful career as a novelist was combined
with the efficient running of a household. She even used a classical
allusion in an attempt to persuade one correspondent that 'the
various household arts' could be made into 'real studies (& there is
plenty of poetry and association about them—remember how the
Greek princesses in Homer washed the clothes &c&c&c&c)'.[54] She
refuses to endorse the traditional combination of the habit of reading
with carelessness in household tasks. There is no reason to suppose
that Phillis is any less capable of doing two things at once than Emily
Brontë, who studied German while kneading dough: 'no study,
however interesting, interfered with the goodness of the bread,
which was always light and excellent'.[55]

Phillis's effort to learn Italian, a language her father does not know,
seems like an attempt to escape his control over her education. It is
initially undertaken, however, using a book that he has bought, and
Phillis explains her interest in Dante's *Inferno* by connecting it with
Virgil, her father's favourite Latin author and Dante's guide. Paul
suggests that Holdsworth, having lived in Italy and read Italian
books, would be a more effective teacher than her father, who can
only endeavour to relate the Italian words to the familiar Latin.
Holdsworth immediately rejects Dante and gives her Manzoni's *I
Promessi Sposi* (1827). Paul, uneasy about the substituted text,

[53] Ibid. 30.

[54] E.G. to unknown correspondent, 25 Sept. [1862]. *The Letters of Mrs. Gaskell*, ed.
J. A. V. Chapple and Arthur Pollard (Manchester: Manchester UP, 1966), 694–5.

[55] Elizabeth Gaskell, *Life of Charlotte Brontë* (1857), ed. Ernest Rhys (London: J. M.
Dent, 1908), 90.

questions whether Phillis's father would approve of her reading a novel. Holdsworth's retort, 'You don't suppose they take *Virgil* for gospel?'(265), shows that he has misunderstood the status of classical literature in the household. Holman (like many other nineteenth-century readers) does not regard the *Georgics* as a work of fiction but as a practical guide to the land: 'It's wonderful ... how exactly Virgil has hit the enduring epithets, nearly two thousand years ago, and in Italy; and yet it describes to a T what is now lying before us' (233). As a regular inmate of the farm Paul understands that Virgil is as much a part of daily life there as the Bible, and it is through his increasingly sensitive narration that 'Gaskell quite insistently stresses the relevance of the minister's and Phillis's classical readings to their own present-day lives'.[56]

Virgil's poem indeed provided some practical guidance for farmers, but the agricultural element is often subordinated to artistic, political, and religious themes. Particularly relevant to Gaskell's plot is the denunciation of sexual passion in book 3 which demonstrates its destructive effects on all animals, including mankind, and there are other subtle correspondences. The 'small, independent farmer' of the *Georgics* was a 'vanishing figure' but 'an important one for Roman sensibility' because of the identification between rural life and the moral life.[57] The Wordsworthian echoes in *Cousin Phillis* incorporate a modern version of a similar narrative, and suggest that the Holmans' way of life is under threat. By helping to bring the railways to Italy, and by giving Phillis *I Promessi Sposi*, Holdsworth allies himself with the forces of modernization and industrialization which will estrange Virgil's country from its agricultural past. Having succeeded there, he moves on to Heathbridge, where he initially encounters some resistance from a landscape which is more suited to farmers than engineers, and then to Canada.

Holdsworth's departure for Canada aligns him with a figure from another poem by Virgil: he, like Aeneas, following 'the commands of empire', deserts the woman he loves, travels to a distant land, and there consolidates his position by marrying a local woman.[58] He

[56] Rogers, 'Education', 37.

[57] See Virgil, *The Eclogues, The Georgics*, tr. C. Day Lewis, ed. R. O. A. M. Lyne (Oxford: OUP, 1983), pp. xxiv–xxxii.

[58] Uglow, *Gaskell*, 542.

abandons Phillis to the fate of a Victorian Dido—not death on a funeral pyre but a near-fatal illness which apparently restores her innocence by returning her to childish dependence on her parents. However, Gaskell's ending suggests that Phillis's hope that a brief absence from her home will complete the healing process and allow her to 'go back to the peace of the old days' (317) is a false one. She cannot bear to look at the Latin and Italian texts whose early domestic associations have been superseded by their connection with Holdsworth. The story is not an encouraging one for a scholarly woman, since it ends by offering Phillis the choice of returning to an artificially extended childhood as her father's pupil or abandoning the texts which recall her sexual temptation. This was not the ending Gaskell had intended; she had planned to have Paul returning years later to find Phillis as a farmer with considerable technical skills and an adoptive mother to several abandoned children, but the publisher George Smith cut the story short, feeling that readers would prefer a deserted, long-suffering romantic heroine.[59]

The patterns established in Gaskell's representation of the classics in relation to daughters of the Church and Nonconformists are reiterated in *Phoebe, Junior* (1876) by Margaret Oliphant. Phoebe (like Gaskell's Phillis) is the daughter of a Nonconformist minister, but one who moves in a more modern and worldly society. She is educated at home by a governess, and attends lectures by eminent men on a wide range of subjects, as well as following 'Mr Ruskin's theory that dancing, drawing, and cooking were three of the higher arts which ought to be studied by girls'. Phoebe is 'very well got up in the subject of education for women' but not allowed to take the Cambridge Local examination because her father feels that when the results are published 'the connection might think it strange to see his daughter's name in the papers', and because he associates such qualifications with the teaching profession.[60] Phoebe is contrasted with Ursula May, the daughter of a perpetual curate, with 'no pretensions to be intellectual', who is excluded from her brother's

---

[59] Linda K. Hughes and Michael Lund, *Victorian Publishing and Mrs. Gaskell's Work* (London: UP of Virginia, 1999), 161–2.

[60] Margaret Oliphant, *Phoebe, Junior* (1876) (London: Virago, 1989), 17–18. Further quotations are given parenthetically in the text.

scholarly interests: 'to hear him talk with his father about Greek poetry and philosophy was a very fine thing indeed; how Phoebe Beecham would have prized it; but Ursula did not enjoy the privilege' (30).

Phoebe, Junior is particularly interesting because it continues Gaskell's intertextual dialogue with novels about scholarly heroines. Oliphant's use of the name May is a deliberate allusion to *The Daisy Chain*, on which Phoebe bases her judgement of members of the May family, although they are eager to point out that they are not 'a set of prigs' like Yonge's characters (141). This is a reminder of Yonge's popularity—she was 'the novelist most middle-class women (and many men) read in childhood and adolescence from the middle of the nineteenth century onwards'.[61] Oliphant's plot alludes to the accusation against Mr Crawley in *The Last Chronicle of Barset*, but in her novel the clergyman is guilty of theft and lacks tragic stature even in his own eyes. Phoebe's name recalls *Cousin Phillis*, and Oliphant, who sought to challenge the traditional distinction between sewing and writing by offering a 'model of the professional originating in and emerging from the domestic', may have wished to endorse Gaskell's combination of domestic duty and intellectual work.[62] The phrase 'she read Virgil at least, if not Sophocles' (18) suggests that Oliphant wishes to align her heroine with Gaskell's gentle classicism (exemplified by the Holmans' reading of the *Georgics*), rather than with Eliot, whose interest in the intractable heroes of Sophoclean tragedy is examined in the following chapter.[63] In choosing to

[61] Valerie Sanders, *Eve's Renegades: Victorian Anti-Feminist Women Novelists* (Basingstoke: Macmillan, 1996), 59.

[62] Linda H. Peterson, 'Margaret Oliphant's *Autobiography* as Professional Artist's Life', *Women's Writing*, 6 (1999), 267.

[63] Oliphant, a competitive writer who resented Eliot's pre-eminence and the comparative financial security which enabled her to concentrate on novels rather than journalism, responded more positively to Gaskell's famous charm and less intimidating literary reputation. Pauline Nestor, *Female Friendships and Communities: Charlotte Brontë, George Eliot, Elizabeth Gaskell* (Oxford: Clarendon, 1985), 28. Gaskell did engage with Sophocles in a short story, 'The Doom of the Griffiths', which draws on *Oedipus Tyrannos* in its depiction of a family curse. Owen Griffiths (who knows that, as the last male of his race, he is fated to kill his father) reads Sophocles' play and identifies with the hero. Like Oedipus, he fulfils his doom in attempting to escape it. Elizabeth Gaskell, *Gothic Tales*, ed. Laura Kranzler (Harmondsworth: Penguin, 2000), 103–38.

place *Phoebe, Junior* so clearly within a tradition of novels about dutiful daughters who do not associate classical studies with personal ambition, in opposition to Eliot's rebellious heroines, Oliphant confirms that Victorian novel readers not only accepted that girls could learn Latin and Greek, but recognized different models of female learning, undertaken for a variety of reasons.

5

Greek Heroines and the Wrongs of Women

When George Eliot enhances the stature of her heroines by likening
the predicament of Victorian women to that of the heroines of Greek
tragedy, such as Antigone and Medea, she is participating in a more
widespread recognition that ancient heroines could speak eloquently
of the wrongs of women in a way which resonated with Victorian
readers. Eliot had seen the powerful effect of Greek tragedy even in a
translation she considered feeble: 'so completely did the poet
triumph over the disadvantages of his medium and of a dramatic
motive foreign to modern sympathies, that the Pit was electrified,
and Sophocles, over a chasm of two thousand years, once more
swayed the emotions of a popular audience'.[1] Serious and burlesque
versions of figures like Medea, Antigone, and Clytemnestra appeared
on the Victorian stage in the 1840s and 1850s, emphasizing
the heroines' vulnerability as well as their violence and rebellion.
Theatrical versions of Medea drew on the issues surrounding divorce
reform and participated in debates which shaped the Divorce and
Matrimonial Causes Act of 1857.[2] Poets also produced translations
and adaptations of Greek tragedy, although choral odes and other
formal features caused difficulties. Matthew Arnold's *Merope* (1858)

---

[1] Eliot, *Selected Critical Writings*, 243.

[2] Fiona Macintosh, 'Medea Transposed: Burlesque and Gender on the Mid-
Victorian Stage', in Edith Hall, Fiona Macintosh, and Oliver Taplin (eds.), *Medea in
Performance 1500–2000* (Oxford: Legenda, 2000), 85–6. Eliot would have known
about these productions, since they were discussed in periodicals like the *Athenaeum*
and the *Illustrated London News*, and G. H. Lewes saw both burlesque and tragic
versions: he wrote that Adelaide Ristori's performance in Legouvé's *Medea* 'surpassed
all expectation': G.H.L. to John Blackwood, 6 Aug. [1857]. *The George Eliot Letters*,
ed. Gordon S. Haight (London: OUP, 1954), ii. 372.

is modelled on Sophocles' *Electra,* but the play is much longer than any surviving Greek tragedy and exchanges emotional intensity for the investigation of moral dilemmas in a manner more reminiscent of *Hamlet.* Arnold himself realized that the play was an academic exercise which would not 'move deeply the present race of humans'.[3] More successful interpretations of the spirit of Greek tragedy tend to be found in newer forms such as the novel and the dramatic monologue. Reframing tragic experience to fit modern literary forms necessitated some reworking of the central characters which both challenged and deferred to Victorian gender ideals. A combination of defiance and submission in terms of gender is articulated through classical figures whose cultural eminence compensated for their scandalous lives: in Eliot's, Augusta Webster's, and Amy Levy's Medeas an infamous figure is toned down to make her more representative. Levy and Eliza Lynn deal with the sufferings of historical women (Socrates' wife and Pericles' mistress) in a similar way, implicitly equating fifth-century Athens and Victorian England in ways that undercut the idealized vision of Greece projected by writers such as Matthew Arnold by recalling the sufferings of women who were excluded from the privileged circles of high culture.

ASPASIA AND XANTIPPE

Like many historical novels, Eliza Lynn's *Amymone: A Romance of the Days of Pericles* (1848) contains criticism of the author's own times. Ironically, given her later career as a scourge of emancipated women (as Eliza Lynn Linton, author of 'The Girl of the Period'), it includes strong indictments of the unjustness of patriarchal society, and exalts Aspasia, Pericles' mistress, the heroine who wants women to become men's equals. Aspasia is an extraordinary choice for a heroine in 1848: she is a 'hetaira' or courtesan. Lynn is keen to emphasize her accomplishments and to downplay any suggestion of sexual

---

[3] Matthew Arnold, *The Complete Poems*, ed. Kenneth Allott and Miriam Allott, 2nd edn. (London: Longman, 1979), 432.

impropriety: 'she was branded with the name of courtesan, because she had learnt those arts of education which had hitherto been reserved for this class; because she had endeavoured to rescue philosophy, learning, and art, from the purposes of seduction'.[4] Some ancient writers, such as Plutarch and Aristophanes, claimed that Aspasia kept a house of courtesans, and the comedian Hermippus accused her of impiety and of procuring women for Pericles; she was brought to trial but acquitted. The novel's preface proclaims Lynn's intention to persuade readers that Aspasia's historical reputation is unmerited and based on prejudice against learned women: 'Her unusual learning and independent life were crimes to the conservatism of social Athens. She was condemned; and posterity has repeated that condemnation, because posterity has the same conservatism to maintain' (i, p. vi). There is an obvious element of self-defence here, since Eliza Lynn herself exemplified 'unusual learning and independent life', and the narrator's statement that the treatment of women in Greece was 'singular' is evidently ironic:

> The condition of women in Greece was singular. Where the hetaira had all love, liberty, and consideration, where her education was most carefully watched, and her mind and person tenderly trained and adorned with accomplishments, the modest woman, the wife and the sister and the daughter were kept in almost prison seclusion; debarred all exercise of free will; denied from almost all but religious amusements; cut off from every means of improvement and self-culture ...   (i. 113)

Amymone was favourably reviewed, although it promotes controversial ideas about free love and women's rights through the character of Aspasia. This was partly due to the patronage of Landor, who was a devotee of historical novels set in the ancient world and had written *Pericles and Aspasia* (1836), a series of imaginary letters. He praised the correctness of Lynn's representation of Athenian life and compared her novel to Becker's *Gallus*, a textbook made up of short fictional passages about daily life in Rome, but claimed that Lynn's narrative was superior in possessing 'a truth of passion, ... a depth of thought which is nowhere to be found in the very admirable work

---

[4] Eliza Lynn [Linton], *Amymone, A Romance of the Days of Pericles* (London: Richard Bentley, 1848), ii. 79. Further references are given parenthetically in the text.

of the erudite and accurate Professor'.[5] Lynn uses the figure of
Aspasia to criticize the sexual double standard shared by Periclean
Athens and Victorian England: 'modest' women are barely educated
and are expected to maintain their purity by staying within the home,
so men consort with public women—actresses, singers, prostitutes—
but are not condemned for impurity. Nevertheless, she weakens her
argument by domesticating Aspasia, who is nearly always referred to
as Pericles' 'wife' and for most of the novel is only a slightly politi-
cized angel in the house. Within her relationship with Pericles, she is
submissive and adoring. Like a Victorian wife, she can only participate in politics through her spiritual influence over her husband: 'She
it was who had made him other and higher than the mere legislator,
the mere politician; leading him to blend poetry and art with
practical government' (i. 59). Although male visitors such as Socrates,
Euripides, and Sophocles visit Pericles and Aspasia, she does not
express her opinions while they are present, although authors like
Xenophon praise her rhetorical skills on the basis of her dialogues
with Socrates. Despite the subversive implications of her attempt to
rehabilitate Aspasia's reputation, Lynn is already suggesting that an
ideal marriage requires submission on the wife's part; 'The Girl of the
Period' expresses her fear that modern girls will not submit.

　Having cast Aspasia merely as a cultured woman and dutiful wife in
the first volume, Lynn makes her a more powerful and controversial
figure in the second. Like the author, Aspasia has rejected the religion
of her childhood, seeing it as having only symbolic value. She also
advocates a kind of marriage which is based on love, and lasts only
while love lasts, although she realizes that her society is not yet ready
for such an ideal. Aspasia makes several long speeches about equality
between the sexes, and a male friend claims to detect her influence in
the funeral oration Pericles delivers after the end of the Samian War.
By the time of her trial, in the third volume, Lynn has suggested that
the charges of impiety and immorality stand for the misrepresenta-
tion of women who dare to think for themselves and to challenge

　[5] [W. S. Landor], 'Harold, and Amymone', *Fraser's Magazine*, 38 (Oct. 1848), 429.
The textbook Landor compares to *Amymone* is Wilhelm Becker, *Gallus; Or, Roman
Scenes of the Time of Augustus*, tr. Frederick Metcalfe (London: J. W. Parker, 1844).
Becker had also written a textbook on Athenian life, *Charicles* (tr. into English
in 1845).

social convention. The trial of Aspasia is also a political challenge to
Pericles, and to democracy, which is defeated when the people respond not to his arguments, but to the more typically feminine
persuasion of tears, another manifestation of Aspasia's influence on
politics through love. Again Lynn hints at daring conclusions and
ends by endorsing a fairly conventional ideal of femininity.

The anti-heroine Amymone shares Aspasia's predicament: she is
the daughter of a foreign woman, so her children cannot be citizens,
and therefore no Athenian will marry her. She marries a Persian and
becomes involved in a plot to gain citizenship for her husband which
involves the murder of his patron and the forging of a will. Amymone
is cold and cannot submit to her loathed husband, but this frigidity
makes her a model for Athenian womanhood: 'She surpassed
Clytemnestra in her hatred, while wanting in the passion, guilty
though it was, which impelled her to her crime. For this the world
called her chaste and virtuous ... bidding their daughters take
example by her' (ii. 78). She hates Aspasia and gives evidence against
her at her trial, although it was not usual for a woman to appear in an
Athenian court. After Aspasia's acquittal, Amymone is tried and
imprisoned for her crimes, and is compared to Medea. When in
prison, Amymone knows that her child will become a slave: 'She
quivered with agony at the thought. A flame of burning fire seemed
lighted in her heart; she could have shrieked aloud writhing in the
tortures of Glauce, as the poisonous thought burst into flames that
consumed her. She had sinned, and now she must suffer' (iii. 337).
Like Medea, she kills her child, but she also kills herself as Medea
destroys Glauce. Lynn's allusions to both Medea and Glauce as
parallels for her heroine may have influenced Eliot's portrayal of
Hetty Sorrel. Whether Eliot recalled Lynn's allusions or not, this
shows how powerfully Greek tragic women, especially Medea,
the vengeful victim, and Glauce, the innocent victim, symbolized
the position of women in a patriarchal society.

In Amy Levy's 'Xantippe' (1881), Aspasia appears as an object of
envy to a woman who has given up her own ambitions. Levy attacks
patriarchal society for thwarting the ambitions of intelligent and
capable women, and for casting those who do not conform to the
ideal of brainless domestic angel as vicious and shrewish. The poem is
obviously influenced by Browning's dramatic monologues in evoking

understanding for an unsympathetic character, Socrates' wife, reputed to be a scold. Levy recasts Xantippe's life as the familiar plot of a woman who attempts to satisfy her craving for intellectual activity by entering into marriage with a man she sees as a mentor, and is disappointed when she realizes that he wants a submissive wife and not an equal:

> ... the high philosopher,
> Pregnant with noble theories and great thoughts,
> Deigned not to stoop to touch so slight a thing
> As the fine fabric of a woman's brain—
> So subtle as a passionate woman's soul.
> I think, if he had stooped a little, and cared,
> I might have risen nearer to his height,
> And not lain shattered, neither fit for use
> As goodly household vessel, nor for that
> Far finer thing which I had hoped to be ...

> (116–25)[6]

Like Dorothea Brooke in *Middlemarch*, Xantippe has a 'soul which yearned for knowledge' (38); when her father tells her she is to marry Socrates she believes that he will enable her to achieve her dreams. Xantippe's exclusion from culture is direct and annihilating: not only is her life restricted to the home but even there Socrates, Alcibiades, and Plato 'cruelly taunt her when she does engage in dialogue with them'.[7] Their mocking of her philosophical aspirations is all the more painful because of the contrast with Aspasia, the 'stranger-woman, bold | With freedom, thought and glib philosophy' (227–8), who is granted a special status by Socrates and his friends. However, the narrative of Xantippe's frustration is interrupted by an incident which recalls the imagery of fire and ice, and the outbursts of the madwoman, in *Jane Eyre*: the 'cold contempt' expressed by Socrates is counteracted by a 'sudden flame, a merciful fury' which releases Xantippe's repressed anger (211, 213). She throws down a full wine-skin, creating a shockingly violent and bloody image of rebellion:

> Then, all unheeding faces, voices, eyes,
> I fled across the threshold, hair unbound—

---

[6] *The Complete Novels and Selected Writings of Amy Levy 1861–1889*, ed. Melvyn New (Gainsville, Fla.: UP of Florida, 1993).

[7] Cynthia Scheinberg, 'Recasting "Sympathy and Judgement": Amy Levy, Women Poets, and the Victorian Dramatic Monologue', *VP* 35 (1997), 182.

> White garment stained to redness—beating heart
> Flooded with the flowing tide of hopes
> Which once had gushed out golden ...
>
> (217–21)

The combination of wine and violence, unbound hair and an altered state of consciousness, suggest that Xantippe's rage makes her like a maenad. However, this outburst represents the end of her defiance, and she decides with great bitterness to become an exemplary house-wife. She does not welcome sympathy from her female companions, whom she had disdained when she was younger—rather, 'such a community is her last resort, and ultimately unsatisfying'.[8] She is speaking to an audience of maids while she sits and performs house-hold tasks such as spinning and weaving (equivalent to the dress-making and embroidery performed by Victorian ladies). It would have been possible to represent this activity in a positive way, since it recalls the artistry and female power associated with weavers like Penelope, yet here spinning and weaving are not seen as creative but as mechanical processes which numb the intellect. Xantippe spins away her soul and intellect until she is overcome by bitterness and can only take pleasure in imposing the same limits on other women. Levy dramatizes the frustration and despair of female intellect and the sacrifice of female self-respect which the institution of marriage had implied since ancient Greece.

TRAGEDY AND THE NOVEL

George Eliot establishes the importance of the novel as a tragic form at a time when stage tragedy was in decline.[9] It was Eliot's novels which finally obtained for her the kind of academic and literary

---

[8] Scheinberg, 'Recasting "Sympathy and Judgement"', *VP* 35 (1997), 182.

[9] See Jeannette King, *Tragedy in the Victorian Novel: Theory and Practice in the Novels of George Eliot, Thomas Hardy and Henry James* (Cambridge: CUP, 1978); P. E. Easterling, 'George Eliot and Greek Tragedy', *George Eliot Review*, 25 (1994), 56–67; Darrel Mansel, jun., 'George Eliot's Conception of Tragedy', *Nineteenth-Century Fiction*, 22 (1967), 155–7; Fred C. Thomson, '*Felix Holt* as Classic Tragedy', *Nineteenth-Century Fiction*, 16 (1961), 47–58.

connections to which a man of her ability would have been admitted
at a far earlier stage. Her writing was praised by classical scholars like
Jebb, who asked Eliot how Sophocles had influenced her fiction: 'he
was startled to hear her say "In the delineation of the great primitive
emotions", which was an impression he had written down privately
long before'.[10] Eliot's erudition did not just exceed that of most
learned women; she also outstripped the products of those educational institutions from which women were excluded. Her knowledge
of Greek and Latin was 'more solid than that Thackeray got at
Charterhouse and Cambridge, probably wider than that Trollope
got at Harrow and Winchester'.[11] The range and depth of Eliot's
classical reading is extraordinary, and it is reflected in her private
writings as well as published works: according to Vernon Rendall, her
fiction, diary, and letters contain references to nine Greek authors
and eight Latin writers. Joseph Wiesenfarth adds eight more Greeks
and four Romans, as well as noting that Eliot's responses to classical
literature were sometimes mediated by German writers such as
Lessing, Goethe, and Heine.[12] Yet the twenty-nine authors identified
by these critics do not include such important influences as Euripides, Lucretius, or Marcus Aurelius (all mentioned in her journals)
or Theophrastus, whose *Characters* inspired Eliot's last book, *The
Impressions of Theophrastus Such* (1879).[13] Her learning was regarded
as a remarkable achievement by contemporary male scholars, as John
Fiske's enthusiastic praise of her knowledge of Homer's texts and the
Homeric question demonstrates: 'I found her thoroughly acquainted
with the whole literature of the Homeric question; and she seems to

---

[10] Caroline Jebb, *Life and Letters of Sir Richard Claverhouse Jebb* (Cambridge: CUP,
1907), 156. Quoted in Gordon S. Haight, *George Eliot: A Biography* (London:
Clarendon, 1968), 464.

[11] Haight, *George Eliot*, 195.

[12] Vernon Rendall, 'George Eliot and the Classics', in Gordon S. Haight (ed.),
A Century of George Eliot Criticism (London: Methuen, 1966), 215–26: Aeschylus,
Aristotle, Epictetus, Homer, Nonnus, Pausanias, Sophocles, Thucydides, Xenophon,
Cicero, Juvenal, Persius, Plautus, Quintilian, Tacitus, Virgil, and Horace. Joseph
Wiesenfarth, 'The Greeks, the Germans and George Eliot', *Browning Institute Studies*,
10 (1982), 91–2, adds the following list (taken from Haight's biography): Aesop,
Aristophanes, Caesar, Hesiod, Menander, Ovid, Plato, Pliny the Elder and Younger,
Plutarch, Theocritus, Zeno.

[13] George Eliot, *The Impressions of Theophrastus Such* (1879), ed. D. J. Enright
(London: Dent, 1995).

have read all of Homer in Greek, too, and could meet me everywhere. She didn't talk like a blue-stocking ... but like a plain woman, who talked of Homer as simply as she would of flat-irons'.[14]

Unlike most of the women writers who read Latin and Greek, Mary Ann Evans was the daughter of a largely self-educated man who never studied the classics—Kathryn Hughes even suggests that, like Mr Tulliver, he was uneasy with the written word.[15] Robert Evans was aware that his children's schooling would elevate their social status, and he sent them to genteel schools which reinforced middle-class gender stereotypes in a pattern familiar to readers of *The Mill on the Floss*. When Isaac Evans was 8 years old, he was sent to school near Coventry to begin learning the Latin and Greek which would mark him as a gentleman, and later on he had a clerical tutor like Tom Tulliver's. Mary Ann attended several girls' schools, of which the last was a cosmopolitan establishment where the formal course of study included music, drawing, French, history, arithmetic, and English literature.[16] Her father encouraged her to read, paid for whatever books she wanted, and arranged for a tutor to teach her Italian and German. His occupation as agent to the Newdegate family gave her access to resources beyond those which would have been available to her friends: Mrs Charles Newdegate invited her to borrow any books she wanted from the library of Arbury Hall. She became interested in classical literature and tried, unsuccessfully, to persuade her friend Martha Jackson 'to follow her example of study-ing Latin by Locke's System of Classical Instruction'. Later she 'got help with her Latin from the Reverend Thomas Sheepshanks, Rector of St John's Church, Coventry, and Headmaster of the Free Grammar School' and read Xenophon with a candidate for the Independent ministry who helped her with Greek during the holidays.[17]

After her father's death, she took the unconventional step of moving alone to London to pursue a literary career, writing for

[14] *Letters of John Fiske*, ed. Ethel Fiske Fisk (New York: Macmillan, 1940), 277–9. Quoted in Haight, *George Eliot*, 468.

[15] Kathryn Hughes, *George Eliot: The Last Victorian* (London: Fourth Estate, 1999), 13.

[16] See Haight, *George Eliot*, 6–13.

[17] Ibid. 25, 35, 62. See also Christopher Stray, 'Locke's System of Classical Instruc-tion', *Locke Newsletter*, 22 (1991), 115–21.

periodicals, and editing ten numbers of the *Westminster Review*. Eliot's career offered a model for a professional woman writer who did not remain at home and write in hours snatched from domestic duties: she might begin with journalism (and editing) as an apprenticeship, and move on to 'serious' writing after achieving financial stability. The convention of anonymity in periodical writing enabled women to adopt a style that was commonly identified as masculine and to express opinions on a wide range of subjects. Eliot expounded the aesthetic and moral principles which were to shape her fiction in reviews and essays such as 'The Natural History of German Life' (1856), which articulates ideas later discussed in *Adam Bede* about realism and the depiction of rural life. She also wrote essays on the classical tradition, such as 'The Art of the Ancients', 'Menander and the Greek Comedy', and 'The Art and Artists of Greece'.[18] In 1854, she defied society and her family to live with the married G. H. Lewes, who shared her intellectual interests and encouraged her to write fiction as well as journalism. The crucial phase of her classical reading was undoubtedly 'the long period of social ostracism when, because of her honest avowal of the union with Lewes, she was not invited to dinner'. Between 1855 and 1858, she read in Greek the second book of the *Iliad*, Sophocles' *Ajax*, *Electra*, *Philoctetes*, and the *Oedipus* trilogy, and the *Oresteia* of Aeschylus.[19]

Eliot's first notable commentary on classical literature appears in 'The *Antigone* and its Moral', published in the *Leader* in 1856. This essay examines the Sophoclean tragedy which supplied one of the archetypes for Eliot's female characters. Throughout the nineteenth century, claims George Steiner, scholars thought *Antigone* the finest Greek tragedy, although in the preface to his *Poems* (1853), Matthew Arnold had claimed that it was no longer possible to feel a deep interest in the conflict because of the remoteness of the religious and moral customs.[20] In Eliot's essay, which reflected the success of an English translation of *Antigone* with music by Mendelssohn at Covent Garden in 1845, the play's powerful appeal to a modern theatre audience and readership is highlighted. Eliot stresses that,

[18] George Eliot, *A Writer's Notebook, 1854–1879*, ed. Joseph Wiesenfarth (Charlottesville, Va.: UP of Virginia, 1981).

[19] Haight, *George Eliot*, 195.

[20] George Steiner, *Antigones* (Oxford: Clarendon, 1984), 1.

although modern readers cannot share the religious belief on which Antigone's rebellion is based, they should respond to the dramatic collision between values based on family responsibilities and duties to the state. The penultimate paragraph of the essay restates the conflict in terms which will be familiar to readers of Eliot's novels, a clash between the individual and society in which neither side can claim a moral victory:

> Wherever the strength of a man's intellect, or moral sense, or affection brings him into opposition with the rules which society has sanctioned, *there* is renewed the conflict between Antigone and Creon; such a man must not only dare to be right, he must also dare to be wrong ... Like Antigone, he may fall a victim to the struggle, and yet he can never earn the name of a blameless martyr any more than the society—the Creon he has defied, can be branded as a hypocritical tyrant.[21]

Rather than describing the novel as 'an anti-classical art form', it is more productive to appreciate, as educated Victorian readers did, that the genre was capable of taking up ancient tropes and characters and rendering them comprehensible, sympathetic, and modern.[22] Mythic features could be recast in realist terms: Nemesis becomes the unpredictable consequences of any action, and the family curse is reworked as the effects of heredity. In *Adam Bede*, the narrator comments: 'Nature, that great tragic dramatist, knits us together by bone and muscle, and divides us by the subtler web of our brains; blends yearning and repulsion; and ties us by our heartstrings to the beings that jar us at every movement'(38). Eliot incorporates tragedy into *The Mill on the Floss* with devices such as the chorus of aunts and uncles who comment on the action, the description of 'the passions at war in Maggie' as 'the essential $\tau\iota$ $\mu\epsilon\gamma\epsilon\theta\sigma\varsigma$ of tragedy' (88), and the title of book 3—'The Downfall'. The suffering of the heroine's family and the reversal of their fortunes invoke the doomed families of Greek tragedy, as do *Wuthering Heights* and *Jude the Obscure*: it is not surprising that G. H. Lewes favoured the title *The House of Tulliver*.[23] Nevertheless, the tragic elements are repeatedly undercut by bathos or by a more positive train of events: Maggie's passions

[21] Eliot, *Selected Critical Writings*, 246.
[22] Jenkyns, *Greece*, 112.
[23] *G.E. Letters*, iii. 240.

lead, at this point, to no more than a muddy dress for Lucy, and Mr Tulliver's reversal of fortune is eventually counteracted by his son's hard work.

Between 1856 and 1858, at the time when Eliot first wrote fiction, she was intensively reading the Greek tragedians and Aristotle's *Poetics*. The three stories which make up *Scenes of Clerical Life* (1858) were intended to illustrate the drama of Evangelicalism, and they establish a connection between Greek tragedy and modern realist fiction by quoting from the works of Sophocles. They are less subtle in their assimilation of the language and themes to the tragedy of everyday life than Eliot's later fictions. In 'The Sad Fortunes of the Rev. Amos Barton', for example, the narrator comments on the Countess Czerlaski's

serious intentions of becoming quite pious—without any reserves—when she had once got her carriage and settlement. Let us do this one sly trick, says Ulysses to Neoptolemus, and we will be perfectly honest ever after—

$$\dot{\alpha}\lambda\lambda' \ \dot{\eta}\delta\dot{\upsilon} \ \gamma\dot{\alpha}\rho \ \tau\iota \ \kappa\tau\tilde{\eta}\mu\alpha \ \tau\tilde{\eta}s \ \nu\dot{\iota}\kappa\eta s \ \lambda\alpha\beta\tilde{\epsilon}\iota\nu$$
$$\tau o\lambda\mu\alpha. \ \delta\dot{\iota}\kappa\alpha\iota o\iota \ \delta' \ \alpha\tilde{\upsilon}\theta\iota s \ \dot{\epsilon}\kappa\varphi\alpha\nuo\dot{\upsilon}\mu\epsilon\theta\alpha.$$

The Countess did not quote Sophocles, but she said to herself, 'Only this little bit of pretence and vanity, and then I will be quite good, and make myself quite safe for another world.'[24]

Here the allusion to lines 81–2 of Sophocles' *Philoctetes* (translated by Jebb as 'yet knowing that victory is a sweet prize to gain, bend thy will thereto. Our honesty shall be shown forth another time'[25]) seems rather self-conscious, as does the quotation from *Electra* in 'Janet's Repentance', another of the *Scenes of Clerical Life*, especially when contrasted with similar references in *The Mill on the Floss*. Yet these stories effectively establish one of Eliot's most important precepts: that tragedy does not necessarily take place in the royal courts which are often represented in drama, but may happen in an English village, and its protagonist might be a poor vicar rather than a mythical king. To the individual, Eliot recognizes, his own life seems magnificent

[24] George Eliot, *Scenes of Clerical Life* (1858), ed. Thomas A. Noble (Oxford: Clarendon, 1985), 40–1. Further references are given parenthetically in the text.
[25] Sophocles, *The Plays and Fragments with Critical Notes, Commentary, and Translation*, ed. Richard Claverhouse Jebb (Cambridge: CUP, 1883), iv. 21.

enough for tragedy, so everyone has the potential to be a tragic hero: this perception extends the Wordsworthian strategy of making humble and rustic life interesting by connecting it to high culture. In 'Amos Barton', the narrator adjures the reader to sympathize with 'a man whose virtues were not heroic, and who … was palpably and unmistakably commonplace' (41). This act of sympathy with a fictional character, Eliot claims, assists the reader in an understanding of everyday life: 'you would gain unspeakably if you would learn with me to see some of the poetry and the pathos, the tragedy and the comedy, lying in the experience of a human soul that looks out through dull grey eyes' (42).

Eliot's recognition that every life has tragic possibilities does not mean that her novels always have tragic endings. It is interesting that the very first Greek quotation in her fiction (in 'Amos Barton') is not from *Antigone* or *Medea*, plays with strong female characters which she was to use to great effect in later novels. Instead, she chose to quote from Sophocles' *Philoctetes*, an unconventional, experimental tragedy with no female characters at all. This play reappears in *The Mill on the Floss* as a story told by Philip Wakem 'about a man who had a very bad wound in his foot, and cried out so dreadfully with the pain that his friends could bear with him no longer, but put him ashore on a desert island, with nothing but some wonderful poisoned arrows' (160). *Philoctetes* ends with the wounded hero setting out from his isolation and agony on Lemnos to Troy, where, according to Heracles' prophecy, he will be cured and will enable the Greeks to capture the city. It is, then, a tragedy in which the hero's suffering will soon be replaced by healing and glory, whereas in most tragedy there can be only defeat without surrender.[26] It is not exactly a happy ending, but is closer to comedy in its focus on the future, and there are no deaths during the play, although the tragedy of the Trojan War is a constant presence in the drama.

The refusal or averting of tragedy is characteristic of Eliot's fiction: the frequency of tragic possibilities is more important than any individual's tragic end. Most characters do not have to die, because they can be exiled, or purged by suffering and returned to society.

---

[26] See Bernard Knox, *The Heroic Temper: Studies in Sophoclean Tragedy* (Berkeley: Calif.: University of California Press, 1964), 117–24, for a discussion of *Philoctetes*.

In *Adam Bede*, Martin Poyser's prophecy that his family will face ostracism or exile is a form of the family curse of Greek tragedy (although Poyser is more likely to interpret it in biblical terms): 'we shall ne'er go far enough for folks not to find out as we've got them belonging to us as are transported o'er the seas, and were like to be hanged. We shall have that flyin' up in our faces, and our children's after us' (433). This doom is averted by Arthur's insistence that they remain in Hayslope while he redeems himself by fighting for his country; only Hetty is never allowed to return.

Eliot consistently seeks to educate the reader's understanding of how tragedy works in everyday life because this kind of awareness may prevent suffering. In almost every one of Eliot's novels there is a tragic episode, although the story as a whole may work against tragedy. In *Felix Holt*, for example, 'such tragic unity as Eliot might have found in the Transome story alone is subordinate to an inclusive study of society'.[27] Esther's recognition of the tragedy of Mrs Transome's life is a final affirmation of her own happier choice, which 'seemed to have come as a last vision to urge her towards the life where the draughts of joy sprang from the unchanging fountains of reverence and devout love'.[28] Such understanding may come from judicious reading: Mr Irwine's disregarded Aeschylean warnings could have averted Hetty's tragedy, had Arthur chosen to accept them. However, most of the readers of classical literature in Eliot's novels do not share Irwine's sympathy and perception.

As a didactic novelist, Eliot remade in a modern form the literature which had taught men like Irwine compassion, so that it could reach and educate a wider readership. In *Middlemarch*, the narrator remarks: 'we do not expect people to be deeply moved by what is not unusual. That element of tragedy which lies in the very fact of frequency, has not yet wrought itself into the coarse emotion of mankind'. If we were aware of just how often lives are tragic, Eliot suggests, we would be sensitized to a degree which might prove unbearable: 'it would be like hearing the grass grow and the squirrel's

---

[27] Alison Booth, 'Not All Men are Selfish and Cruel: *Felix Holt* as a Feminist Novel', in Anthony H. Harrison and Beverly Taylor (eds.), *Gender and Discourse in Victorian Literature and Art*, (DeKalb, Ill.: Northern Illinois UP, 1992), 150.

[28] George Eliot, *Felix Holt, the Radical* (1866), ed. Fred C. Thomson (Oxford: Clarendon, 1980), 393–4.

heart beat, and we should die of that roar which lies on the other side of silence' (189). Yet a sympathetic reader should (like Esther Lyon or Mr Irwine) feel the 'pathos' of a situation, although it may seem to be 'below the level of tragedy'; a reader who properly appreciates *Middlemarch* must feel for Casaubon: 'are there many situations more sublimely tragic than the struggle of the soul with the demand to renounce a work which has been all the significance of its life ... which is to vanish as the waters which come and go where no man has need of them?' (413).

Eliot's adaptation of the themes and situations of Greek tragedy to realist fiction has been extensively discussed by critics, but it is also worth focusing on the ways in which she translates motifs and images into realist narrative. One of the recurring motifs of Greek tragedy which Eliot reworks in her fictions is that of a poisoned garment or jewels. In 'Mr Gilfil's Love-Story', one of the *Scenes of Clerical Life*, Eliot 'alludes to the poisoned garment in the *Trachiniae*'.[29] Sophocles' play represents Deianeira, hearing that her husband Heracles has brought home a captive princess to replace his wife, and seeking to regain his love by sending him a tunic soaked in the blood of the dead Centaur Nessus. (Heracles had killed Nessus with an arrow poisoned with the venom of the Lernaean Hydra; the dying Centaur persuaded Deianeira to keep the blood and use it as a love charm.) Having sent the tunic to her husband, she sees the effect of the envenomed blood on a fragment of wool, which shrivels into powder, and realizes the trick Nessus had perpetrated. The remorseful Deianeira stabs herself. In Sophocles' version, then, the plot works through a deserted wife's desire to reclaim her husband's love, not through her wish to kill him, and Heracles unwittingly provides the means by which he is killed. In Eliot's story, Captain Wybrow, like Heracles, is a potential husband to two women. He flirts with his uncle's protégée Caterina Sarti out of boredom, and becomes engaged to Beatrice Assher, a suitable match for the heir to an estate. Eliot emphasizes that her aristocratic protectors do not consider Caterina an equal—her status as the family pet is underlined by references to her as a bird or a monkey—and her guardian expects her to marry Maynard Gilfil, a poor curate. Incapable of loving

---

[29] Jenkyns, *Greece*, 114.

anyone except himself, but unable to 'withstand the temptation of a woman to fascinate, and another man to eclipse', Wybrow finds that 'matters had reached a point which he had not at all contemplated. Gentle tones had led to tender words, and tender words had called forth a response of looks which made it impossible not to carry on the *crescendo* of love-making' (114). His vanity is gratified by the feeling that he is caught 'between two jealous women, and both of them ready to take fire as tinder' (138). However, he has a morbid consciousness that the self-imposed tension of his situation acts badly on his weak heart, and eventually decides to give up Caterina to Gilfil. Feeling that he has betrayed her, Caterina prepares to enact the role of a vengeful and violent heroine of Greek tragedy, a Medea or a Clytemnestra, snatching up a dagger and hurrying to confront Wybrow: she 'rushes noiselessly, like a pale meteor ... Those gleaming eyes, those bloodless lips, that swift silent tread, make her look like the incarnation of a fierce purpose, rather than a woman' (155).[30] Her murderous resolve is never tested, because she finds him already dead 'from long-established disease of the heart ... accelerated by some unusual emotion' (171). Like Heracles, he is killed by the incalculable effects of his actions. This is Eliot's version of Nemesis: 'Consequences are unpitying. Our deeds carry their terrible consequences, quite apart from any fluctuations that went before—consequences that are hardly ever confined to ourselves'.[31] Caterina is explicitly linked with the motif of the poisoned garment, when she is told that Wybrow has prompted Sir Christopher to arrange her engagement to Gilfil: 'With the poisoned garment upon him, the victim writhes under the torture—he has no thought

---

[30] Eliot's description of Caterina is reminiscent of Becky Sharp playing Clytemnestra, when she 'glides swiftly into the room like an apparition—her arms are bare and white,—her tawny hair floats down her shoulders,—her face is deadly pale,—and her eyes are lighted up with a smile so ghastly, that people quake as they look at her'. Thackeray, *Vanity Fair*, 645–6. The charade is echoed in the main narrative when Rawdon is arrested by the bailiffs and Becky betrays him by not sending the money for his release—he returns home, like Agamemnon, to find his wife with another man. Later in the novel, the illustration 'Becky's Second Appearance in the Character of Clytemnestra' shows Becky hiding behind a curtain while Jos Sedley begs Dobbin to protect him from her. See Maria DiBattista, 'The Triumph of Clytemnestra: The Charades in *Vanity Fair*', PMLA 95 (1980), 827–37.

[31] Eliot, *Adam Bede*, 161.

of the coming death' (149). Weakened by her excessive emotion, Caterina dies after a brief period of married happiness. However, as the story's title suggests, neither Wybrow nor Caterina is the hero of this tale. Their melodramatic 'days and nights of anguish, and ... unspeakable joys' (186) are contained within a frame narrative (as the mementoes of Caterina are in a locked room). The elderly Mr Gilfil is initially represented as a prosaic, parsimonious figure, and finally as a man 'crushed and maimed' by sorrow. His life is not a tragedy, but a sympathetic reader should be able to see that, although it seems so ordinary, its thwarted possibilities give it a tragic aspect.

Eliot employs the poisoned garment plot in two later fictions which draw more on Euripides' *Medea* than the *Trachiniae*. Threatened with exile as a result of her husband's second marriage, Medea resolves to kill her rival with the gift of a poisoned robe and coronet, and to break Jason's heart by murdering their children. In *Adam Bede* (1859), Hetty Sorrel admiring herself in the mirror is like Jason's young wife Glauce when she puts on the poisoned robe and coronet which Medea's sons bring as a gift. However, there is no Medea figure as a rival for Arthur's attentions. Hetty unknowingly acts both parts herself: 'a woman spinning in young ignorance a light web of folly and vain hopes which may one day close round her and press upon her, a rancorous poisoned garment, ... a life of deep human anguish' (249). P. E. Easterling suggests that 'the notion of the creator being destroyed by her own creation is closer to Deianeira in *Trachiniae*' than to Medea, and notes the comparison of Arthur to 'a river god', which recalls Deianeira's unsuccessful suitor Achelous.[32] The fight between Arthur and Adam may allude to Achelous' defeat by Heracles, although Adam's victory does not win him a bride. Nevertheless, it is the Euripidean parallel which is crucial, precisely because Hetty comes to resemble Medea as well as Glauce: she kills her own child. Edith Hall demonstrates that the increasingly frequent representations of Medea on the stage from the mid-1840s opened up the question of 'the plausibility of Medea's calculating infanticide', whereas in eighteenth-century productions the idea of a mother deliberately killing her child could not be entertained without the

[32] Easterling, 'George Eliot', 58.

mitigating circumstances of temporary insanity.[33] Eliot felt that the subject of infanticide should be treated like other 'tragic incidents in the human lot', and refused to give her publisher an outline of the plot of *Adam Bede*, since it might 'give rise ... to objections which would lie far away from my treatment'; she offered as a distinguished precedent the handling of infanticide in Sir Walter Scott's *The Heart of Midlothian*.[34] Eliot allows some sympathy for Hetty by making her innocent of murderous intent—her baby does not die as the result of a vengeful and violent act, but after being abandoned. The baby's death is an extreme consequence of Hetty's neglect of the needs of others, motivated by fear and her desire to return to her former life without the disgrace of an illegitimate child.

Eliot's final version of the poisoned garment motif in *Daniel Deronda* (1876) is the most sophisticated, an effective use of the materials of Greek tragedy in the context of the realist novel. Gwendolen, who had wanted to act tragic parts on the stage, is placed by her marriage in the role of Creüsa (an alternative name for Glauce): ' "It's rather a piquant picture," said Mr Vandernoodt— "Grandcourt between two fiery women ... It's a sort of Medea and Creüsa business" ' (403). Euripides' Glauce receives on her wedding night a gift from her rival which sends her mad with pain:

> For both the golden crown set round her head
> Was sending marvellous streams of eating fire,
> And the fine-webbed robe, the offering of thy sons,
> Was gnawing at the hapless one's white flesh.
> But she, sprung from her couch, now flies, ablaze,
> Tossing her head and curls this way and that,
> Fain to dash off the crown.[35]

Grandcourt's cast-off mistress also sends the bride a poisonous gift. Although Eliot uses the tragic image of 'poisoned gems', the myth is deftly adapted to its realist context. There is no venom eating into Gwendolen's skin, to which a nineteenth-century parallel might be

---

[33] Edith Hall, 'Medea and British Legislation before the First World War', *Greece & Rome*, 46 (1999), 54–64.

[34] *G.E. Letters*, viii. 201.

[35] Augusta Webster, *The Medea of Euripides, Literally Translated into English Verse* (London: Macmillan, 1868), 1183–9.

the attack on Clara Hewett in George Gissing's *The Nether World* (1889), when a rival actress throws acid at her face: 'something that ate into her flesh, that frenzied her with pain, that drove her shrieking she knew not whither'.[36] The letter which accompanies the family diamonds seems to Gwendolen like 'an adder': the venom is in the words with which Lydia Glasher curses Grandcourt and his wife: 'those written words kept repeating themselves in her. Truly here were poisoned gems, and the poison had entered into this poor young creature' (331). Again, the consequences of the action are incalculable, since Gwendolen, being temperamentally predisposed to hysteria, reacts violently:

Gwendolen screamed again and again with hysterical violence. He had expected to see her dressed and smiling, ready to be led down. He saw her pallid, shrieking as it seemed with terror, the jewels scattered around her on the floor. Was it a fit of madness?

In some form or other the Furies had crossed his threshold.   (331)

'In some form or other': the incidents and themes of Greek tragedy are eternal, but their names have changed. In Greek tragedy 'the Furies' avenge violence and hatred within the family. The death of Grand-court does not end the family curse, although since his legal marriage produces no children its effects are curtailed. As part of her general strategy of muting or averting tragedy, Eliot's Medea is not an evil sorceress: Lydia Glasher is a powerless woman who attacks her rival to protect her children using the only means available to her, and, like Deianeira, injures herself in doing so. The Creüsa is not simply an innocent victim: Gwendolen might be said, like Hetty, to have prepared the poisoned garment for herself, in accepting Grandcourt's offer despite her knowledge about his illegitimate family.

Gwendolen had imagined herself a tragic heroine—Mrs Davilow is worried by her penchant for the kind of roles played by the tragedi-enne Rachel Félix (the model for Vashti in *Villette*)[37]—but her tragic propensities are contained within the larger narrative of the novel. Rex suggests the subject of the tableau she appears in, the concubine

[36] George Gissing, *The Nether World* (1889), ed. Stephen Gill (Oxford: OUP, 1992), 209.

[37] Gail Marshall, *Actresses on the Victorian Stage: Feminine Performance and the Galatea Myth* (Cambridge: CUP, 1998), 48.

Briseis being led away to Agamemnon's camp (*Iliad* 1. 392).[38] Rex is
Achilles, who is forced to give her up to the king and commander of
the Greek forces, Agamemnon (although she is later given back to
persuade Achilles to re-enter the war). This episode foreshadows
Gwendolen's rejection of Rex and her marriage to Grandcourt:
Agamemnon claimed Briseis after losing his own prize, Chryseis,
which suggests that women are interchangeable as far as men like
Grandcourt are concerned. What this tableau does not show is that
Briseis has already endured the fate that Andromache foresees for
herself: Achilles acquired her as a war prize after killing her husband
and brothers. The tableau reflects a different response to women's
powerlessness from the violent rebellion associated with tragic heroines like Clytemnestra or Medea. In *Daniel Deronda*, women suffer at
the hands of men, but they survive (in contrast to Maggie Tulliver,
both Mirah and Gwendolen are saved from drowning) and adapt to
their straitened circumstances. At the end of the novel, Gwendolen is
beginning to understand that she must give up the narcissistic su-
premacy of the tragic hero and adopt a more novelistic perspective
which recognizes that hers is only one of many plots.

VICTORIAN MEDEAS

It may seem strange that Eliot should liken her heroines to one of the
most notoriously evil female characters in Greek literature, yet
women writers unquestionably found Medea a powerful and not
entirely repugnant model. Greek tragic women, especially Medea,
the vengeful victim, and Glauce, the innocent victim, powerfully

---

[38] The tableau is based on a print Rex has seen, perhaps one of Flaxman's
illustrations of the *Iliad* (1793), or a drawing of the sculptor Thorwaldsen's *Briseis
Led Away from Achilles by Agamemnon's Heralds* (1803). See Jane Davidson Reid and
Chris Rohmann, *The Oxford Guide to Classical Mythology in the Arts, 1300–1990s*
(Oxford: OUP, 1993), i. 9–12. Eliot may also have known of George Frederick Watts's
Achilles and Briseis (1858), a fresco painted at Bowood House in Wiltshire. Eliot
owned a copy of Watts's famous sculpture, *Clytie*, based on a story from the
Metamorphoses: Christopher Wood, *Olympian Dreamers: Victorian Classical Painters,
1860–1914* (London: Constable, 1983), 88. Wilfrid Blunt, *England's Michelangelo: A
Biography of George Frederic Watts* (London: Hamilton, 1975), 100, 191.

symbolized the position of women in a patriarchal society. Works like Augusta Webster's translation of *Medea* (1868), her dramatic monologue 'Medea in Athens' (1870), and Amy Levy's 'Medea (A Fragment in Drama Form, After Euripides)' (1891) draw on Eliot's characterization of Medea to make her a more comprehensible character, although not a sympathetic one. Given the number and quality of novels available particularly in the second half of the nineteenth century, poets who rework classical characters from a feminist point of view unsurprisingly draw on novelistic conventions: the Medea poems are clearly influenced by the depiction of strong female characters in Victorian fiction as well as the heroines of Greek tragedy. As a figure of female rage, Medea resembles the madwoman in the attic, a double who acts out the unconscious anger of more conventional heroines; a similar figure is Dickens's Miss Havisham, whose betrayed passion turns to vengeful cruelty and her own version of the poisoned garment (she is burnt to death by her decayed wedding dress).

Augusta Webster's translations of Greek tragedy and closet dramas were classed by her contemporaries with the works of Barrett Browning. *Medea* dealt with a controversial figure which the earlier poet had tackled in her poem 'The Runaway Slave at Pilgrim's Point'—a mother who kills her child. These poems were particularly subversive since Victorian women poets rarely represented mothers negatively—Kathleen Hickok remarks that 'women poets in general tended to reinforce the conventional image of motherhood or else not to depict mothers at all'.[39] Her rendering of the speech in which Medea pleads with the women of Corinth for sympathy and appeals to their common experience is a powerful statement which addresses the situation of women in Victorian England as well as in fifth-century Athens. Webster's translation makes clear the relevance of Medea's speech to contemporary debates on marriage and divorce:

> Aye, of all living and of reasoning things
> Are women the most miserable race:
> Who first needs buy a husband at great price,

---

[39] Kathleen Hickok, *Representations of Women: Nineteenth-Century British Women's Poetry* (London: Greenwood, 1984), 90.

> To take him then for owner of our lives:
> For this ill is more keen than common ills.
> And of essays most perilous is this,
> Whether one good or evil do we take.
> For evil-famed to women is divorce,
> Nor can one spurn a husband.

> (225–33)

Webster's dramatic monologue 'Medea in Athens' picks up the theme of women's powerlessness, casts Medea as a woman who challenges her situation, and explains her motivation for killing her children in terms of a rebellion against patriarchy, depriving the husband who deserted her of his heirs. Jason's second marriage is seen as a union undertaken for political reasons and 'Medea's drama is a critique of Jason's motives and an explanation of [her] actions as a repudiation of those motives.'[40] Hearing of Jason's death, Medea fantasizes that he came to regret his choice and to recognize that she could have furthered his ambitions. However, the supernatural attributes with which Medea is often endowed are not emphasized here—her power is located in 'man's wisdom, woman's craft, her rage of love' (85)—her magic is seen as an exaggerated version of feminine qualities, and is related to nursing. Looking back on her girlhood, Medea begins to sound surprisingly like a familiar Victorian character, and one who features prominently in Webster's *Portraits*, the fallen woman rebuking her seducer for ruining her innocence:

> Oh smooth adder,
> who with fanged kisses changedst my natural blood
> to venom in me, say, didst thou not find me
> a grave and simple girl in a still home,
> learning my spells for pleasant services
> or to make sick beds easier? ...
> all things glad and harmless seemed my kin,
> and all seemed glad and harmless in the world.
> Thou cam'st, and from the day thou, finding me
> in Hecate's dim grove to cull my herbs,

[40] Christine Sutphin, 'The Representation of Women's Heterosexual Desire in Augusta Webster's "Circe" and "Medea in Athens" ', *Women's Writing*, 5 (1998), 386.

didst burn my cheeks with kisses hot and strange,
the curse of thee compelled me.

(199–204; 212–17)[41]

Medea claims that the responsibility for all her transgressions—such
as her 'treacherous flight' from her father's kingdom and the killing
of her brother—lies with Jason, whom she calls 'soul of my crimes'
(229). She goes on to cast the killing of her children in the same light,
blaming him for their deaths and claiming sympathy for herself as a
bereaved mother—'what is thy childlessness to mine?' (243). Medea's
traditional associations with sorcery and evil are muted, so that she
appears as a victim of her own sexuality and of Jason's control over
her. Like Eliot, Webster examines Medea as a figure for women's utter
powerlessness in patriarchal society.

In her 'Medea', subtitled 'A Fragment in Drama Form, After
Euripides', the poet and novelist Amy Levy highlights the wasted
talents of women in a misogynistic society. Medea is represented as
a woman whose love is thwarted by her husband's indifference, and
who is tormented by her inability to change in her affections despite
Jason's inconstancy: it is her desperate need for love which makes her
a 'monster'. She is powerful because of her intelligence and craft:
when she hears the rumour of Jason's marriage she reminds him that
it was through her agency that he escaped death and acquired the
Golden Fleece. Levy chooses an epigraph from Euripides (printed in
Greek), taken from Medea's speech to the women of Corinth. This is
the famous statement that women must devote their lives to finding a
husband and then defer to him in everything and have no other
interests. Medea describes this as slavery; by rejecting her, Jason
actually liberates her:

> Now behold me free,
> Ungyved by any chains of this man wrought ...
> Strong, stronger than the blast of wintry storms;
> And lifted up into an awful realm
> Where is nor love, nor pity, nor remorse,
> Nor dread, but only purpose.

(240–1, 244–7)

[41] Augusta Webster, *Portraits* (London: Macmillan, 1870).

In Levy's version, there are no women to respond to her speech or offer any kind of sympathy to Medea, but only Jason and two male citizens of Corinth who perform a function similar to that of the Greek chorus, explaining the offstage action and commenting on the speeches of the protagonists. Unlike the chorus in Euripides, however, they do not speak to Medea; this increases her isolation, as her only dialogue is with Jason and then only in the first scene, before the murders.

Euripides' play opens with a speech by the Nurse, who explains the origin of the tragedy from the cutting down of the trees which were used in building the *Argo*, up to Jason's betrayal of Medea, and foreshadows the coming action by expressing her fear of Medea's violent response. In contrast, Levy's 'Fragment' begins with a speech by Medea, emphasizing her isolation in Corinth and her otherness in terms of race:

> Alas, alas, this people loves me not!
> This strong, fair people, marble-cold and smooth
> As modelled marble. I, an alien here,
> That well can speak the language of their lips,
> The language of their souls can never learn.

> (21–5)

In foregrounding the issue of Medea's alienation from the people of the country she lives in, her incomprehension of the 'language of their souls', Levy's treatment of Medea differs from Eliot's allusions and Webster's 'Medea in Athens', emphasizing racism and making the oppression of all women a less noticeable theme. The physical contrast between Medea's 'swart' skin and 'purple hair' (65) and her rival Glauce's 'gold hair, lithe limbs, and gracious smiles' (73) seem to represent Levy's encounters with anti-Semitism, particularly acute during her time at Newnham. Lorna Hardwick remarks that Levy both unmasks the racist subtext of Euripides' contrast between Greek and barbarian, and 'demonstrate[s] how the nineteenth century might voice' anti-Semitic sentiments.[42] The physical contrast also

---

[42] Lorna Hardwick, 'Theatres of the Mind: Greek Tragedy in Women's Writing in England in the Nineteenth Century', *Theatre: Ancient and Modern* (Open University Department of Classical Studies, 2000), <http://www2.open.ac.uk/ClassicalStudies/GreekPlays/Conf99/Hardwck.htm>, accessed 5 June 2005.

allies Medea to numerous dark heroines with unusual intelligence and artistic powers who are inevitably abandoned by their lovers in favour of virtuous golden-haired maidens in nineteenth-century novels such as *Corinne* and *Ivanhoe* (in which the dark heroine Rebecca is a Jewess). Maggie Tulliver's wish for a narrative in which 'the dark woman triumphs' is satisfied here, although, as in *The Mill on the Floss*, the triumph is brief and the heroine is 'vanquished' by fate. Her final soliloquy is made as she leans on a rock, alone, outside the city.

The murder of Medea's children takes place in the time between two scenes, and is narrated by the citizens. One of them says that Medea was like a tigress protecting her cubs, but the other recalls an earlier incident which shows that she was always an unnatural mother, and follows this by explaining how she killed her children. Although Levy appears to want the reader to understand Medea's actions, she takes away the confrontation with Jason in which it becomes clear how her sense of women's powerlessness in marriage led her to defend her position by violence. This is a weakness in dramatic terms, but emphasizes that Medea's vengefulness arises from her marginalization: Isobel Armstrong remarks that 'Medea' explores 'the destructive impulse of the rejected'.[43] It is reminiscent of the violent outbursts of the madwoman in the attic, also a dark foreigner associated with imprisonment and slavery, whose husband seeks to replace her with a new wife. In writing of Medea, Levy experienced 'a catharsis that came from speaking behind the mask of a female character, a stranger in a foreign land, whose rage has become archetypal in the literary tradition of the West'.[44]

The racial alienation Levy highlights in the Medea story is rarely given prominence by other women writers, for whom the feminist issues raised by the play seemed perpetually relevant. Mary Elizabeth Coleridge identifies Medea as a *fin de siècle* femme fatale whose violent acts align her rather too closely with the crime-ridden White-chapel slums associated with Jack the Ripper:

I read some of Medea; it stiffens one's mind to do a bit of Greek. Classic folk despise Euripides, but after all he was Milton's man. Medea is thoroughly *fin*

---

[43] Isobel Armstrong, *Victorian Poetry: Poetry, Poetics and Politics* (London: Routledge, 1993), 375.
[44] Beckman, *Amy Levy*, 114.

de siècle, says she would rather go into battle three times than have a baby once, pitches into men like anything. But there's too much Whitechapel about her. How are you to be seriously interested in a woman who has murdered her father and boiled her father-in-law before the play begins? So different from the gentle Phædra, and the wonderful Antigone and Helen.[45]

After the First World War, Dora Russell, in *Hypatia, or Woman and Knowledge* (1925) recasts the Greek heroine as a more political figure: 'Medea, driven mad—like so many able and remarkable women—by the contempt and ingratitude of men as individuals or in the mass, ... expressed herself in savage protest after the manner of a militant suffragette.' She comments bitterly that women had won the vote in 1918 'as a reward for our services in helping the destruction of our offspring. Had we done it after the fashion of Medea, the logical male would have been angry.'[46]

A NEW ALCESTIS

Performances of Euripidean plays in the 1880s suggest the popularity of heroines such as Medea, violently but to some extent justifiably rebelling against the injustices of marriage, and her opposite Alcestis, the selfless wife who takes her husband's place when Death comes to claim him.[47] Changing ideas about women's role and questions about marriage rendered Alcestis a more problematic model than the infamous Medea, and the selfish husband Admetus who allows her to die for him a figure even less admirable than Jason (the model for Jermyn in *Felix Holt* and Grandcourt in *Daniel Deronda*). Mary Coleridge's 1884 dramatic monologue in sonnet form 'Alcestis to Admetus' is influenced by Robert Browning's *Balaustion's Adventure, including a Transcript from Euripides* (1871). This poem is a promising influence for a woman writer since, in her praise of Euripides'

---

[45] Coleridge, *Gathered Leaves*, 235.

[46] Dora Russell, *Hypatia: Or, Woman and Knowledge* (London: Kegan Paul, Trench, Trubner, 1925), 1–3.

[47] For productions of *Alcestis* and related plays such as *The Winter's Tale* from the 17th cent. onwards, see Edith Hall and Fiona Macintosh, *Greek Tragedy and the British Theatre 1660–1914* (Oxford: OUP, 2005).

psychological insight and in her poetic gift, Balaustion recalls Elizabeth Barrett Browning: lines from her poem 'Wine of Cyprus' provide the poem's epigraph, praising Euripides, her favourite dramatist. Balaustion describes her memory of a performance of *Alkestis*, giving a recitation of the play interspersed with ironic comments on Admetos' selfishness before the death of his wife initiates his moral regeneration. After the recitation, she remarks that Euripides' play is only one way of treating the story, that Sophocles will create a new play with different characters, and that Balaustion herself, or anyone else, can also 'mould a new | Admetos, new Alkestis' (2145–6).[48] In her version, both Admetos and Alkestis are willing to die, and love triumphs over death without any need for interference by the gods or by Herakles. Coleridge's 'Alcestis to Admetus', however, is a characteristically ironic representation of a failed relationship from the woman's point of view. Resigned to the inevitability of her husband's speedy remarriage, she tells him not to build her a tomb or create any kind of art in her memory, since any work of art would outlast his affection and devalue her sacrifice:

> The lasting stone would mock thy brief lament
> Witness thy short affection over long …
> Live and forget me. Farewell! Better so,
>
> Than that I should be made the scorn of men,
> Who mark the pageantry of grief, the show
> Of feeling lighter than the wind, and then,
> With lifted eyebrows, smile and whisper, 'Lo!
> A year is past, Admetus weds again!'
>
> (5–6, 9–14)[49]

Coleridge's cynical Alcestis is very different from those of Euripides and Browning, being strikingly bitter about the consequences of her self-sacrifice. Instead of taking a scandalous heroine and making her actions comprehensible in realist terms, Coleridge examines the frustration of a supposedly exemplary woman (like the self-subdued

[48] Robert Browning, *The Poems*, ed. John Pettigrew and Thomas J. Collins (Harmondsworth: Penguin, 1981).
[49] *The Collected Poems of Mary Coleridge*, ed. Theresa Whistler (London: Rupert Hart-Davis, 1954).

Xantippe in Levy's poem) to suggest that the sacrifices women are supposed to make will never be rewarded. Far from the saintly self-abnegation of the heroine's earlier incarnations, the new Alcestis' jaded views suggest that she is not so different from Medea after all, and that if women are to escape the oppression they have suffered since ancient Greece, they must create a new kind of marriage.

6

Revising the Victorians

In the early twentieth century the stories of heroines like Dorothea Brooke, Maggie Tulliver, and Jane Eyre are repeatedly reworked by novelists struggling to reconcile the notions of femininity they absorbed in their late Victorian childhoods with the increase in educational and professional opportunities for women.[1] Despite her negative representations of the classics as instruments of patriarchal oppression, George Eliot's novels and her own sibylline persona inspired women to adopt the study of Latin and Greek as a token of their potential; in producing their own versions of Eliot's heroines, writers such as May Sinclair and Vera Brittain perceive Greek as a crucial symbol for all that is denied to women, and they preserve its centrality in their narratives. Sinclair concentrates on the mother–daughter relationship, and chooses to explore the maternal hostility to a daughter's classical studies which Gaskell and Trollope had mostly smoothed over, as well as freedom from family life in the context of school, and the necessity of a room of one's own. Drawing attention to the need for a new plot for university-educated women like themselves, Vera Brittain, Dorothy L. Sayers, Winifred Holtby, and the other 'Somerville novelists' of the 1930s question what kind of books a woman who has enjoyed the privilege of an Oxford education should be writing. Brittain and Holtby 'compromised with the tutorial opinion which deplored our inexplicable preference for popular forms of literature by promising to collaborate in a work of historical research, which we thankfully abandoned as soon as we discovered how unfavourable were its chances of

---

[1] Diana Wallace, *Sisters and Rivals in British Women's Fiction, 1914–39* (Basingstoke: Macmillan, 2000), 8; e.g. Winifred Holtby's *South Riding* evokes *Jane Eyre* and *Middlemarch*.

making any impression'.[2] They did not choose to fulfil the scholarly
ambitions projected onto them by an older generation of feminists, but
(like Sayers's heroine Harriet Vane) to write fiction.

Brittain and Sayers studied the classics in Somerville's hurried and
incomplete version of the masculine curriculum; for them, readings
and reimaginings of classical characters and images were mediated by
other literatures, and the feminist awareness which women students
at Oxford learnt from their position within the university. Although
their knowledge of the classics is acknowledged as fragmentary, they
display confidence in reworking classical literature to reflect modern
women's experience; frequently they choose to do this in novels, the
literary form in which Victorian women writers had been so con-
spicuously successful. Despite the diversity of their interests in the
classics, the adaptation of epic themes to modern forms is an important similarity in Sayers's and Brittain's responses to classical
literature. Brittain's writings repeatedly interrogate and reshape
elements of Homer's *Iliad* in the context of the First World War;
part of Virgil's *Aeneid* provides a clue to the mystery in one of
Sayers's detective stories and another part becomes a mock-epic
narrative of the Second World War. This humorous appropriation
of Virgilian material contrasts with Vera Brittain's anguished rejection of the Homeric values of the First World War. Both writers use
classical epic, modified by the influence of the nineteenth-century
novel, as a source of inspiration in genres which neither endorse the
heroic code nor attempt to gain the traditionally high status of epic
poetry but subvert literary hierarchies by pointing out that a modern
detective story or personal narrative, and a classical epic or tragedy,
deal with essentially the same emotions and actions.

MAY SINCLAIR

An intriguing combination of Victorian repression and self-
abnegation with feminism and interest in the developing science of
psychology, May Sinclair is also a transitional figure in terms

---

[2] Vera Brittain, *Testament of Friendship: The Story of Winifred Holtby* (1940;
London: Virago, 1981), 108.

of literary history.[3] She attempted, in fiction and criticism, to build on the work of Victorian women novelists, and wrote both a biography of the Brontës (*The Three Brontës*, 1912) and a novel about the three daughters of a clergyman in a remote Yorkshire parish (*The Three Sisters*, 1914).[4] Influenced by Freud and Jung, she revised the plots of Victorian women's novels to fit her own generation: the repression and passivity demanded of the Angel in the House are imposed on daughters by mothers who are themselves victims of the same ideologies and can exercise power only by emotional manipulation. In *Mary Olivier: A Life* (1919) the conflict between generations is exacerbated by the daughter's desire to learn Greek, since George Eliot's novels are crucial to Sinclair's thinking about the problems facing intellectual women. Lyn Pykett comments that *Mary Olivier* is a version of *The Mill on the Floss*, in which Sinclair's heroine achieves some of the successes denied to Eliot's— Mary learns Greek, survives the death of her beloved brother and her lover's desertion, and becomes a writer—but is ultimately defeated by the same ingrained self-renunciation and repression.[5] As a child, Mary has a governess while her five brothers are educated by a tutor, but one of her brothers offers her a chance to share their cultural background by giving her copies of Shakespeare, Pope's *Iliad*, and Milton. She finds the Greek text of the *Iliad* more attractive than the English version and wants to learn Greek because she likes the patterns made by the sounds: '"Silent he wandered by the sounding sea" was good, but the Greek that Mark showed her went: "Be d'akeon para thina poluphloisboio thalasses"; that was better.'[6]

---

[3] She encouraged the work of the Imagists H.D., Richard Aldington, and Ezra Pound, particularly their combination of classicism and artistic innovation, and bequeathed her Greek books to these three poets: Aristophanes and poetry to Pound, Aeschylus to Aldington, and Euripides to H.D.: Raitt, *May Sinclair*, 266.

[4] See Miller, *Brontë Myth*, esp. 92–4, 119–22, 221–4.

[5] Lyn Pykett, 'Writing around Modernism: May Sinclair and Rebecca West', in Lynne Hapgood and Nancy L. Paxton (eds.), *Outside Modernism: In Pursuit of the English Novel, 1900–30*, (Basingstoke: Macmillan, 2000), 114.

[6] May Sinclair, *Mary Olivier: A Life* (1919; London: Virago, 1980), 77. Further references are given parenthetically in the text. The quotation referred to here is from Pope's *Iliad*, 1. 50: 'Silent he wander'd by the sounding Main', a translation of the Homeric phrase transliterated by Sinclair (*Iliad* 1. 34). Readers of the *Iliad* evidently

Unlike Eliot, who incorporates Greek quotations in her fiction without any help for the non-classical reader, Sinclair links the Homeric phrase with Pope's familiar translation and accurately transliterates the Greek to allow her readers to try making the 'hard and still' Greek sounds for themselves. This technique diminishes, although it does not entirely erase, the alienating effect of finding a Greek phrase in an English novel about a Victorian woman's life.

Sinclair repeatedly sets up the expected conflict between a heroine with intellectual aspirations and the confining ideology of separate spheres for men and women, but reduces the impact by presenting it in an unexpected way. For example, Mary's mother (like Mrs Tulliver, Aurora Leigh's aunt, and any number of Victorian mothers) believes that it is more important for a girl to sew than to read, and rewards Mary with affection when she sees her bloodstained needlework. The commonplace opposition of sewing and Greek is introduced but evaded by Mary's politic decision to spend more time on another feminine accomplishment: by repeatedly practising a hated piece of music, Mary buys her mother's temporary acceptance of her Greek studies, which have to remain secret, and are accomplished in 'the hour after breakfast':

There was something queer about learning Greek. Mamma did not actually forbid it, but she said it must not be done in lesson time or sewing time, or when people could see you doing it, lest they should think you were showing off. You could see that she didn't believe that you *could* learn Greek, and that she wouldn't like it if you did. (78)

The departure for school of Mary's sympathetic brother Mark does not mean an end to her classics, as it might have done in a Victorian novel, because he leaves her some Greek textbooks and the *Lays of Ancient Rome*. Despite her hostility to the idea of her daughter learning Greek, Mrs Olivier likes Mary to read aloud from the *Lays*

found the sound of the phrase *poluphloisboio thalasses* particularly resonant (see below, n. 52). In the short story 'The Incredible Elopement of Lord Peter Wimsey' Sayers's hero uses his knowledge of classical literature to deceive an uneducated audience, reciting passages from the *Aeneid* and the *Iliad* (and other classical tags) to convince a community of Basque peasants that he is a magician: ' "Tendebantque manus ripae ulterioris amore," said the wizard with emphasis. "Poluphloisboio thalasses. Ne plus ultra. Valete. Plaudite." ' Dorothy L. Sayers, *Hangman's Holiday* (London: Gollancz, 1933), 77.

and Pope's *Iliad* at sewing time, and buys her the kind of books about ancient history and mythology which had traditionally been used in girls' seminaries as a substitute for the classical languages.

After the comparative freedom of childhood, Mary's adolescence is increasingly constricted by Victorian gender ideologies, and her story begins to resemble those of Maggie Tulliver and Ethel May. Mary's mother becomes a 'powerful and rather cruel' deity: 'You could only appease her with piles of hemmed sheets and darned stockings' (124). Mary's Greek texts—Homer, Aeschylus, Sophocles, Aristophanes, Euripides, a Greek Testament, and the Anthology—are lost for five years when a younger brother takes them to school with him. When the books are returned, Mary encounters more determined opposition to her studies: 'Her mother's face shivered with repugnance. It was incredible that anybody should hate a poor dead language so' (126). She describes Mary's desire to learn Greek as a 'tiresome affectation', which could be tolerated in a child but is unsuitable for a woman. Although she resents her mother's need to control and limit her, Mary also colludes in it by turning against the books which seem to alienate her from her mother and Mark, who no longer sympathizes with her intellectual ambitions. Mary finds solace in a translation of Plato, although it lacks the Greek sounds she loved as a child. At school, however, she is allowed to learn Greek and to have a room of her own, however small and poorly lit. There she reads Plato and the funeral song for Bion. That Mary is of the generation of women born too early to benefit from educational reforms is emphasized when a professor of English literature takes her to a lecture and she realizes it is too late for her to become a student. Sinclair herself obtained access to university resources through influential friends. 'In effect, she was having informal tutorials with one of Cambridge's most eminent professors, a privilege she would not have had even if she had been able to enrol at Girton or Newnham.'[7]

When she returns home, Mary continues to hide in her room and read Greek alone while her mother is in the garden (mainly tragedies with rebellious female characters, such as *Antigone* and the *Bacchae*). Her mother's reservations about Greek and philosophy are

---

[7] Raitt, *May Sinclair*, 67.

reinforced when Mary's fiancé jilts her after finding that he cannot persuade her to concentrate on clothes rather than ideas. However, the end of her engagement does not force Mary into the more overtly feminine behaviour her mother wishes her to adopt. Instead, as Terry Phillips points out, Mary accepts her mother's belief that marriage is entirely separate from intellectual fulfilment, which paradoxically ensures that she chooses to remain single.[8] Her Greek texts become an instrument of her psychological separation from her mother: 'When she looked at them she could still feel her old, childish lust for possession, her childish sense of insecurity, of defeat. And something else. The beginning of thinking things about Mamma' (301).

Sinclair's revisionary aim is again in evidence when Mary becomes secretary and mistress to Richard Nicholson, who has written a book on Euripides. By selecting the controversial tragedian who had been out of favour for much of the nineteenth century, rather than Eliot's favourite Sophocles, Sinclair associates her heroine with modernity and radicalism: the classical scholar (and member of the Fabian Society) Gilbert Murray commented on his own identification with Euripides, whose beliefs he considered 'rational, liberal, humane, feminist'.[9] Instead of suffering a life of intellectual drudgery as the wife of a modern Casaubon or Professor Forth, Mary is empowered by her Greek. Believing that her translation of the *Bacchae*, influenced by Whitman's poetry, proves that his theories about Euripides are correct, Nicholson arranges for its publication and encourages Mary to publish her poetry as well. Her professional triumphs are offset by her inability to escape from the dutiful self-abnegation of the Victorian daughter: she refuses to marry Nicholson and take her place in London literary society as a poet because of her mother, who dies ten days before Nicholson's marriage to another woman. There is a powerful sense of wasted potential at the end of the novel, yet there is also a sense of psychological resilience deriving from Sinclair's interest in the Brontës. As Lyn Pykett notes, *Mary Olivier*'s rewriting of the romance plot echoes *Villette* in representing a brief episode of emotional and

8 Terry Phillips, 'Battling with the Angel: May Sinclair's Powerful Mothers', in Sarah Sceats and Gail Cunningham (eds.), *Image and Power: Women in Fiction in the Twentieth Century* (London: Longman, 1996), 134.

9 Francis West, *Gilbert Murray: A Life* (London: Croom Helm, 1984), 69.

sexual fulfilment followed by the achievement of a sense of identity as a single woman.[10] Like Lucy Snowe (and Jane Eyre), Mary is enabled by her education to see herself as a woman whose vocation may be work rather than marriage: Sinclair was 'convinced that there was a close kinship between celibacy and creativity in the female artist'.[11] Her revision of the tragic fates imposed on George Eliot's heroines (and frequently resented by readers) suggested that 'odd women' or 'superfluous' females would gain by preferring intellectual fulfilment to the constraints of Victorian marriage.

'MAENADS DANCING BEFORE THE MARTYRS' MEMORIAL'

The solution Sinclair proposes, choosing the life of the intellect and rejecting marriage, was one which appeared increasingly problematic for the next generation of women writers, who wanted to go on from university to a literary career combined with a fulfilling domestic life. They had no models for this kind of existence: 'there are no myths about ... the successful married career woman or the woman who has children and remains an individual. This lack has a profound effect on everyone who learns about life through literature.'[12] Dora Russell's *Hypatia: Or Woman and Knowledge* (1925) pays tribute to the previous generation of virgin feminists who achieved a cultural revolution equivalent to that of the Renaissance by the 'opening of high school and university to the feminine mind of today'. Her examination of gender roles in terms of archetypes deriving from Greek mythology and history figures these Victorian spinsters as members of a pagan cult of virginity, 'votaries, hanging the tablet of each achievement in the temple of Athene or Artemis, pressing on breathless, swift of foot, sure of aim, in dread of the fate of Atalanta whom the Golden Apples lured to destruction and the marital embrace'. Despite living 'in an atmosphere of swoons and ringlets',

[10] Pykett, 'Modernism', 115.
[11] Miller, *Brontë Myth*, 120.
[12] Mary R. Lefkowitz, *Heroines and Hysterics* (London: Duckworth, 1981), 41–2.

they gave future generations of women 'schools and colleges, free limbs, health and the open air, ... the classics, science, medicine, the history of the world... They, these pioneers, childless, unwed, created and bore thousands of women.'[13] Russell's celebration of the unmarried pioneers of women's education was not without risk: when popular ideas about psychology made chastity deplorable, 'learned women' were again perceived as unwomanly. Sayers writes of 'the ancient dread of Artemis, moon-goddess, virgin-huntress, whose arrows are plagues and death'.[14] Pervasive ideas about the psychological damage inflicted by prolonged celibacy undermined women at Oxford in their attempts to gain equality with men. During the First World War rigid notions of propriety had been relaxed; the mothers of illegitimate 'war-babies' were treated less harshly than the 'fallen women' of the Victorian period. The need to replace the men who had been killed meant that the post-war spinster became a symbol of the nation's decline, and popular versions of Freudian theories caused the repression of sexual desire to be seen as unhealthy.[15] Winifred Holtby observes 'the unmarried woman is surrounded by doubts cast not only upon her attractiveness or her common sense, but upon her decency, her normality, even her sanity'.[16] Having recognized the achievements of Victorian spinsters, Russell emphasizes that 'the important task of modern feminism is to accept and proclaim sex'. Encouraging post-war women to see their sexuality and potential for motherhood as a source of power, she reminds them of another classical model of femininity: 'the call of Demeter the Fruitful is insistent'.[17]

The need to find some compromise between the dread Artemis and the fruitful Demeter and to counter prejudice against learned women in Oxford (which was often couched in a classical idiom) is at the core of Sayers's *Gaudy Night* (1935). The appearance of women students in caps and gowns, once women had achieved full membership of the University in 1920, provoked much ridicule, often

[13] Russell, *Hypatia*, 16–17.

[14] Dorothy L. Sayers, *Gaudy Night* (London: Gollancz, 1935), 276.

[15] Ingman, *Women's Fiction*, 10.

[16] Vera Brittain and Winifred Holtby, *Testament of a Generation: The Journalism of Vera Brittain and Winifred Holtby*, ed. Paul Berry and Alan Bishop (London: Virago, 1985), 91.

[17] Russell, *Hypatia*, 24–5.

expressed through literary parody. Vera Brittain quotes in *Testament of Youth* (1933) an example by a 'typical humorist' which involves a quotation from *Aeneid* 3. 658. 'The woman undergraduate stood revealed. Two senile, placid dons passed me. "*Monstrum horrendum informe*," I heard one murmur.'[18] Here the woman student in cap and gown is described by a phrase ('a terrible, deformed monster') which refers in the original to the Cyclops Polyphemus. 'Michael Field' and Jane Ellen Harrison may have adopted the 'Greek maenad' as 'an imaginary alternative to the Victorian spinster', but for Brittain it was a derogatory image.[19] She responded with heavy irony to a leading article in *The Times* in 1919 which had suggested that women should be subjected to stricter discipline if they were admitted to full membership of the University.[20] Brittain shows how ridiculous the assumption that women were undisciplined seemed to those students who were constantly advised to behave with the utmost feminine propriety and who found it hard to return to the strictly Victorian standards of decorum demanded by Somerville after the greater freedoms of wartime society. She comments on the imagined fears of *The Times* writer by juxtaposing violent, uncontrolled female characters from Greek mythology with Oxford landmarks: 'Is it generally presumed outside the precincts of this university that ... women students are free to wander whithersoever they will from darkness to dawn? ... Or are we pictured as Maenads dancing before

[18] Brittain, *Youth*, 508–9. Further references are given parenthetically in the text. I have been unable to locate the source of the anecdote, which does not appear in the *Oxford Magazine* (which generally supported women's membership) or *Isis* (which opposed women's degrees and ridiculed women students).

[19] Prins, 'Maenads', 46. Katherine Bradley and Edith Cooper proclaimed themselves maenads; Cooper wrote to Robert Browning that Bradley was an 'enthusiastic student of the *Bacchae*': Michael Field, *Works and Days: From the Journal of Michael Field*, ed. T. Sturge Moore and D. C. Sturge Moore (London: J. Murray, 1933), 3. They do not use the maenad image to identify themselves as members of a female group but 'seem to have functioned in a cultural vacuum with regard to other women writers, being both so male-identified that they felt little affinity with their female contemporaries': Blain, *Victorian Women Poets*, 6.

[20] A quotation from *The Times* leading article 'Women at Oxford and Cambridge' was printed in *Isis*. 'If the women and their colleges are prepared to face the responsibilities of full membership, we can see no reason why it should not be granted to them. But if they or their friends in the Universities seek to procure for them an extension of their present advantages without the corresponding obligations, opposition may not unnaturally be expected': *Isis*, 544 (5 Nov. 1919), 8.

the Martyrs' Memorial, or as Bacchantes revelling in the open spaces of Carfax and the High?' (505). Another response to the maenad image is a poem by N. M. Haldane (later Naomi Mitchison). She rewrites a negative image of uncontrolled, violent female force to reassure readers that the women liberated by the First World War will not abuse their unwonted freedom. The first stanza establishes a pastoral setting which represents the awakening as taking place in the English countryside. This idyllic scene recalls accounts of the summer of 1914, which came to represent the Golden Age of classical pastoral in First World War literature:

> We were asleep in sleepy fields,
> In summer-scented fields of hay,
> Or where that heavy oak-copse shields
> Pale bracken from the light of day—
> We were asleep and dreaming endlessly.
> No breath of May or June us from our dreams could sever—
> Dreams like long furrows in a crested sea.
> We were asleep, but now are awake for ever.
>
>   (1–8)[21]

The second stanza describes the dawn which brings 'new life', and the final stanza concentrates on the details of Bacchic rituals: 'the dappled skin | The thyrsus twining wondrously | The wine we steeped our faces in'. The Bacchae of this poem are not savage or destructive, unlike the Bacchae of Euripides' play who tear a man to pieces in their frenzy. Their awakening does not endanger anyone, the god who 'endows' them with 'wisdom' does not inspire violence or loss of control. Haldane suggests that women have experienced a decisive awakening after the long and sleepy summer of pre-war life.

'ARISTOTLE ON DETECTIVE FICTION'

As the daughter of a clergyman and former headmaster of a boys' school, Dorothy L. Sayers began her classical education in a traditional way: she was taught Latin by her father from the age

---

[21] N. M. Haldane, 'Awakening of the Bacchae', in G. D. H. Cole and T. W. Earp (eds.), *Oxford Poetry 1915* (Oxford: Blackwell, 1915), 22.

of 6.[22] She was interested in the teaching of classics and the wider reception of the subject. In 'The Teaching of Latin: A New Approach', she recalls a consciousness even at 6 that a knowledge of Latin would set her apart from the women of her family, associating her more closely with her father. She describes her own experience of learning the language and asserts that 'the committing to memory of meaningless syllables and inconsequent lists of things' is as easy for children as learning nursery rhymes.[23] Her experience of Latin at school did not improve on this early training, and perhaps even detracted from it by introducing the difficulty of changes in Latin pronunciation. While at Oxford, she studied Virgil's *Aeneid* (she had already read the second book with her father), a text which is echoed in *Gaudy Night* and the mock-epic 'Aeneas at the Court of Dido'. She also read Greek tragedies, and enjoyed translating passages into English verse. After passing Responsions, Sayers did not continue to study classics, except the New Testament Greek required for Divinity Mods, which then 'followed the Latin down the drain' (183). She later complained that the haphazard teaching of classical Latin to women (and the teaching she received from her father had equipped her better than most of her Somerville contemporaries) had left her 'after close on twenty years' teaching, unable to read a single Latin author with ease or fluency, unable to write a line of Latin without gross error, unfamiliar with the style and scope of any Latin author' (185). Nevertheless, she did not envy the kind of Latin teaching which the public schools had been practising for four hundred years 'in a more leisured age, and for one sex only of a privileged professional class, and in schools which concentrated on the teaching of classical languages and uncommonly little else' (193–4).

Sayers's attitude towards the curriculum is unorthodox and clearly derives from her experience as a modern linguist—she declares that Augustan texts are too difficult for language learners. Her 'New Approach' includes controversial advice: 'Throw that dreary man

[22] See *The Letters of Dorothy L. Sayers 1899–1936: The Making of a Detective Novelist*, ed. Barbara Reynolds (London: Hodder & Stoughton, 1995), 2–3.
[23] Sayers, *Poetry of Search*, 178–9. Further references are given parenthetically in the text.

Cicero out of the window, and request the divine Virgil (with the utmost love and respect) to take a seat ... until your pupils are ready to be ushered into the presence' (197). She is preoccupied with Latin as a spoken language and is particularly concerned to contradict the stiff, statuesque image of the ancients, to present them as ordinary people: 'The language of Cicero was not spoken in the streets ... of ancient Rome. The legions did not tramp their way to victory chanting the Hellenic quantitative measures which delighted the ears of the cognoscenti' (193). Far from endorsing the traditional literary curriculum and the hierarchy of genres with epic and tragedy at the top, Sayers asserts the importance of non-classical Latin and wishes the language to be taught like French, not with exaggerated reverence. She describes how her interest in French was stimulated by books which were suitable for children and by speaking the language every day. She lays particular stress on the usefulness of Latin as a key to correct English and to the Romance languages (she studied Old French and the Italian of Dante), and promotes medieval Latin as a practical alternative to the classical language.

She wrote irreverent poetry on classical themes, offering unusual perspectives on familiar stories. The most interesting of these is the mock-epic 'Aeneas at the Court of Dido', written in 1945 as a Christmas greeting for her friends. The hero and heroine are cats, he a 'lean, hard-bitten Tom' who has escaped from 'an enemy-occupied sea-coast town' on a British gunboat. The poem is prefaced by an 'Argument' in the epic style and a quotation from Dido's request that Aeneas tell her the story of the fall of Troy.[24] Sayers recalls Aeneas' story and many phrases from the Virgilian original but skilfully adapts them to the species of the hero and the historical circumstances of 1945. The cats who are weakened by hunger after a five-year war (like the ten-year siege of Troy) are defeated by their traditional enemies (the Greeks become mice and rats). The cats' owners take the place of the unfathomable and sometimes callous Olympian gods:

[24] *Aeneid* 1. 615–16, 630, *Quis te, nate dea, per tanta pericula casus* | *insequitur?* *Quae vis, immanibus applicat oris?...* | *non ignara mali miseris succurrere disco.* 'Son of the goddess, what fortune pursues you through such dangers? What force has flung you on these wild shores? ... Being not unacquainted with suffering, I have learned to help the wretched.'

'Huge starving hordes of mice and rats
Rushed in; we fought—lo, now, the scars
On ear and eyebrow! but our cats
Were grown too few, too weak for wars.

The household oracles fell mute;
In vain we wailed; the high gods went
Wrapped up in some divine pursuit,
Preoccupied, indifferent.'

(29–36)[25]

Aeneas escapes alone after the fall of the French town which takes the place of Troy, and is welcomed onto the ship by a 'sleek-coat, tabby, guardian-priest', the counterpart of Helenus in the third book of the *Aeneid*, who prophesies the Trojans' future in Italy. Dido tells her foreign guest that the cats in England (Carthage) have also suffered privation: 'There is less cream now in the bowl | And less tinned salmon on the plate' (71–2). Sayers also incorporates topical references—for example, air-raids become Jupiter's thunderbolts:

'We too have seen the vengeful brand
Strike from the sky; but yet we live
Favoured of Heaven, and what our land
Can offer you, we freely give.'

(73–6)

Although in novels and poems she was more often inspired by Latin literature than by Greek, there are a few key passages of Greek literature which recur in Sayers's critical work. She encouraged teachers to introduce the Greek myths to children in English translations, as she had first learnt them, and she responds to the archetypal narrative patterns of the myths rather than to Greek language and literature. Her hostility to Freudian theories in *Gaudy Night* might simply be read as a reaction against the demonization of spinsterhood in the 1930s, yet her real objection to Freud was that his allegorical interpretations of Greek myth were becoming accepted as canonical versions of the stories themselves by a generation increasingly remote from the Greek classics: 'So powerful is the impression made upon our minds by the devotional literature of

[25] Dorothy L. Sayers, *The Poetry of Dorothy L. Sayers*, ed. Ralph E. Hone (Cambridge: Dorothy L. Sayers Society, 1996), 145–9.

the Freudian cult that if you were to ask the first person you met what the story of Oedipus was about, he would quite probably reply that it was about incest.'[26] The topos which Sayers finds most important in the Oedipus myth is man's attempt to thwart oracles, especially those prophecies which foretell the killing of an old king by a young rival, or the birth of a child who will bring about some disaster: she classes it with *Macbeth* or the story of Perseus.

Sayers's essays and lectures also show her fascination with narrative patterns which could be taken out of their original context and represented from a different point of view or in an unexpected genre. The most striking examples are usually employed to support analogies between classical epic and tragedy, and the despised modern form of which she was a famous exponent. She edited an anthology of detective fiction which included the story of Cacus, the cattle thief, in which Hercules acts as detective and executioner (*Aeneid* 8) and three other stories from antiquity. In 'Aristotle on Detective Fiction' (1935) Sayers reads the *Poetics* as a treatise on the detective story—'tragedy being the form which the detective story took in his day'.

Aristotle, with no better mysteries for his study than the sordid complications of the Agamemnon family, no more scientific murder-methods than the poisoned arrow of Philoctetes or the somewhat improbable medical properties of Medea's cauldron; above all, with detective heroes so painfully stereotyped and unsympathetic as the inhuman array of gods from the machine, yet contrived to hammer out from these unpromising elements a theory of detective fiction so shrewd, all-embracing and practical that the *Poetics* remains the finest guide to the writing of such fiction that could be put, at this day, into the hands of an aspiring author.[27]

Sayers was not the first novelist to apply Aristotle's *Poetics* to fiction: George Eliot invokes Aristotle when she argues that ordinary people deserve sympathy for their sufferings, which are as great to them as the reversals of fortune suffered by the kings which are represented on the tragic stage. John Kerrigan's phrase for the detective story—'a form of tragic romance'—might also apply to

[26] Sayers, *Poetry of Search*, 243.
[27] Dorothy L. Sayers, *Unpopular Opinions* (London: Gollancz, 1946), 179.

Eliot's *The Mill on the Floss*.[28] Eliot's ironic description of 'the passions at war in Maggie' as 'the essential τι μέγεθος of tragedy' is relevant here, because it is in a similar tone that Sayers's detective, Lord Peter Wimsey, quotes from the *Poetics* (1460a): 'The great advantage about telling the truth is that nobody ever believes it— that is at the bottom of the ψευδη λέγειν ὡς δεῖ.'[29] Sayers translates this phrase as 'the art of framing lies in the right way': the narrator of detective fiction tells the truth in such a way that the reader will draw false conclusions based on sound evidence.[30]

Sayers was concerned to advance the detective story from a puzzle to something that would be acknowledged as a novel of psychological depth and complexity, to promote detective fiction as a literary genre, to confound those readers who believed that 'a detective plot cannot bear any relation to a universal theme'.[31] Critics like Q. D. Leavis, who felt that no student of literature should read Sayers's books, responded by strenuously reinforcing the distinction between serious and popular literature. This debate is enacted in *Gaudy Night* in the opinions about Harriet Vane's detective novels which are expressed by members of the Senior Common Room: eager readers of detective stories are represented as more intellectually rigorous than those who automatically condemn popular writing. Sayers sets up the solving of a detective story, the writing of psychologically accurate fiction, and scholarly research as different aspects of the same search for truth, in which the most important quality is integrity. A university education, as Sayers represents it in this novel, is a training in intellectual honesty, which can then be applied to any kind of work. In *Gaudy Night*, the detective story which Harriet is writing begins to subvert the superficiality of the genre, as she pursues literary excellence even at the cost of personal pain. Harriet's work reflects what Sayers was trying to achieve: it 'elucidates and asserts the experimental status of *Gaudy Night* itself and the import-

---

[28] John Kerrigan, *Revenge Tragedy: Aeschylus to Armageddon* (Oxford: Clarendon, 1996), 65.

[29] Eliot, *Mill*, 88; Sayers, *Gaudy Night*, 348.

[30] Sayers, *Unpopular Opinions*, 185.

[31] Dorothy L. Sayers, 'Gaudy Night', *Titles to Fame*, ed. Denys Kilham Roberts (London: Thomas Nelson, 1937), 88.

ance of such experiments'.[32] Sayers's determination to write a detective story which would also be a novel with literary merit was based on
the work of nineteenth-century novelists as well as the theories of
Aristotle. She particularly admired Wilkie Collins's novels *The
Woman in White* and *The Moonstone,* and worked on a biography
of Collins, which she never completed. Her use of epigraphs from
earlier literature is a stylistic device which recalls nineteenth-century
writers such as George Eliot and is not typical of detective fiction.
Gaudy Night persistently refers to genres more established and
respected than the detective story, placing Sayers's narrative in a
prestigious literary tradition: the novel's title alludes to the 'gaudy
night' of Shakespeare's *Antony and Cleopatra* (3.5) as well as to a
college gathering of former students.

   Gaudy Night fulfils the requirements of the twentieth-century
detective novel: taking place in a closed setting, providing all the
facts of the case, increasing suspense and retarding the conclusion by
misleading the detective and the reader, and finally the scene in which
the detective explains the solution to an audience of suspects. However, the crucial feature of the detective story is missing: there is no
body in the library. The 'crimes' which are to be investigated include
poison pen letters and the destruction of academic paraphernalia
such as books and gowns, and in each attack the individual victim is
less important than the assault on the increasingly fragile confidence
of the community of academic women. Sayers brought the problems
facing women at Oxford to the attention of a wide range of readers,
and participated in debates about women's education and marriage.

   The plotting of *Gaudy Night,* the framing of lies to deceive the
reader, successfully plays on the willingness of the reader and of the
characters who try to solve the mystery to accept the view that celibate
life in an all-female college does not promote normality or sanity: 'the
solution to the mystery of *Gaudy Night* does not involve massive
ingenuity, but only a freedom on the part of the investigators from
the internalization of sexual myths'.[33] Harriet Vane is unable to solve
the mystery because she allows the 'popular Freudian suspicion of

[32] Susan J. Leonardi, *Dangerous by Degrees: Women at Oxford and the Somerville
College Novelists* (London: Rutgers UP, 1989), 99.
[33] Heilbrun, *Hamlet's Mother,* 240.

spinsterhood' to influence her reading of the evidence she collects. Her suspects also believe that their way of life may lead to mental disturbance: the 'possibility of incipient madness is thoroughly ingrained' in the members of the SCR.[34] Sayers encourages the reader to participate in the increasingly hysterical reaction against the celibate life, yet there is a counter-narrative of the malign effects of marriage and motherhood which points to the correct solution of the mystery. Harriet's first impressions on returning to the college for the Gaudy suggest that married life is more likely to thwart a woman than to give her a fulfilling role, since the married former students who have returned for the Gaudy are ill or wasting their abilities on mundane work.

The use of classical literature to express masculine scorn of women at Oxford was something Sayers had probably encountered in Oxford journals around 1920, when she was one of the first women to be awarded a degree. She took her revenge in *Gaudy Night* by increasing the number of women students and the space allotted to them in her fictional Oxford, and by building Shrewsbury College on Balliol's cricket ground, a location closer to the centre of Oxford than any of the existing women's colleges. Vera Brittain's anecdote of the don who referred to a woman in cap and gown as *monstrum horrendum informe* seems particularly relevant to *Gaudy Night*. The evidence which convinces Harriet that the culprit must be an educated woman is a quotation from a Latin poem, which is attached to an effigy dressed in a cap and gown.

The message upon it was pasted up in the usual way, and ran

> *tristius haud illis monstrum nec saevior ulla*
> *pestis et ira deum Stygiis sese extulit undis.*
> *virginei volucrum vultus foedissima ventris*
> *proluvies uncaeque manus et pallida semper*
> *ora fame.*

'Harpies,' said Harriet aloud. 'Harpies. That seems to suggest a train of thought. But I'm afraid we can't suspect Emily or any of the scouts of expressing their feelings in Virgilian hexameters'.[35]

---

[34] Leonardi, *Dangerous*, 94; Rossen, *University*, 38.
[35] Sayers, *Gaudy Night*, 180. The quotation is from Virgil, *Aeneid* 3. 214–18. 'No monster more vile than these, nor more pitiless plague ever rose by divine wrath from

Her initial reading is more accurate than the conclusion she draws from the fact that the quotation is in Latin: her 'train of thought' must suggest that the likening of college women to some of the least attractive female characters in ancient mythology is not something that a female academic would be inclined to do. Harriet's assumption that the use of the quotation frees from suspicion those who do not belong to her own educated class is reinforced by a member of the SCR. '"Would any of the scouts quote Virgil?" "No," said the Dean, examining the "Harpy" passage. "No; it doesn't seem likely"' (210). The idea that only an educated woman could have used this negative female image from a Latin poem is another example of framing evidence to mislead the reader. Sayers plants the correct solution in the narrative knowing that the reader will not recognize it. Another member of the SCR reads the document correctly, as evidence of a (masculine) spite against women in the universities. Miss Hillyard's conjecture is proved right when Wimsey demonstrates that the immediate source of the Latin quotation was a tirade against educated women, and one member of the Shrewsbury College SCR in particular, so that the Virgilian context was irrelevant.

The use of Latin poetry to express misogynistic sentiments which endanger the community of women, and Harriet's misreading of the Latin, have caused some critics to find the final pages of the novel troubling: Wimsey chooses to make the last of his many marriage proposals to Harriet in Latin. 'Surely some misgiving must haunt Harriet as she hears the Latin words that Wimsey has chosen' writes Miriam Brody.[36] The assumption that any utterance in Latin indicates misogyny is no more accurate than Harriet's mistaken perception that a note in Latin means that the writer is a scholar. Sayers chose the form of words for the final proposal with particular care, and explicitly rejected the idea that Harriet would be placed in the helpless position of the virgin heroines of antiquity: 'I could not marry Peter off to the young woman he had (in the conventional

the Stygian waves. They are like birds, but with girls' faces; there is a disgusting discharge from their bellies, they have hands with crooked claws, and their faces are always pale with hunger.'

[36] Miriam Brody, 'The Haunting of *Gaudy Night*: Misreadings in a Work of Detective Fiction', *Style*, 19 (1985), 114.

Perseus manner) rescued from death and infamy, because I could find no form of words in which she could accept him without a loss of self-respect.'[37] In the 'form of words' she finally chose, the Latin of the proposal is not a classical quotation, but taken from an Oxford degree ceremony.

> With a gesture of submission he bared his head and stood gravely, the square cap dangling in his hand.
> '*Placetne, magistra?*'
> '*Placet.*'   (482)

As Carolyn Heilbrun points out, 'Peter gains her consent in the words of the great, long-male, ceremony of the granting of degrees': the ceremony and the Latin discourse of the University are no longer exclusively male.[38] Sayers was (as she suspected when she began to learn Latin at the age of 6) privileged in a way that most women were not, by her ability to read and understand a language from which women had traditionally been excluded, and which made them, if not quite the acknowledged equals of their male contemporaries, certainly closer to the dominant culture than other women. Harriet Vane uses this Latin to define her own status in the University when she is less certain about her social position elsewhere:

> 'They can't take this away, at any rate. Whatever I may have done since, this remains. Scholar; Master of Arts; Domina; Senior Member of this University (*statutum est quod Juniores Senioribus debitam et congruam reverentiam tum in privato tum in publico exhibeant*); a place achieved, inalienable, worthy of reverence.'   (14)

As an MA, a Senior Member of the University (Sayers quotes in Latin from the University Statutes 'it is decreed that Junior Members must show the due and fitting reverence to Seniors both in private and in public'), Harriet does not appear to feel any 'misgiving' about this use of Latin. This is not to say that University Latin is any more feminist than classical texts, but that a woman of Harriet's generation at least has the chance to share in the prestige it bestows: she might legitimately feel concerned about what her status as a woman in Oxford would be were she not a member of the University. Harriet's position in Oxford is so secure that she initially feels tempted to leave

---

[37] Sayers, 'Gaudy Night', 79.   [38] Heilbrun, *Hamlet's Mother*, 256.

the tumultuous literary world of London and to become a scholar. However, Sayers chooses to end the novel with her acceptance of Wimsey's proposal, after several dialogues which deal with the problem of creating a new kind of marriage which will allow Harriet to continue with her career. Despite the lack of a classical role model, Harriet is to become a woman who can embody the positive characteristics of both Artemis and Demeter. During the novel she matures into the ideal product of the women's college, as the wedding in *Busman's Honeymoon* (1937) suggests. In a significant modification of marriage traditions, Harriet chooses to be married from her college and given away by the Warden: she is the true daughter of those pioneers who 'childless, unwed, created and bore thousands of women'.

'THE EPIC OF THE WOMEN WHO WENT TO THE WAR'

Vera Brittain did not choose to study Greek and Latin from the desire for enlightenment which had inspired nineteenth-century women writers, but they are an important influence on her writing. The intertwining of her classical education and the events of the First World War is demonstrated by her letters and diaries, both in their original form, and in their reworking as her memoir, *Testament of Youth* (1933); had her degree begun with English literature as she anticipated, her war diaries and the use she later made of them would have been very different. *Testament of Youth* is a unique account of a woman whose classical studies were imposed on her because she wanted to study English at Oxford, and were almost entirely compressed into a brief period, yet which attained enormous significance through being connected with a war in which the men of her generation followed Hector and Achilles to their deaths. The social and intellectual restrictions of Buxton, the provincial town where Brittain grew up, and the gendered difference between her brief schooling and her brother Edward's anticipated career of public school followed by Oxford Greats resemble *The Mill on the Floss*. Brittain found the classics attractive because of their associations with Eliot, a writer whose influence on her is clear: 'Sometimes [Edward] reminds me very much of Tom Tulliver ... And I suppose I am like Maggie—who was probably George Eliot.'[39] Although her parents certainly had not expected their daughter to go to university, Brittain exaggerates their opposition to fit her self-fashioning as Maggie Tulliver, and emphasizes the difficulties she encountered in trying to win a place at Oxford, writing that the private girls' school she had attended did not offer Latin: because of the difficulty in finding a tutor in Buxton she was coached by the 'classical assistant' at 'a small institution for backward boys' (70–1). Deborah Gorham's biography of Brittain provides a useful corrective, noting that her father was (as many of his contemporaries might not have been) prepared to pay for coaching, and then college fees and expenses, and that her mother arranged the Latin lessons which were a necessary preparation for Oxford entrance.[40] The prosperity of Brittain's family, the University Extension Lectures which offered provincial middle-class women some contact with higher education, and the establishment of women's colleges enabled her to study at Oxford, an opportunity which was not available to Maggie or to Eliot herself.

Brittain chose to apply to non-denominational Somerville, with its reputation for high academic standards. Somerville seems to have attracted writers, and has often been recreated in fiction, for example as Shrewsbury College in Sayers's *Gaudy Night* (1935), and Drayton College in Brittain's *The Dark Tide* (1923). She arrived in Oxford in 1914 to read English, not realizing that she would have to study Greek as well as the Latin she had painstakingly acquired at home. She strongly associated the Oxford of 1914–15 with Plato and the *Iliad*, yet by the time of her return to Oxford in 1919, Brittain's rapidly acquired Greek had been 'completely forgotten'. While 'Convocation at Oxford was wrangling hotly on the subject of compulsory Greek', leading to its abolition, Brittain was learning the translation of set passages by heart for Divinity Mods (483).

Greek initially figures in *Testament of Youth* as a ridiculous academic hurdle for which Brittain's patchy education proves

[39] Brittain, *Chronicle*, 93–4.
[40] Deborah Gorham, *Vera Brittain: A Feminist Life* (Oxford: Blackwell, 1996), 43, 48.

inadequate: 'the prosaic demands of Greek verbs and the tedium of ploughing with a "crib" through the *Alkestis* of Euripides almost before I knew the Greek alphabet' (108). She felt that life at Oxford was inferior to active service, particularly as she was experiencing a sketchy approximation of masculine classical education which her correspondents (former public school pupils) regarded as amusingly basic. 'I shall think of you tomorrow wrestling with Greek verbs' wrote her fiancé Roland Leighton, who had been awarded a prestigious classical scholarship, adding rather patronizingly 'I do hope you will get the ones you know.' Having reiterated his academic superiority, he crushingly states that 'All Classics seem to me incredibly far away now. I am not at all sure that I shall go to Oxford when this war is finished.'[41] War, it seems, has replaced Oxford as the site of a desirable and worthwhile education from which women are excluded. For Vera Brittain's brother Edward and Roland Leighton, educated at Uppingham, 'in the forefront of public-school militarism',[42] the thought of remaining in Oxford 'in inglorious safety' while others went to fight would be a disgrace.[43] Roland's letters reflect the success of the public school ideology of manliness: 'I don't think in the circumstances I could easily bring myself to endure a life of scholastic vegetation. It would seem a somewhat cowardly shirking of my obvious duty.'[44] The morally charged language he employs here demonstrates how difficult it was for a woman at Oxford to feel that her work was worthwhile if it would be so great a disgrace for a man to undertake it.

The circumstances of the war were unusual in giving soldiers time to read during long periods of inactivity in the trenches; an excellent postal service to France meant that books were available. Literary stereotypes helped to give shape to the unfamiliarity of trench warfare and gas attacks, which might be transformed into knightly 'battles' by the persistently chivalric discourse of the war.[45] Interest

---

[41] R.L. to V.B., 8 Dec. 1914, *Lost Generation*, 38–9.

[42] Paul Berry and Mark Bostridge, *Vera Brittain: A Life* (London: Chatto & Windus, 1995), 29.

[43] Brittain, *Chronicle*, 89–90.

[44] R.L. to V.B., 29 Sept. 1914, *Lost Generation*, 30.

[45] See Paul Fussell, *The Great War and Modern Memory* (1975; Oxford: OUP, 2000), 21–2.

in classical literature was mainly, but by no means exclusively, part of the public school and university tradition.[46] Brittain thought that the exceptional literariness of the war could be attributed to the large number of civilians who enlisted, whose ideas of war had been largely shaped by their reading. Late Victorian and Edwardian boys' adventure stories had made fighting foreigners seem likely to result in the victory of British heroes; public school mythology represented war as sport (as in Newbolt's poem 'Vitaï Lampada'); the historical remoteness of any major conflict for those who went to war in 1914 meant that war could be treated with cheerful irony: Rupert Brooke wrote to a friend 'Come and die! It'll be great fun.'[47]

Brittain felt that her classical studies were a tedious routine, and her letters refer to the least exhilarating aspects of that work: 'To sit at my table & do a Latin prose feels not only a physical but a mental impossibility.'[48] Despite her success in the Responsions Greek examination, which she passed 'in record time', she remained conscious that her work would have seemed easy to Roland: 'I can't help thinking all this week ... how charming you would have been to me over Pass Mods., and how tactfully condescending. You would have left your level of forty-eight books of Homer to talk to me about my five ... And I should have felt that it wasn't quite as absurd as I thought to try and do Pass Mods. on nine months Greek' (160). Classical literature became irksome not because it seemed pointless but because it allowed no escape from the war. Brittain 'joined the Pass Mods. class and studied the *Cyropædia* and Livy's *Wars* with a resentful feeling that there was quite enough war in the world without having to read about it in Latin' (124). Despite this reluctance, she later appreciated her tutor's attempts to relate the classical literature they were reading to contemporary events: 'During her coachings for "Pass Mods." [Miss Lorimer] faced the realities of the

[46] One of the most famous classical allusions in First World War poetry is Wilfred Owen's bitter condemnation of Horace's 'old Lie', *dulce et decorum est pro patria mori*. Owen, who had been to neither public school nor university, records his reading of the poets Theocritus, Bion, and Moschus in Dec. 1917, suggesting an interest in pastoral elegy rather than epic heroism. Fussell, *The Great War*, 232.

[47] Quoted in Nosheen Khan, *Women's Poetry of the First World War* (London: Harvester Wheatsheaf, 1988), 11.

[48] V.B. to R.L., 25 Apr. 1915. *Lost Generation*, 88.

War in terms of the Siege of Troy, and from Plato's account of the trial and death of Socrates sought to impart to her students the strength to conquer grief.'[49] Brittain wrote in *Testament of Youth*:

A phrase from my Pass Mods. days at Oxford slipped into my mind; I had quoted it not long ago in a letter to Edward in a letter from Malta: 'The gods are not angry for ever …'
It came, I thought, from the *Iliad* and those quiet evenings with my Classical tutor in reading of the battles for sorrowful Troy. How like we were to the fighters of those old wars… (368–9)

Having decided that she would leave Oxford to become a nurse, she resolved to remain until she had done enough work to be able to return after the war without having to start again from the beginning of the degree course. Her letters reiterate her desire to get away from Oxford and emulate her male contemporaries: she left after just nine months and began nursing at the 1st London General Hospital in Camberwell. Nevertheless, the time she spent at Oxford was crucial: as well as reading classical texts which shaped her view of the war, Brittain received a literary and linguistic training at Oxford which differentiated her from the women she had grown up with. However inferior she felt her classical attainments to be, they were sufficient to initiate her into the private codes used by officers which could circumvent the army's censorship of letters. She arranged with Roland that he should use the phrase '*Hinc illae lacrimae*' in his letters if he thought he would be going into action or would otherwise be in danger, since 'the Censor would not of course pass any precise information of that kind.'[50] Since the phrase was arranged in advance, it easily could have been written in a letter to someone who knew no Latin; later in the war Edward Brittain employed the prose composition skills acquired at Uppingham to warn his sister not to be afraid if she did not hear from him for some time. This letter is quoted in Latin, and not translated, in *Testament of Youth*: 'Calling desperately upon the elusive shades of Pass Mods.,' Brittain writes,

[49] Brittain, *Women*, 142.
[50] *Brittain, Chronicle*, 273. *Hinc illae lacrimae* (hence arose those tears) is a phrase from Terence's *Andria* (99) which was quoted by Cicero (*pro Caelio* 25. 61) and Horace (*Epistles*, 1. 19. 41).

'I managed to gather that Edward's battalion had been ordered ... to reinforce the Italian army' (391).

Brittain's increasing alienation from the classical culture which seemed to have inspired so many men to fight and be killed becomes clear as the references to Homer in *Testament of Youth* become more bitter. Her decision to change from English to history after the war arose from 'a desire to understand ... why it had been possible for me and my contemporaries, through our own ignorance and others' ingenuity, to be used, hypnotised and slaughtered' (471). *Testament of Youth* suggests that the masculine literary culture of the public school and university, particularly the 'forty-eight books of Homer' she set against her five, bears a share of the responsibility for the slaughter. The most important victim of the classics is Roland Leighton: Brittain suggests that he was betrayed by the epic ideal that so many soldiers had believed in. The reward of eternal glory for an early death, like that of Achilles, could not be attached to a gradual death from wounds not received in battle: 'so painful, so unnecessary, so grimly devoid of that heroic limelight which Roland had always regarded as ample compensation for those who were slain, like Kingsley's *Heroes*, "in the flower of youth on the chance of winning a noble name"' (241). Kingsley's retelling of the lives of the heroes of Greek mythology translates into English literary terminology the traditional Greek hero's willingness to exchange a long life for post-humous glory.

The *Iliad* was a familiar text for classically educated soldiers; its aristocratic code of male friendship and individual glory resembled the public school culture from which Brittain initially felt excluded by her gender, and which she later condemned for sending so many young men to ignominious and unnecessary deaths. Officers straight out of public school or university read Homer in the trenches, but soon discovered the ideal of epic heroism to be far removed from the squalid realities of the conflict in which they found themselves. 'Like Rupert Brooke, [Vera Brittain's] young men may have set off in expectation of a Greek epic; as Roland Leighton tried to make clear to her, they did not find it.'[51] Those who, like Brooke, set off for the

---

[51] Claire M. Tylee, *The Great War and Women's Consciousness: Images of Militarism and Feminism in Women's Writings, 1914–64* (Basingstoke: Macmillan, 1990), 214.

Dardanelles (named after Dardanus, the legendary founder of Troy, and famous from ancient times as the Hellespont) or other locations which were familiar from Greek literature, felt especially close to the heroes whose adventures had formed an important part of their education.[52] Ironically, by the time Vera Brittain travelled towards the same area, on her way to nurse at a hospital in Malta, these literary associations had been displaced by memories of more recent suffering: 'Rupert Brooke's "corner of a foreign field"' on the island of Skyros (299). It was with the victorious army of Greeks rather than with the devastated inhabitants of Troy that fighting men understandably chose to identify themselves, so Homer's version of the Trojan War was far more influential than that of Virgil.

Brittain's diaries and letters, as well as *Testament of Youth*, make it clear that her perception of contemporary events was mediated by the classical texts she encountered at Oxford, yet critics have tended to ignore this significant influence both on her thinking at the time and on the later writings based on the diaries and letters of 1914–18. *Testament of Youth* is seen as a text which 'promote[s] and validate[s] the woman's story of the war' but Brittain's engagement with and rejection of the dominant literary discourse of war poets, based on classical literature, is not sufficiently appreciated.[53] 'Brittain's personalization of the war ... involved a shift from male to female identification', comments Lynne Layton, noting that Brittain's pre-war intimates were men, and her closest friend after the war was Winifred Holtby.[54] However, Layton does not discuss the literary consequences of this shift, which gave *Testament of Youth* its distinctive character. Brittain's 'male identification' at the start of the war was due not only to her close relationship with her brother and male friends, but to the literary culture they shared, in which the

---

[52] Brooke speculated in Homeric terms which seem remote from the reality of the Gallipoli campaign: 'Do you think *perhaps* ... they'll make a sortie and meet us on the plains of Troy? It seems to me strategically so possible. ... Will the sea be polyphloisbic and wine-dark and unvintageable?' RB to Violet Asquith, [Feb. 1915], *The Letters of Rupert Brooke*, ed. Geoffrey Keynes (London: Faber, 1968), 662.

[53] Sharon Ouditt, *Fighting Forces, Writing Women: Identity and Ideology in the First World War* (London: Routledge, 1994), 4.

[54] Lynne Layton, 'Vera Brittain's Testament(s)', *Behind the Lines: Gender and the Two World Wars*, ed. Margaret Randolph Higonnet, Jane Jenson, Sonya Michel, and Margaret Collins Weitz (London: Yale UP, 1987), 82.

conceptual frame for a war story was classical epic. Nearly twenty years later Brittain reinscribed the epic narrative in terms of the female participants in the war:

I began to ask: 'Why should these young men have the war all to themselves? Didn't women have their war as well? ... Does no one remember the women who began their war work with such high ideals, or how grimly they carried on when that flaming faith had crumbled into the grey ashes of disillusion? Who will write the epic of the women who went to the war?'[55]

Testament of Youth was Vera Brittain's own answer to her challenge. When Brittain demanded 'the epic of the women who went to the war', what she meant was a war book which would attain the cultural status of ancient epic but have at the centre of its narrative the women who had remained marginal in men's war narratives, whether the *Iliad* or *Goodbye to All That* (1929). This did not mean that she believed that the 'epic' of women's experiences in the First World War should be a poem in twelve or twenty-four books on the lines of the *Iliad*. Brittain describes a narrative of the destruction of faith and ideals, and women's dogged determination to carry on with war work despite their disillusionment; her choice of the word 'epic' is a challenge to a prestigious and traditionally masculine genre which focuses on physical courage and glorious death rather than the struggle to preserve life. *Testament of Youth* records the devastating effects on the survivors of the gradual erosion of a whole generation of British men. There was no obvious genre or model for war literature focused on women. The traditional formulae of epic themes suggest masculine subjects and preoccupations—*arma virumque* (arms and the man: Virgil, *Aeneid*, 1. 1), *reges et proelia* (kings and battles: Virgil, *Eclogues* 6. 3). Brittain's choice of the term 'epic' reflects her awareness of the importance of the classics, and particularly of the *Iliad*, in the literary culture of the First World War. Her later references to the *Iliad* reveal another side of the poem, the scenes and images which act as a reminder of domestic life and the effects of war on women and children. Remembering the time she spent studying classics at Oxford during the war, Brittain significantly

---

[55] Vera Brittain, *Testament of Experience: An Autobiographical Story of the Years 1925–1950* (1957; London: Virago, 1980), 77.

focuses on 'the lovely lines from the *Iliad* which describe Andromache holding out the child Astyanax to Hector before Troy and "smiling through her tears," ' which she associates with 'the poignant early days of the War' (151).

Brittain was not sure what form the 'epic of the women who went to the war' should take. Since she particularly admired the women novelists of the nineteenth century, she initially imagined her war narrative as a novel, but found that she could not accommodate her ideas to that form. Some years later she successfully recast her diaries in the form of a Victorian *Bildungsroman* in *Testament of Youth.* She wrote a narrative of epic scale to point out the futility of the masculine code of honour which saw death as the only achievement to be commemorated: 'immortality—as so many of the disabled and the unemployed have since come to realize—is the reward only of a life laid down. In wartime it is necessary to die in order that one's name shall live for evermore.'[56] She subverts the epic tradition by questioning the ideals on which it is based. 'It is not by accident', she wrote, 'that what I have written constitutes, in effect, the indictment of a civilisation' (12). In *Testament of Friendship,* writing of her relationship with Winifred Holtby, Brittain places women in a relationship which she felt had been characterized as masculine. 'From the days of Homer the friendships of men have enjoyed glory and acclamation, but the friendships of women ... have usually been not merely unsung, but mocked, belittled and falsely interpreted.' Brittain notes that her husband 'suggested the title ... inspired by his recollection of Cicero's *De Amicitia*'. She defines her project in terms of a classical literary form mediated by the work of a Victorian woman novelist: lacking any model in ancient literature for an account of women's friendship, Brittain found that 'Mrs. Gaskell's *Life of Charlotte Brontë,* which Winifred and I had read and admired together' was a text to which she turned for 'help and advice'.[57] Brittain does not propose a complete rejection of Homer, but a feminist reading which emphasizes the women whose lives are obscured in the epic tradition.

---

[56] Brittain, *Testament of a Generation,* 206.
[57] Brittain, *Testament of Friendship,* 2.

Conclusion

'ON NOT KNOWING GREEK'

For it is vain and foolish to talk of knowing Greek, since in our ignorance we should be at the bottom of a class of schoolboys, since we do not know how the words sounded, or where precisely we ought to laugh, or how the actors acted ... All the more strange, then, is it that we should wish to know Greek, try to know Greek, feel for ever drawn back to Greek, and be for ever making up some notion of the meaning of Greek ... [1]

The title and opening sentences of Virginia Woolf's essay 'On Not Knowing Greek' (1925) seem to suggest that the author is another Dorothea Brooke, seeing the classics as a source of wisdom denied to women and regretting her exclusion from those masculine institutions where such knowledge could be acquired. Yet if she lacks formal schooling, she is familiar enough with Greek tragedy to quote from Sophocles in the original language, and to comment on the playwright's handling of myth.[2] Like many women, she wants to read Aeschylus, Plato, and Sophocles in Greek 'quickly, even if inaccurately', and is weaker in traditionally masculine areas of classical study such as grammar and accents.[3] It quickly becomes obvious that the 'ignorance' Woolf claims is far from straightforward: what she does not know about the Greeks cannot really be known, whether by schoolboys, scholars, or female autodidacts. Not knowing the Greeks is not a gendered deprivation after all, but a limitation which can only be overcome by using the imagination (as Charlotte Brontë and

---

[1] Virginia Woolf, *A Woman's Essays*, ed. Rachel Bowlby (Harmondsworth: Penguin, 1992), 93. Further references are given parenthetically in the text.

[2] For details of Woolf's classical reading, see William Herman, 'Virginia Woolf and the Classics: Every Englishman's Prerogative Transmuted into Fictional Art', in Elaine K. Ginsberg and Laura Moss Gottlieb (eds.) *Virginia Woolf: Centennial Essays* (Troy, NY: Whitston, 1983), 257–68; Henry M. Alley, 'A Rediscovered Eulogy: Virginia Woolf's "Miss Janet Case: Classical Scholar and Teacher" ', *Twentieth-Century Literature*, 28 (1982), 290–301.

[3] Fowler, 'Moments and Metamorphoses', 220.

Lucy Snowe did). Acknowledging the gap between ancient Greece and modern England, her response to Greek literature is not mediated by the classroom, but draws instead on the fictional tradition.

After quoting a line of Sophocles in English, Woolf imagines the surroundings in which a Greek tragedy might now take place, and suggests an isolated country village in one of 'the wilder parts of England' (94) as a possible setting. This juxtaposition of an insular rural location (with everyday characters depicted realistically) and tragic emotion is strongly reminiscent of Victorian fiction: it recalls *The Mill on the Floss*, *Wuthering Heights*, and Thomas Hardy's Wessex, 'where, from time to time, dramas of a grandeur and unity truly Sophoclean are enacted in the real, by virtue of the concentrated passions and closely knit interdependence of the lives therein'.[4] Yet Woolf finds the English background inappropriate after all, because of the climate: life in Italy and Greece is 'transacted out of doors ... small incidents are debated in the street, not in the sitting room, and become dramatic' (94). Like Mary Shelley's, her reading of ancient texts is enriched by the memory of Mediterranean sunlight. Woolf emphasizes the contrast between seeing a tragedy performed and reading in private. She does not attempt to synthesize ancient and modern literature, but performs imaginative leaps which link Sophocles and Jane Austen through the 'shape' of *Electra* and *Emma*, the constricted lives of the protagonists and 'the dangerous art where one slip means death' (96).

Obliquely introducing the novel as a modern form of equal status with tragedy by referring to Austen, Woolf is clearly indebted to Eliot: she quotes a phrase from *Electra*—δεινὸν τὸ τίκτειν ἐστιν—and translates it 'there is a strange power in motherhood'; Eliot had quoted the same words in 'Janet's Repentance', and rendered them as 'Mighty is the force of motherhood!' Woolf is interested in the formal features of the tragedy and the novel, commenting on the development of the stage chorus into the fictional narrator. She notes that Euripides' interest in psychology makes his dramas more like modern fiction, so that he 'suffers less than Sophocles and less than Aeschylus from being read privately in a room, and not seen

---

[4] Thomas Hardy, *The Woodlanders* (1877), ed. Dale Kramer (Oxford: Clarendon, 1981), 8.

on a hill-side in the sunshine. He can be acted in the mind; he can comment upon the questions of the moment' (99). This reflects Euripides' increasing popularity at the end of the nineteenth century and the beginning of the twentieth, in contrast to the mid-Victorian appeal of Sophocles.

Unlike those Victorian heroines who thought that they could acquire wisdom along with the Greek alphabet, Woolf stresses that the inscrutability and the siren appeal of Greek increase on further acquaintance. She emphasizes the impossibility of knowing Greek and the continuing attraction of a language which retains mystery: 'Chief among these sources of glamour and perhaps misunderstanding is the language ... We cannot hear it, now dissonant, now harmonious, tossing sound from line to line across a page ... Nevertheless, it is the language that has us most in bondage; the desire for that which perpetually lures us back' (103). 'Not Knowing Greek' means not being drilled in the language at school, not identifying the ancient Greeks with modern Englishmen (as the unsympathetic representatives of classical scholarship in Woolf's novels do), not assuming that Greek culture is recoverable. Woolf does not place her classical studies in opposition to but alongside her preoccupation with women writers in the nineteenth century and earlier: in her essays on Elizabeth Barrett Browning, Sara Coleridge, and George Eliot, she discusses their education, how they came to learn Latin and Greek, and what use they made of their knowledge. 'On Not Knowing Greek' makes clear what Woolf learnt from her predecessors, that finding pleasure in the strangeness of a new language and creating contemporary forms of literature in response to ancient myth are crucial to the development of the woman writer.

Bibliography

Adams, Pauline, *Somerville for Women: An Oxford College, 1879–1993*. Oxford: OUP, 1996.

Agorni, Mirella, 'The Voice of the "Translatress": From Aphra Behn to Elizabeth Carter', *RES* 28 (1998), 181–95.

A.H.S., 'A Note on the Teaching of Greek in Translations', *Oxford Magazine*, 38 (5 Mar. 1920), 259–60.

Alexander, Christine, 'Readers and Writers: *Blackwood's* and the Brontës', *Gaskell Society Journal*, 8 (1994), 54–69.

Allen, Grant, 'The Girl of the Future', *Universal Review*, 7 (1890), 56.

—— *The Woman who Did*. London: John Lane, 1895.

Alley, Henry M., 'A Rediscovered Eulogy: Virginia Woolf's "Miss Janet Case: Classical Scholar and Teacher" ', *Twentieth-Century Literature*, 28 (1982), 290–301.

A.M.S., 'Fragment of a Lost MS', *The Daisy*, 7 (1891), 3–4.

An Introduction to the Latin Tongue, 1758. Menston: Scolar Press, 1970.

Anderson, Nancy F., *Woman against Women in Victorian England: A Life of Eliza Lynn Linton*. Bloomington: Indiana UP, 1987.

Arlen, Shelley, ' "For Love of an Idea": Jane Ellen Harrison, Heretic and Humanist', *Women's History Review*, 5 (1996), 165–90.

Armstrong, Isobel, *Victorian Poetry: Poetry, Poetics and Politics*. London: Routledge, 1993.

Arnold, Matthew, *On the Classical Tradition*, ed. R. H. Super. Ann Arbor: University of Michigan Press, 1960.

—— *Philistinism in England and America*, ed. R. H. Super. Ann Arbor: University of Michigan Press, 1974.

—— *The Complete Poems*, ed. Kenneth Allott and Miriam Allott, 2nd edn. London: Longman, 1979.

Austen, Jane, *Catharine and Other Writings*, ed. Margaret Anne Doody and Douglas Murray. Oxford: OUP, 1993.

Avery, Gillian, *The Best Type of Girl: A History of Girls' Independent Schools*. London: Deutsch, 1991.

Bailey, Gemma, *Lady Margaret Hall: A Short History*. London: OUP, 1923.

Baldick, Chris, *The Social Mission of English Criticism 1848–1932*. Oxford: Clarendon, 1987.

Barbera, Jack, and William McBrien, *Stevie: A Biography of Stevie Smith*. London: Heinemann, 1985.

Barker, Juliet, *The Brontës*. London: Phoenix, 1995.

Bassnett, Susan, *Translation Studies*, 3rd edn. London: Routledge, 2002.

Bayne, Peter, *Two Great Englishwomen, Mrs. Browning and Charlotte Brontë*. London: James Clarke, 1881.

Beard, Mary, *The Invention of Jane Harrison*. London: Harvard UP, 2000.

Bebbington, D. W., *The Mind of Gladstone: Religion, Homer, and Politics*. Oxford: OUP, 2004.

Becker, Wilhelm, *Gallus; Or, Roman Scenes of the Time of Augustus*, tr. Frederick Metcalfe. London: J. W. Parker, 1844.

Beckman, Linda Hunt, *Amy Levy: Her Life and Letters*. Athens, Ohio: Ohio UP, 2000.

Berry, Paul, and Mark Bostridge, *Vera Brittain: A Life*. London: Chatto & Windus, 1995.

Bianchi, Petra, ' "Hidden Strength": The Poetry and Plays of Augusta Webster', D.Phil. University of Oxford, 1999.

Bilston, Sarah, *The Awkward Age in Women's Popular Fiction, 1850–1900: Girls and the Transition to Womanhood*. Oxford: Clarendon, 2004.

Birch, Dinah, 'The Scholar Husband', *Essays in Criticism*, 54 (2004), 205–15.

Blain, Virginia, *Victorian Women Poets: A New Annotated Anthology*. Harlow: Longman, 2001.

Blunt, Wilfrid, *England's Michelangelo: A Biography of George Frederic Watts*. London: Hamilton, 1975.

Bock, Carol A., 'Gender and Poetic Tradition: The Shaping of Charlotte Brontë's Literary Career', *TSWL* 7 (1988), 49–67.

Booth, Alison, 'Not All Men are Selfish and Cruel: *Felix Holt* as a Feminist Novel', in Anthony H. Harrison and Beverly Taylor (eds.), *Gender and Discourse in Victorian Literature and Art*, 143–60. DeKalb Ill.: Northern Illinois UP, 1992.

Boswell, James, *Journal of a Tour to the Hebrides with Samuel Johnson, LL.D., 1773*, ed. Frederick A. Pottle and Charles H. Bennett. London: Heinemann, 1963.

Bowen, James, 'Education, Ideology and the Ruling Class: Hellenism and English Public Schools in the Nineteenth Century', in G. W. Clarke (ed.), *Rediscovering Hellenism: The Hellenic Inheritance and the English Imagination*, 161–86. Cambridge: CUP, 1989.

Braddon, Mary Elizabeth, *Lady Audley's Secret* (1862), ed. David Skilton. Oxford: OUP, 1987.

—— *Aurora Floyd*. (1863), ed. P. D. Edwards. Oxford: OUP, 1996.

Breay, Claire, 'Women and the Classical Tripos 1869–1914', in Christopher Stray (ed.), *Classics in 19th- and 20th-Century Cambridge: Curriculum,*

Culture and Community, 48–70. Cambridge: Cambridge Philological Society, 1999.

Bremner, Christina S., *The Education of Girls and Women in Great Britain.* London: Sonnenschein, 1897.

Bridges, Robert, *Demeter: A Mask.* Oxford: Clarendon, 1905.

Brittain, Vera, *Chronicle of Youth: Great War Diary, 1913–1917* (1918), ed. Alan Bishop. London: Phoenix, 2000.

—— *On Becoming a Writer.* London: Hutchinson, 1947.

—— *Testament of Experience: An Autobiographical Story of the Years 1925–1950* (1957). London: Virago, 1980.

—— *Testament of Friendship: The Story of Winifred Holtby* (1940). London: Virago, 1981.

—— *Testament of Youth: An Autobiographical Study of the Years 1900–1925* (1933). London: Virago, 1978.

—— *The Women at Oxford: A Fragment of History.* London: Harrap, 1960.

—— and Winifred Holtby, *Testament of a Generation: The Journalism of Vera Brittain and Winifred Holtby,* ed. Paul Berry and Alan Bishop. London: Virago, 1985.

Brittain, Vera, *et al.*, *Letters from a Lost Generation: The First World War Letters of Vera Brittain and Four Friends, Roland Leighton, Edward Brittain, Victor Richardson, Geoffrey Thurlow,* ed. Alan Bishop and Mark Bostridge. London: Abacus, 1999.

Brock, M. G., 'The Oxford of Peel and Gladstone, 1800–1833', *The History of the University of Oxford,* vi. *Nineteenth-Century Oxford, Part 1,* ed. M. G. Brock and M. C. Curthoys, 7–71. Oxford: Clarendon, 1997.

Brody, Miriam, 'The Haunting of *Gaudy Night*: Misreadings in a Work of Detective Fiction', *Style,* 19 (1985), 94–116.

Brontë, Anne, *Agnes Grey* (1847), ed. Hilda Marsden and Robert Inglesfield. Oxford: Clarendon, 1988.

—— *The Tenant of Wildfell Hall* (1848), ed. Herbert Rosengarten. Oxford: Clarendon, 1992.

Brontë, Charlotte, *Jane Eyre* (1847), ed. Jane Jack and Margaret Smith. Oxford: Clarendon, 1969.

—— *Shirley* (1849), ed. Herbert Rosengarten and Margaret Smith. Oxford: Clarendon, 1979.

—— *Villette* (1853), ed. Herbert Rosengarten and Margaret Smith. Oxford: Clarendon, 1984.

—— *The Poems of Charlotte Brontë,* ed. Tom Winnifrith. Oxford: Blackwell, 1984.

—— and Emily Brontë, *The Belgian Essays,* tr. Sue Lonoff. London: Yale UP, 1996.

Brontë, Emily, *Wuthering Heights* (1847), ed. Hilda Marsden and Ian Jack. Oxford: Clarendon, 1976.

Brooke, Rupert, *The Letters of Rupert Brooke*, ed. Geoffrey Keynes. London: Faber, 1968.

Broughton, Rhoda, *Belinda*, 3 vols. London: Richard Bentley, 1883.

—— *Cometh Up as a Flower*, 2 vols. London: Richard Bentley, 1867.

Brown, Sarah Annes, *Devoted Sisters: Representations of the Sister Relationship in Nineteenth-Century British and American Literature*. Aldershot: Ashgate, 2003.

Browning, Elizabeth Barrett, *Aurora Leigh*, ed. Margaret Reynolds. Athens, Ohio: Ohio UP, 1992.

—— *Casa Guidi Windows*, ed. Julia Markus. New York: Browning Institute, 1977.

—— *Diary by E.B.B.: The Unpublished Diary of Elizabeth Barrett Barrett, 1831–1832*, ed. Philip Kelley and Ronald Hudson. Athens, Ohio: Ohio University Press, 1969.

—— *The Battle of Marathon: A Poem.* (1820), ed. H. Buxton Forman. London, 1891.

—— *The Letters of Elizabeth Barrett Browning*, ed. Frederic G. Kenyon, 2nd ed., 2 vols. London: Smith Elder, 1897.

—— *The Poetical Works of Elizabeth Barrett Browning*, ed. H. W. Preston. Boston: Houghton Mifflin, 1974.

—— *The Letters of Elizabeth Barrett Browning to Mary Russell Mitford, 1836–1854*, ed. Meredith B. Raymond and Mary Rose Sullivan, 3 vols. Waco, Tex.: Armstrong Browning Library of Baylor University, 1983.

—— and Robert Browning, *The Brownings' Correspondence*, ed. Ronald Hudson and Philip Kelley, 14 vols. Winfield, Kan.: Wedgestone, 1984– .

Browning, Robert, *Learned Lady: Letters from Robert Browning to Mrs. Thomas FitzGerald, 1876–1889.* Ed. Edward C. McAleer. Cambridge, MA: Harvard UP, 1966.

—— *The Poems*, ed. John Pettigrew and Thomas J. Collins, 2 vols. Harmondsworth: Penguin, 1981.

Brownstein, Rachel M., *Becoming a Heroine: Reading about Women in Novels*. Harmondsworth: Penguin, 1984.

Burstall, S. A., *English High Schools for Girls: Their Aims, Organisation and Management*. London: Longmans, Green, 1907.

Burstyn, Joan N., *Victorian Education and the Ideal of Womanhood*. London: Croom Helm, 1980.

Bush, Douglas, *Mythology and the Romantic Tradition in English Poetry*. Cambridge, Mass.: Harvard UP, 1937.

Butler, Samuel. *The Authoress of the 'Odyssey': Where and When She Wrote, Who She Was, The Use She Made of the 'Iliad', And How the Poem Grew Under Her Hands*. London: A.C. Fifield, 1897.

—— *The Humour of Homer and Other Essays*, ed. R. A. Streatfeild. London: A. C. Fifield, 1913.

Buzard, James, *The Beaten Track: European Tourism, Literature, and the Ways to Culture, 1800–1918*. Oxford: Clarendon, 1993.

Byrd, Deborah, 'Combating an Alien Tyranny: Elizabeth Barrett Browning's Evolution as a Feminist Poet', in Sandra Donaldson (ed.), *Critical Essays on Elizabeth Barrett Browning*, 202–17. New York: G. K. Hall, 1999.

Byrne, M. St Clare, and Catherine Hope Mansfield, *Somerville College, 1879–1921*. London: OUP, 1922.

Byron, George Gordon, *Byron's Letters and Journals*, ed. Leslie A. Marchand, viii. London: John Murray, 1978.

—— *Poetical Works*, ed. Frederick Page, 3rd edn. London: OUP, 1970.

Cadogan, Mary, 'Lamburn, Richmal Crompton (1890–1969)', *Oxford Dictionary of National Biography*. Oxford: OUP, 2004, <http://www.oxforddnb.com/view/article/34386>, accessed 3 June 2005.

Carnell, Jennifer, *The Literary Lives of Mary Elizabeth Braddon: A Study of her Life and Work*. Hastings: Sensation Press, 2000.

Chapman, Alison, 'Mary Elizabeth Coleridge, Literary Influence and Technologies of the Uncanny', in Ruth Robbins and Julian Wolfreys (eds.), *Victorian Gothic: Literary and Cultural Manifestations in the Nineteenth Century*, 109–28. Houndmills: Palgrave, 2000.

Chapple, J. A. V., *Elizabeth Gaskell: The Early Years*. Manchester: Manchester UP, 1997.

Chitham, Edward, *The Birth of Wuthering Heights: Emily Brontë at Work*. Basingstoke: Palgrave, 1998.

Chorley, H. F., '*Aurora Leigh*', *Athenaeum*, 1517 (22 Nov. 1856), 1425–7.

Clarke, Charles Cowden, and Mary Cowden Clarke, *Recollections of Writers*. London: Sampson Low Marston Searle & Rivington, 1878.

Clarke, G. W. (ed.), *Rediscovering Hellenism: The Hellenic Inheritance and the English Imagination*. Cambridge: CUP, 1989.

Clarke, M. L., *Classical Education in Britain, 1500–1900*. Cambridge: CUP, 1959.

—— 'Classical Studies', *The History of the University of Oxford*, v. *The Eighteenth Century*, ed. L. S. Sutherland and L. G. Mitchell, 513–33. Oxford: Clarendon, 1986.

Clarke, Norma, *Dr Johnson's Women*. London: Hambledon & London, 2000.

Cole, G. D. H., and T. W. Earp. (eds.), *Oxford Poetry 1915*. Oxford: Blackwell, 1915.

Cole, G. D. H., G. P. Dennis, and W. S. Vines. (eds.), *Oxford Poetry, 1910–1913*. Oxford: Blackwell, 1913.

Coleridge, Christabel, *Charlotte Mary Yonge: Her Life and Letters*. London: Macmillan, 1903.

Coleridge, Edith (ed.), *Memoir and Letters of Sara Coleridge*, 3rd edn. London: Henry S. King & Co., 1873.

Coleridge, Mary Elizabeth, *Gathered Leaves from the Prose of Mary E. Coleridge*, ed. Edith Sichel. London: Constable, 1910.

—— *The Collected Poems of Mary Coleridge*, ed. Theresa Whistler. London: Rupert Hart-Davis, 1954.

Coleridge, Samuel Taylor, *Collected Letters of Samuel Taylor Coleridge*, ed. Earl Leslie Griggs, vi. Oxford: Clarendon, 1956.

—— *Shorter Works and Fragments*, ed. H. J. Jackson and J. R. de J. Jackson, 2 vols. London: Routledge, 1995.

Coleridge, Sara, *Pretty Lessons in Verse for Good Children: With Some Lessons in Latin, in Easy Rhyme*, 4th edn. London: J. W. Parker, 1845.

Collins, John Churton, *Greek Influence on English Poetry*, ed. Michael Macmillan. London: I. Pitman, 1910.

Collins, Wilkie, *Antonina: Or, The Fall of Rome*. London: Richard Bentley, 1850.

Cooper, Helen, *Elizabeth Barrett Browning: Woman and Artist*. London: University of North Carolina Press, 1988.

Corson, Hiram, 'A Few Reminiscences of Robert Browning', in Martin Garrett (ed.), *Elizabeth Barrett Browning and Robert Browning: Interviews and Recollections*, 136–7. Basingstoke: Macmillan, 2000.

Cory, William, *Extracts from the Letters and Journals of William Cory*, ed. Francis Warre Cornish. Oxford: privately printed, 1897.

Cronin, Richard, *Romantic Victorians: English Literature, 1824–1840*. Basingstoke: Palgrave, 2002.

Crosse, Victoria, *The Woman who Didn't*. London: John Lane, 1895.

Cunningham, Valentine (ed.), *The Victorians: An Anthology of Poetry and Poetics*. Oxford: Blackwell, 2000.

Currie, H. MacL., 'English Translations of the Classics in the Nineteenth Century', in H. D. Jocelyn (ed.), *Aspects of Nineteenth-Century British Classical Scholarship*, 51–8. Liverpool: Liverpool Classical Monthly, 1996.

Currie, Robert, 'The Arts and Social Studies, 1914–1939'. *The History of the University of Oxford*, viii. *The Twentieth Century*, ed. Brian Harrison, 109–38. Oxford: Clarendon, 1994.

Dennis, Barbara, *Elizabeth Barrett Browning: The Hope End Years*. Bridgend: Seren, 1996.

Deutsch, Helen, *Resemblance and Disgrace: Alexander Pope and the Deformation of Culture*. London: Harvard UP, 1996.

DiBattista, Maria, 'The Triumph of Clytemnestra: The Charades in *Vanity Fair*', *PMLA* 95 (1980), 827–37.

Dickens, Charles. *Dombey and Son* (1846–8), ed. Alan Horsman. Oxford: Clarendon, 1974.

—— *Little Dorrit* (1857), ed. Harvey Peter Sucksmith. Oxford: Clarendon, 1979.

Doherty, Lilian E., 'The Snares of the Odyssey: A Feminine Narratological Reading', in S. J. Harrison (ed.), *Texts Ideas, and the Classics: Scholarship, Theory, and Classical Literature*, 117–33. Oxford: OUP, 2001.

Donaldson, M. F., 'A Day at Girton College', *Lady's World* (Nov 1886), 142–3.

Dorman, Susann, '*Hypatia* and *Callista*: The Initial Skirmish between Kingsley and Newman', *Nineteenth-Century Fiction*, 34 (1979) 173–93.

Dowling, Linda C., *Hellenism and Homosexuality in Victorian Oxford*. London: Cornell UP, 1994.

Downes, Jeremy M., *Recursive Desire: Rereading Epic Tradition*. London: University of Alabama Press, 1997.

Dryden, John, *Dryden's Aeneid: A Selection with Commentary*, ed. Robin Sowerby. Bristol: Bristol Classical Press, 1986.

Dyhouse, Carol, *Girls Growing up in Late Victorian and Edwardian England*. London: Routledge & Kegan Paul, 1981.

—— *No Distinction of Sex? Women in British Universities, 1870–1939*. London: UCL Press, 1995.

Eagleton, Terry, *Sweet Violence: The Idea of the Tragic*. Oxford: Blackwell, 2003.

Easterling, P. E., 'George Eliot and Greek Tragedy', *George Eliot Review*, 25 (1994), 56–67.

Edwards, Catharine. (ed.), *Roman Presences: Receptions of Rome in European Culture, 1789–1945*. Cambridge: CUP, 1999.

Elfenbein, Andrew, *Byron and the Victorians*. Cambridge: CUP, 1995.

Eliot, George, *Scenes of Clerical Life*. 1858. Ed. Thomas A. Noble. Oxford: Clarendon, 1985.

—— *Adam Bede* (1859), ed. Carol A. Martin. Oxford: Clarendon, 2001.

—— *A Writer's Notebook, 1854–1879*, ed. Joseph Wieserfarth, Charlottesville, Va.: UP of Virginia, 1981

—— *Daniel Deronda* (1876), ed. Graham Handley. Oxford: Clarendon, 1984.

—— *Felix Holt, the Radical* (1866), ed. Fred C. Thomson. Oxford: Clarendon, 1980.

Eliot, George, *Middlemarch: A Study of Provincial Life* (1871–2), ed. David Carroll. Oxford: Clarendon, 1992.

—— *Romola* (1862–3), ed. Andrew Brown. Oxford: Clarendon, 1993.

—— 'Notes on the Spanish Gypsy and Tragedy in General', *George Eliot's Life: As Related in her Letters and Journals*, ed. J. W. Cross, iii. 42–9. Edinburgh: Blackwood, 1885.

—— *Selected Critical Writings*, ed. Rosemary Ashton. Oxford: OUP, 1992.

—— *The George Eliot Letters*, ed. Gordon S. Haight, 9 vols. London: OUP, 1954.

—— *The Impressions of Theophrastus Such* (1879), ed. D. J. Enright. London: Dent, 1995.

—— *The Journals of George Eliot*, ed. Margaret Harris and Judith Johnston. Cambridge: CUP, 1998.

—— *The Lifted Veil; Brother Jacob*, ed. Helen Small. Oxford: OUP, 1999.

—— *The Mill on the Floss* (1860), ed. Gordon S. Haight. Oxford: Clarendon, 1980.

Elkin, Susan, 'Rossetti, Maria Francesca (1827–1876)', *Oxford Dictionary of National Biography*. Oxford: OUP, 2004, <http://www.oxforddnb.com/view/article/24142>, accessed 3 June 2005.

Ellis, Sarah Stickney, *The Women of England: Their Social Duties and Domestic Habits*. London: Fisher, Son & Co., 1839.

Euripides, *Medea*, ed. Donald J. Mastronarde. Cambridge: CUP, 2002.

Falk, Alice, 'Elizabeth Barrett Browning and Her Prometheuses: Self-Will and a Woman Poet', *TSWL* 7 (1988), 69–85.

—— 'Lady's Greek without the Accents: Aurora Leigh and Authority', *Studies in Browning and his Circle*, 19 (1991), 84–92.

Field, Michael, *Works and Days: From the Journal of Michael Field*, ed. T. Sturge Moore and D. C. Sturge Moore. London: J. Murray, 1933.

FitzGerald, Edward, *Selected Works*. London: Hart-Davis, 1962.

Flaxman, John, *The Iliad of Homer*. London, 1805.

Flint, Kate, *The Woman Reader, 1837–1914*. Oxford: Clarendon, 1993, 1999.

Fowler, Alastair, *Kinds of Literature: An Introduction to the Theory of Genres and Modes*. Oxford: Clarendon, 1982.

Fowler, Rowena, '*Cranford*: Cow in Grey Flannel or Lion Couchant?', *SEL* 24 (1984), 717–29.

—— 'Moments and Metamorphoses: Virginia Woolf's Greece', *Comparative Literature*, 51 (1999), 217–42.

—— ' "On Not Knowing Greek": The Classics and the Woman of Letters', *Classical Journal*, 78 (1983), 337–49.

Friedman, Susan Stanford, 'Gender and Genre Anxiety: Elizabeth Barrett Browning and H.D. as Epic Poets', *TSWL* 5 (1986), 203–28.

Fussell, Paul, *The Great War and Modern Memory* (1975). Oxford: OUP, 2000.

Garnett, Richard, 'Shelley, Mary Wollstonecraft (1797–1851)', *Dictionary of National Biography on CD-ROM*. Oxford: OUP, 1995.

Gaskell, Elizabeth, *Cranford and Cousin Phillis*, ed. Peter Keating. Harmondsworth: Penguin, 1976.

—— *Gothic Tales*, ed. Laura Kranzler. Harmondsworth: Penguin, 2000.

—— *Life of Charlotte Brontë* (1857), ed. Ernest Rhys. London: J. M. Dent, 1908.

—— *North and South* (1854–5), ed. Angus Easson. Oxford: OUP, 1982.

—— *The Letters of Mrs. Gaskell*, ed. J. A. V. Chapple and Arthur Pollard. Manchester: Manchester UP, 1966.

—— *Wives and Daughters* (1866), ed. Pam Mason. Harmondsworth: Penguin, 1996.

Gilbert, Sandra M., 'From *Patria* to *Matria*: Elizabeth Barrett Browning's Risorgimento'. *PMLA* 99 (1984), 194–211.

—— and Susan Gubar, *The Madwoman in the Attic: The Woman Writer and the Nineteenth-Century Literary Imagination*, 2nd edn. New Haven: Yale UP, 2000.

—— and—— *No Man's Land: The Place of the Woman Writer in the Twentieth Century*, 3 vols. London: Yale UP, 1988.

Gillespie, Stuart (ed.), *The Poets on the Classics: An Anthology of English Poets' Writings on the Classical Poets and Dramatists from Chaucer to the Present*. London: Routledge, 1988.

Gissing, George, *New Grub Street* (1891), ed. Bernard Bergonzi. Harmondsworth: Penguin, 1985.

—— *The Nether World* (1889), ed. Stephen Gill. Oxford: OUP, 1992.

Goldhill, Simon, *Who Needs Greek? Contests in the Cultural History of Hellenism*. Cambridge: CUP, 2002.

Gorham, Deborah, *The Victorian Girl and the Feminine Ideal*. London: Croom Helm, 1982.

—— *Vera Brittain: A Feminist Life*. Oxford: Blackwell, 1996.

Graduate of Girton, A, 'Greek Plays at the Universities', *Woman's World* (Jan. 1888), 121–8.

Graham, Colin, *Ideologies of Epic: Nation, Empire and Victorian Epic Poetry*. Manchester: Manchester UP, 1998.

Gray, Donald J., 'Macaulay's *Lays of Ancient Rome* and the Publication of Nineteenth-Century British Poetry', in James R. Kincaid and Albert J. Kuhn, (eds.), *Victorian Literature and Society: Essays Presented to Richard D. Altick*, 74–93. Columbus: Ohio State UP, 1983.

Greene, Ellen, *Re-Reading Sappho: Reception and Transmission*. London: University of California Press, 1996.

Griffin, Penny, *St Hugh's: One Hundred Years of Women's Education in Oxford*. Basingstoke: Macmillan, 1986.

Haggard, H. Rider, *She* (1887), ed. Daniel Karlin. Oxford: OUP, 1991.

Haight, Gordon S., *George Eliot: A Biography*. London: Clarendon, 1968.

Hainsworth, J. B., *The Idea of Epic*. Oxford: University of California Press, 1991.

Hall, Edith, 'Greek Plays in Georgian Reading'. *Greece & Rome*, 44 (1997), 59–81.

—— 'Medea and British Legislation Before the First World War', *Greece & Rome*, 46 (1999), 42–76.

—— 'Sophocles' *Electra* in Britain', in Jasper Griffin (ed.), *Sophocles Revisited: Essays Presented to Sir Hugh Lloyd-Jones*, 261–306. Oxford: OUP, 1999.

—— and Fiona Macintosh, *Greek Tragedy and the British Theatre 1660–1914*. Oxford: OUP, 2005.

Hanson, Lawrence, and Elisabeth Hanson, *Necessary Evil: The Life of Jane Welsh Carlyle*. London: Constable, 1952.

Hardwick, Lorna, 'Theatres of the Mind: Greek Tragedy in Women's Writing in England in the Nineteenth Century', *Theatre: Ancient and Modern*. Open University Department of Classical Studies, 2000, <http://www2.open.ac.uk/ClassicalStudies/GreekPlays/Conf99/Hardwck.htm>, accessed 5 June 2005.

—— *Translating Words, Translating Cultures*. London: Duckworth, 2000.

—— 'Women, Translation and Empowerment', in Joan Bellamy, Anne Laurence, and Gillian Perry (eds.), *Women, Scholarship and Criticism: Gender and Knowledge c.1790–1900*, 180–203. Manchester: Manchester UP, 2000.

Hardy, Thomas, *Jude the Obscure* (1895), ed. C. H. Sisson. Harmondsworth: Penguin, 1978.

—— *The Woodlanders* (1887), ed. Dale Kramer. Oxford: Clarendon, 1981.

Harraden, Beatrice, *Ships that Pass in the Night*. London, 1893.

Harrison, Jane Ellen, *Aspects, Aorists and the Classical Tripos*. Cambridge: CUP, 1919.

—— *Myths of the Odyssey in Art and Literature*. London: Rivingtons, 1882.

—— *Prolegomena to the Study of Greek Religion*. Cambridge: CUP, 1903.

—— *Reminiscences of a Student's Life*. London: Hogarth Press, 1925.

—— 'The Pictures of Sappho', *Woman's World* (Apr. 1888), 274–8.

Hawley, Judith, 'Carter, Elizabeth (1717–1806)', *Oxford Dictionary of National Biography*. Oxford: OUP, 2004, <http://www.oxforddnb.com/view/article/4782>, accessed 3 June 2005.

Haynes, Kenneth, *English Literature and Ancient Languages*. Oxford: OUP, 2003.

Heilbrun, Carolyn G., *Hamlet's Mother and Other Women*. New York: Columbia UP, 1990.

Herman, William, 'Virginia Woolf and the Classics: Every Englishman's Prerogative Transmuted into Fictional Art', in Elaine K. Ginsberg and Laura Moss Gottlieb (eds.), *Virginia Woolf: Centennial Essays*, 257–68. Troy, NY: Whitston, 1983.

Hickok, Kathleen, *Representations of Women: Nineteenth-Century British Women's Poetry*. London: Greenwood, 1984.

Highet, Gilbert, *The Classical Tradition: Greek and Roman Influences on Western Literature*. London: OUP, 1949.

Hill-Miller, Katherine, ' "The Skies and Trees of the Past": Anne Thackeray Ritchie and William Makepeace Thackeray', in Lynda E. Boose and Betty S. Flowers (eds.), *Daughters and Fathers*, 361–83. London: Johns Hopkins UP, 1989.

Hirsch, Pam, *Barbara Leigh Smith Bodichon 1827–1891: Feminist, Artist and Rebel*. London: Chatto & Windus, 1998.

Hoberman, Ruth, *Gendering Classicism: The Ancient World in Twentieth-Century Women's Historical Fiction*. Albany, NY: SUNY Press, 1997.

Hogg, Thomas Jefferson, *The Life of Percy Bysshe Shelley*. London: E. Moxon, 1858.

Holmes, Richard, *Shelley: The Pursuit*, 2nd edn. London: Flamingo, 1995.

Holtby, Winifred, *South Riding: An English Landscape* (1936). London: Virago, 1988.

Horne, R. H., *A New Spirit of the Age* (1844), 2 vols. New York: Garland, 1986.

Howarth, Janet, ' "In Oxford But … Not of Oxford": The Women's Colleges', *The History of the University of Oxford*, vii. *Nineteenth-Century Oxford, Part 2*, ed. M. G. Brock and M. C. Curthoys, 237–307. Oxford: OUP, 2000.

—— 'Women', *The History of the University of Oxford*, viii. *The Twentieth Century*, ed. Brian Harrison, 345–75. Oxford: Clarendon, 1994.

Hughes, Kathryn, *George Eliot: The Last Victorian*. London: Fourth Estate, 1999.

Hughes, Linda K., and Michael Lund, *Victorian Publishing and Mrs Gaskell's Work*. London: UP of Virginia, 1999.

Hughes, M. V., *A London Child of the 1870s* (1934). Oxford: OUP, 1977.

—— *A London Family Between the Wars* (1940). Oxford: OUP, 1979.

—— *A London Girl of the 1880s* (1936). Oxford: OUP, 1978.

—— *A London Home in the 1890s* (1937). Oxford: OUP, 1978.

—— *Vivians: A Family in Victorian Cornwall* (1935). Oxford: OUP, 1980.

Hughes, Thomas, *Tom Brown's School Days*. Cambridge: Macmillan, 1857.

234   *Bibliography*

Hunt, Felicity (ed.), *Lessons for Life: The Schooling of Girls and Women 1850–1950*. Oxford: Blackwell, 1987.

Hutchinson, Lucy, *Lucretius: De Rerum Natura*, ed. Hugh De Quehen. London: Duckworth, 1996.

Ingman, Heather, *Women's Fiction between the Wars: Mothers, Daughters and Writing*. Edinburgh: Edinburgh UP, 1998.

Jameson, Anna, *Diary of an Ennuyée*. London: Henry Colburn, 1826.

—— *The Loves of the Poets*, 2 vols. London: Henry Colburn, 1829.

Jay, Elisabeth, *Mrs Oliphant: 'A Fiction to Herself'*. Oxford: Clarendon, 1995.

—— 'Yonge, Charlotte Mary (1823–1901)', *Oxford Dictionary of National Biography*. Oxford: OUP, 2004, <http://www.oxforddnb.com/view/article/37065>, accessed 3 June 2005.

Jebb, Caroline, *Life and Letters of Sir Richard Claverhouse Jebb*. Cambridge: CUP, 1907.

Jenkyns, Richard, 'Classical Studies, 1872–1914', *The History of the University of Oxford*, vii. *Nineteenth-Century Oxford, Part 2*, ed. M. G. Brock and M. C. Curthoys, 237–307. Oxford: Clarendon, 2000.

—— 'The Beginnings of Greats, 1800–1872: Classical Studies', *The History of the University of Oxford*, vi. *Nineteenth-Century Oxford, Part 1*, ed. M. G. Brock and M. C. Curthoys, 513–20. Oxford: OUP, 1997.

—— *The Victorians and Ancient Greece*. Oxford: Blackwell, 1980.

Johnson, Samuel, *Lives of the English Poets*, ed. George Birkbeck Hill. Oxford: Clarendon, 1905.

Jones, John, *A Grammar of the Greek Tongue, On a New Plan*. London, 1808.

Jones, Kathleen, *A Passionate Sisterhood: The Sisters, Wives and Daughters of the Lake Poets*. London: Virago, 1998.

Jowett, Benjamin, *Dear Miss Nightingale: A Selection of Benjamin Jowett's Letters to Florence Nightingale*, ed. Vincent Quinn and John Prest. Oxford: Clarendon, 1987.

Keele, Mary (ed.), *Florence Nightingale in Rome: Letters Written by Florence Nightingale in Rome in the Winter of 1847–1848*. Philadelphia, Pa.: American Philosophical Society, 1981.

Keith, A. M., *Engendering Rome: Women in Latin Epic*. Cambridge: CUP, 2000.

Kerrigan, John, *Revenge Tragedy: Aeschylus to Armageddon*. Oxford: Clarendon, 1996.

Khan, Nosheen, *Women's Poetry of the First World War*. London: Harvester Wheatsheaf, 1988.

King, Jeannette, *Tragedy in the Victorian Novel: Theory and Practice in the Novels of George Eliot, Thomas Hardy and Henry James*. Cambridge: CUP, 1978.

Kipling, Rudyard, *Puck of Pook's Hill and Rewards and Fairies*, ed. Donald Mackenzie. Oxford: OUP, 1993.

Knellwolf, Christa, *A Contradiction Still: Representations of Women in the Poetry of Alexander Pope*. Manchester: Manchester UP, 1998.

Knoepflmacher, U. C., 'On Exile and Fiction: The Leweses and the Shelleys', in Ruth Perry and Martine Watson Brownley (eds.), *Mothering the Mind: Twelve Studies of Writers and their Silent Partners*, 102–21. London: Holmes & Meier, 1984.

Knox, Bernard, *The Heroic Temper: Studies in Sophoclean Tragedy*. Berkeley: University of California Press, 1964.

—— *The Oldest Dead White European Males and Other Reflections on the Classics*. London: W. W. Norton, 1993.

Laird, Holly, 'Aurora Leigh: An Epical Ars Poetica', in Sandra Donaldson (ed.), *Critical Essays on Elizabeth Barrett Browning*, 275–90. New York: G. K. Hall, 1999.

Lamb, Charles, *The Letters of Charles Lamb*, ed. T. N. Talfourd, 2 vols. London, 1837.

Landor, W. S., 'Harold, and Amymone', *Fraser's Magazine*, 38 (1848), 429–33.

Lang, Andrew, *The Poetical Works of Andrew Lang*, 4 vols. London: Longmans Green, 1923.

Lawrence, D. H., *The Rainbow* (1915), ed. Kate Flint. Oxford: OUP, 1998.

Layton, Lynne, 'Vera Brittain's Testament(s)', in Margaret Randolph Higonnet *et al.* (eds.), *Behind the Lines: Gender and the Two World Wars*, 70–83. London: Yale UP, 1987.

Ledger, Sally, *The New Woman: Fiction and Feminism at the Fin de Siècle*. Manchester: Manchester UP, 1997.

Lefkowitz, Mary R., *Heroines and Hysterics*. London: Duckworth, 1981.

Leighton, Angela, *Victorian Women Poets: Writing Against the Heart*. Hemel Hempstead: Harvester Wheatsheaf, 1992.

—— and Margaret Reynolds, *Victorian Women Poets: An Anthology*. Oxford: Blackwell, 1995.

Leonardi, Susan J., *Dangerous by Degrees: Women at Oxford and the Somerville College Novelists*. London: Rutgers UP, 1989.

Levy, Amy, 'Readers at the British Museum', *Atalanta*, 2 (1889), 449.

—— *The Complete Novels and Selected Writings of Amy Levy 1861–1889*, ed. Melvyn New. Gainsville: UP of Florida, 1993.

Lloyd-Jones, Hugh, 'Jane Ellen Harrison, 1850–1928', in Edward Shils and Carmen Blacker (eds.), *Cambridge Women: Twelve Portraits*, 29–72. Cambridge: CUP, 1996.

Lonsdale, Roger (ed), *Eighteenth-Century Women Poets: An Oxford Anthology*. Oxford: OUP, 1989.

Lupton, Mary Jane, 'A Little Hemming and More Greek', in Sandra Donaldson (ed.), *Critical Essays on Elizabeth Barrett Browning*, 32–7. New York: G. K. Hall, 1999.

Lynn Linton, Eliza, *Amymone: A Romance of the Days of Pericles*. London: Richard Bentley, 1848.

—— *My Literary Life*. London: Hodder & Stoughton, 1899.

—— *The Autobiography of Christopher Kirkland*. London: Richard Bentley, 1885.

Lyons, Patrick, 'Burnett, Dame Ivy Compton- (1884–1969)', *Oxford Dictionary of National Biography*. Oxford: OUP, 2004, <http://www.oxforddnb.com/view/article/32524>, accessed 3 June 2005.

Macaulay, Thomas Babington, *Lays of Ancient Rome*. London: Longman Brown Green, 1842.

McClure, Laura, 'On Knowing Greek: George Eliot and the Classical Tradition', *Classical and Modern Literature*, 13 (1993), 139–56.

—— 'The Shavian Murray and the Euripidean Shaw: *Major Barbara* and the *Bacchae*', *Classics Ireland*, 5 (1998), 64–84.

Macintosh, Fiona, 'Medea Transposed: Burlesque and Gender on the Mid-Victorian Stage', in Edith Hall, Fiona Macintosh, and Oliver Taplin (eds.), *Medea in Performance 1500–2000*, 75–99. Oxford: Legenda, 2000.

Mackenzie, Faith Compton, *William Cory: A Biography*. London: Constable, 1950.

Macpherson, Gerardine, *Memoirs of the Life of Anna Jameson*. London: Longmans, Green, 1878.

Mangnall, Richmal, *Historical and Miscellaneous Questions, for the Use of Young People*, 3rd edn. London: Thomas Hurst, 1803.

Mansel, Darrel, jun., 'George Eliot's Conception of Tragedy', *Nineteenth-Century Fiction*, 22 (1967), 155–71.

Marandon, Sylvaine, 'Duclaux, (Agnes) Mary Frances (1857–1944)', *Oxford Dictionary of National Biography*. Oxford: OUP, 2004, <http://www.oxforddnb.com/view/article/59577>, accessed 3 June 2005.

Marcus, Jane, 'Critical Response, I: Quentin's Bogey', *Critical Inquiry*, 11 (1985), 486–97.

—— (ed.), *Virginia Woolf and Bloomsbury: A Centenary Celebration*. Basingstoke: Macmillan, 1987.

—— *Virginia Woolf and the Languages of Patriarchy*. Bloomington: Indiana UP, 1987.

Marsh, Jan, *Christina Rossetti: A Literary Biography*. London: Pimlico, 1995.

Marshall, Emma, *No. XIII; Or, The Story of the Lost Vestal*. London: Cassell, 1885.

Marshall, Gail, *Actresses on the Victorian Stage: Feminine Performance and the Galatea Myth*. Cambridge: CUP, 1998.

Martindale, Charles (ed.), *Ovid Renewed: Ovidian Influences on Literature and Art from the Middle Ages to the Twentieth Century*. Cambridge: CUP, 1988.

—— and David Hopkins (eds.), *Horace Made New: Horatian Influences on British Writing from the Renaissance to the Twentieth Century*. Cambridge: CUP, 1993.

Maslen, Elizabeth, 'Mitchison, Naomi Mary Margaret, Lady Mitchison (1897–1999)', *Oxford Dictionary of National Biography*. Oxford: OUP, 2004, <http://www.oxforddnb.com/view/article/50052>, accessed 3 June 2005.

Mavor, W. F., *The Eton Latin Grammar, Or An Introduction to the Latin Tongue*, 11th edn. London, 1822.

Maxwell, Catherine, *The Female Sublime from Milton to Swinburne: Bearing Blindness*. Manchester: Manchester UP, 2001.

Mayor, F. M., *The Rector's Daughter* (1924). Harmondsworth: Penguin, 1985.

Meade, L. T., *A Sweet Girl Graduate*. London: Cassell, 1891.

Mellor, Anne K., *Mary Shelley: Her Life, Her Fiction, Her Monsters*. London: Routledge, 1988.

Mermin, Dorothy, *Elizabeth Barrett Browning: The Origins of a New Poetry*. London: University of Chicago Press, 1989.

—— *Godiva's Ride: Women of Letters in England, 1830–1880*. Bloomington: Indiana UP, 1993.

Miller, Lucasta, *The Brontë Myth*. London: Vintage, 2002.

Milton, John, *The Poetical Works of John Milton*, ed. David Masson, 2nd edn., 3 vols. London: Macmillan, 1890.

Mitchell, Charlotte, '*The Gosling Society, 1859–1877*', Charlotte Mary Yonge Fellowship website. Available: <http://www.dur.ac.uk/c.e.schultze/context/goslings.html>, 7 June 2005.

Mitchell, Sally. *The New Girl: Girls' Culture in England, 1880–1915*. New York: Columbia UP, 1995.

Moers, Ellen, *Literary Women: The Great Writers*. London: Women's Press, 1978.

Moody, Clement, *The New Eton Grammar, in which that Popular Introduction to the Latin Tongue is Rendered into English*. London: Smith, Elder, 1838.

Morlier, Margaret M., 'The Death of Pan: Elizabeth Barrett Browning and the Romantic Ego', in Sandra Donaldson (ed.), *Critical Essays on Elizabeth Barrett Browning*, 258–74. New York: G. K. Hall, 1999.

Mudge, Bradford Keyes, *Sara Coleridge: A Victorian Daughter.* London: Yale UP, 1989.

Munich, Adrienne, *Andromeda's Chains: Gender and Interpretation in Victorian Literature and Art.* New York: Columbia UP, 1989.

Murray, Gilbert, *The Place of Greek in Education: An Inaugural Lecture.* Glasgow, 1889.

Myers, Sylvia Harcstark, *The Bluestocking Circle: Women, Friendship, and the Life of the Mind in Eighteenth-Century England.* Oxford: Clarendon, 1990.

Nardo, Anna, '*Romola* and Milton: A Cultural History of Rewriting', *Nineteenth-Century Literature*, 53 (1998), 238–63.

Nelson, James G., *The Sublime Puritan: Milton and the Victorians.* Madison: University of Wisconsin Press, 1963.

Nestor, Pauline, *Female Friendships and Communities: Charlotte Brontë, George Eliot, Elizabeth Gaskell.* Oxford: Clarendon, 1985.

Nichol, John, *Byron.* London: Macmillan, 1880.

Nuttall, A. D., *Dead from the Waist Down: Scholars and Scholarship in Literature and the Popular Imagination.* London: Yale UP, 2003.

Ogilvie, R. M., *Latin and Greek: A History of the Influence of the Classics on English Life from 1600 to 1918.* London: Routledge & Kegan Paul, 1964.

Oliphant, Margaret, *Phoebe, Junior* (1876). London: Virago, 1989.

—— 'The Ancient Classics', *Blackwood's Edinburgh Magazine*, 116 (1874), 365–86.

Ouditt, Sharon, *Fighting Forces, Writing Women: Identity and Ideology in the First World War.* London: Routledge, 1994.

Pascoe, Charles Eyre, *Schools for Girls and Colleges for Women: A Handbook of Female Education Chiefly Designed for the Use of Persons of the Upper Middle Class.* London: Hardwicke & Bogue, 1879.

Peterson, Linda H., 'Margaret Oliphant's *Autobiography* as Professional Artist's Life', *Women's Writing*, 6 (1999), 261–78.

—— 'Sappho and the Making of Tennysonian Lyric', *ELH* 61 (1994), 121–37.

Peterson, M. Jeanne, *Family, Love, and Work in the Lives of Victorian Gentlewomen.* Bloomington: Indiana UP, 1989.

Phillips, Terry, 'Battling with the Angel: May Sinclair's Powerful Mothers', in Sarah Sceats and Gail Cunningham (eds.), *Image and Power: Women in Fiction in the Twentieth Century*, 128–38. London: Longman, 1996.

Plutarch, *Lives*, tr. Bernadotte Perrin. Loeb Classical Library. London: Heinemann, 1914.

Pope, Alexander, *Iliad I–IX*, ed. Maynard Mack. London: Methuen, 1967.

Prins, Yopie, 'Elizabeth Barrett, Robert Browning and the *Différance* of Translation', *VP* 29 (1991), 435–51.

—— 'Greek Maenads, Victorian Spinsters', in Richard Dellamora (ed.), *Victorian Sexual Dissidence*, 43–81 Chicago: University of Chicago Press, 1999.

—— *Victorian Sappho*. Princeton: Princeton UP, 1999.

'Public Schools of England—Eton', *Edinburgh Review*, 51 (1830).

Purkis, John, 'Reading Homer Today', in C. Emlyn-Jones, Lorna Hardwick, and J. Purkis, (eds.), *Homer: Readings and Images*, 1–18. London: Duckworth, 1992.

Pykett, Lyn, 'Writing around Modernism: May Sinclair and Rebecca West', in Lynne Hapgood and Nancy L. Paxton (eds.), *Outside Modernism: In Pursuit of the English Novel, 1900–30*, 103–22. Basingstoke: Macmillan, 2000.

Quint, David, *Epic and Empire: Politics and Generic Form from Virgil to Milton*. Princeton: Princeton UP, 1993.

Raby, Peter, *Samuel Butler: A Biography*. London: Hogarth, 1991.

Raitt, Suzanne, *May Sinclair: A Modern Victorian*. Oxford: Clarendon, 2000.

Raphaely, Judith, 'Nothing But Gibberish and Shibboleths? The Compulsory Greek Debate 1870–1919', in Christopher Stray (ed.), *Classics in 19th- and 20th-Century Cambridge: Curriculum, Culture and Community*, 71–94. Cambridge: Cambridge Philological Society, 1999.

Reid, Jane Davidson, and Chris Rohmann, *The Oxford Guide to Classical Mythology in the Arts, 1300–1990s*, 2 vols. Oxford: OUP, 1993.

Reid, Tim, 'Bookish Girl Nourished on a Diet of History and Grammar', *The Times* (28 Apr. 2001).

—— 'Victoria, Princess in a Class of her Own', *The Times* (28 Apr. 2001).

Rendall, Vernon, 'George Eliot and the Classics', in Gordon S. Haight (ed.), *A Century of George Eliot Criticism*, 215–26. London, Methuen, 1966.

Reynolds, Barbara, *Dorothy L. Sayers: Her Life and Soul*. London: Sceptre, 1994.

Reynolds, Margaret (ed.), *The Sappho Companion*. London: Chatto & Windus, 2000.

Reynolds, William, 'Literature, Latin, and Love: Dorothy L. Sayers' *Gaudy Night*', *Clues*, 6 (1985), 67–78.

Ripman, Walter, and M. V. Hughes, *A Rapid Latin Course*. London: J. M. Dent, 1923.

Roberts, W. J., *Mary Russell Mitford: The Tragedy of a Bluestocking*. London, 1913.

Robinson, Annabel, *The Life and Work of Jane Ellen Harrison*. Oxford: OUP, 2002.

Rogers, Philip, 'The Education of Cousin Phillis', *Nineteenth-Century Literature*, 50 (1995), 27–50.

Ronnick, Michele Valerie, 'Epictetus' Liberation of Elizabeth Carter', *Res Publica Litterarum*, 18 (1995), 169–71.

Rose, Jonathan, *The Intellectual Life of the British Working Classes*. London: Yale UP, 2001.

Rossen, Janice, *The University in Modern Fiction: When Power is Academic*. Basingstoke: Macmillan, 1993.

Rossetti, Christina, *The Complete Poems*, ed. R. W. Crump and Betty S. Flowers. London: Penguin, 2001.

—— *The Letters of Christina Rossetti*, ed. Antony H. Harrison. 3 vols. London: UP of Virginia, 1997.

Rowbotham, Judith, *Good Girls Make Good Wives: Guidance for Girls in Victorian Fiction*. Oxford: Blackwell, 1989.

Russell, Dora, *Hypatia: Or, Woman and Knowledge*. London: Kegan Paul, Trench, Trubner, 1925.

Sanders, Valerie, *Eve's Renegades: Victorian Anti-Feminist Women Novelists*. Basingstoke: Macmillan, 1996.

—— 'Marriage and the Anti-Feminist Woman Novelist', in Nicola Diane Thompson (ed.), *Victorian Women Writers and the Woman Question*, 24–41. Cambridge: CUP, 1999.

—— (ed.), *Records of Girlhood: An Anthology of Nineteenth-Century Women's Childhoods*. Aldershot: Ashgate, 2000.

Sayers, Dorothy L., *Gaudy Night*. London: Gollancz, 1935.

—— 'Gaudy Night', in Denys Kilham Roberts (ed.), *Titles to Fame*, 75–95. London: Thomas Nelson, 1937.

—— *Hangman's Holiday*. London: Gollancz, 1933.

—— *The Letters of Dorothy L. Sayers 1899–1936: The Making of a Detective Novelist*, ed. Barbara Reynolds. London: Hodder & Stoughton, 1995.

—— *The Poetry of Dorothy L. Sayers*, ed. Ralph E. Hone. Cambridge: Dorothy L. Sayers Society, 1996.

—— *The Poetry of Search and the Poetry of Statement*. London: Gollancz, 1963.

—— *Unpopular Opinions*. London: Gollancz, 1946.

—— *Wilkie Collins: A Critical and Biographical Study*, ed. E. R. Gregory. [Toledo, Ohio]: The Friends of the University of Toledo Libraries, 1977.

Schaffer, Talia, *The Forgotten Female Aesthetes: Literary Culture in Late-Victorian England*. London: UP of Virginia, 2000.

Scheinberg, Cynthia, 'Recasting "Sympathy and Judgement": Amy Levy, Women Poets, and the Victorian Dramatic Monologue', *VP* 35 (1997), 173–92.

Schor, Hilary M., *Scheherezade in the Marketplace: Elizabeth Gaskell and the Victorian Novel*. Oxford: OUP, 1992.

Schultze, Clemence, 'Manliness and the Myth of Heracles in Charlotte M. Yonge's *My Young Alcides*', *International Journal of the Classical Tradition*, 5 (1998–9) 383–414.

Scott, John A., *Homer and his Influence*. London: G. G. Harrap, 1925.

Shelley, Mary Wollstonecraft, *Collected Tales and Stories*, ed. Charles E. Robinson. Baltimore: John Hopkins UP, 1976.

—— *The Journals of Mary Shelley, 1814–1844*, ed. Paula R. Feldman and Diana Scott-Kilvert, 2 vols. Oxford: Clarendon, 1987.

—— *The Letters of Mary Wollstonecraft Shelley*, ed. Betty T. Bennett, 3 vols. London: Johns Hopkins UP, 1980.

Showalter, Elaine, *A Literature of their Own: British Women Novelists from Brontë to Lessing* (1977). Rev. edn. Princeton: Princeton UP, 1999.

—— *Sexual Anarchy: Gender and Culture at the Fin de Siècle*. London: Bloomsbury, 1991.

Sinclair, May, *Mary Olivier: A Life* (1919). London: Virago, 1980.

—— *The Three Sisters* (1914). London: Virago, 1982.

Skilton, David, 'Schoolboy Latin and the Mid-Victorian Novelist: A Study in Reader Competence', *Browning Institute Studies*, 16 (1988), 39–55.

Smith, Stevie, *Novel on Yellow Paper: Or, Work it out for Yourself*. London: Jonathan Cape, 1936.

Sophocles, *Antigone*, ed. Mark Griffith. Cambridge: CUP, 1999.

—— *The Plays and Fragments with Critical Notes, Commentary, and Translation*, ed. Richard Claverhouse Jebb, 7 vols. Cambridge: CUP, 1883.

Spalding, Frances, *Stevie Smith: A Biography*. Stroud: Sutton, 2002.

St Aubyn, Alan, *A Proctor's Wooing*, 3 vols. London, 1897.

—— *The Junior Dean*, 3 vols. London, 1891.

Stanley, Arthur Penrhyn, *The Life and Correspondence of Thomas Arnold*, 2 vols. London: Ward Lock, 1844.

Steele, Jeremy, 'Classics'. *Oxford Reader's Companion to Hardy*, ed. Norman Page, 58–66. Oxford: OUP, 2000.

Stodart, M. A., *Female Writers: Thoughts on their Proper Sphere, and on their Powers of Usefulness*. London: R. B. Seeley & W. Burnside, 1842.

Stone, Marjorie, *Elizabeth Barrett Browning*. Basingstoke: Macmillan, 1995.

—— 'Genre Subversion and Gender Inversion: *The Princess* and *Aurora Leigh*', *VP* 25 (1987), 101–27.

Stray, Christopher, *Classics Transformed: Schools, Universities, and Society in England, 1830–1960*. Oxford: Clarendon, 1998.

—— 'Locke's System of Classical Instruction', *The Locke Newsletter*, 22 (1991), 115–21.

—— 'The First Century of the Classical Tripos (1822–1922): High Culture and the Politics of Curriculum', in Christopher Stray (ed.), *Classics in*

19th- and 20th-Century Cambridge: Curriculum, Culture and Community, 1–14. Cambridge: Cambridge Philological Society, 1999.

Sturrock, June, *'Heaven and Home': Charlotte M. Yonge's Domestic Fiction and the Victorian Debate over Women.* Victoria, BC: University of Victoria Press, 1995.

Super, R. H., 'Landor's "Dear Daughter", Eliza Lynn Linton', *PMLA* 59 (1944), 1059–85.

Sutherland, Gillian, ' "Girton for Ladies, Newnham for Governesses" ', in Jonathan Smith and Christopher Stray (eds.), *Teaching and Learning in Nineteenth-Century Cambridge*, 139–49. History of the University of Cambridge: Texts and Studies, 4. Woodbridge: Boydell Press in association with Cambridge University Library, 2001.

Sutherland, John, *Mrs Humphry Ward: Eminent Victorian, Pre-Eminent Edwardian.* Oxford: Clarendon, 1990.

—— *The Longman Companion to Victorian Fiction.* London: Longman, 1988.

Sutphin, Christine, 'The Representation of Women's Heterosexual Desire in Augusta Webster's "Circe" and "Medea in Athens" '. *Women's Writing*, 5 (1998), 373–92.

Suzuki, Mihoko, *Metamorphoses of Helen: Authority, Difference, and the Epic.* Ithaca, NY: Cornell UP, 1989.

Swinburne, Algernon Charles, *Lesbia Brandon*, ed. Randolph Hughes. London: Falcon, 1952.

Syrett, Netta, *The Sheltering Tree.* London: G. Bles, 1939.

Tennyson, Hallam, *Alfred, Lord Tennyson: A Memoir*, 2 vols. London: Macmillan, 1897.

Thackeray, William Makepeace, *Vanity Fair: A Novel Without a Hero.* (1847), ed. John Sutherland. Oxford: OUP, 1998.

Thompson, Nicola Diane, 'Responding to the Woman Questions: Rereading Noncanonical Victorian Women Novelists', in Nicola Diane Thompson (ed.), *Victorian Women Writers and the Woman Question*, 1–23. Cambridge: CUP, 1999.

Thomson, Fred C., *'Felix Holt* as Classic Tragedy', *Nineteenth-Century Fiction*, 16 (1961), 46–58.

Thomson, J. A. K., *The Classical Background of English Literature.* London: G. Allen & Unwin, 1948.

Tracy, Robert, *'Lana Medicata Fuco*: Trollope's Classicism', in John Halperin (ed.), *Trollope Centenary Essays*, 1–23. London: Macmillan, 1982.

Trimmer, Mrs, *New and Comprehensive Lessons: Containing a General Outline of the Roman History.* London: John Harris, 1835.

Trodd, Anthea, *Women's Writing in English: Britain, 1900–1945.* Harlow: Longman, 1998.

Trollope, Anthony, *An Autobiography* (1883), ed. Michael Sadleir and Frederick Page. Oxford: OUP, 1980.

—— 'Ancient Classics for English Readers', *Saint Pauls*, 5 (1870).

—— *Barchester Towers* (1857), ed. Michael Sadleir and Frederick Page. Oxford: OUP, 1996.

—— *Framley Parsonage* (1860–1), ed. P. D. Edwards. Oxford: OUP, 1980.

—— *The Last Chronicle of Barset* (1867), ed. Stephen Gill. Oxford: OUP, 1980.

Tucker, Herbert F., 'Aurora Leigh: Epic Solutions to Novel Ends', in Alison Booth (ed.), *Famous Last Words: Changes in Gender and Narrative Closure*, 62–85. London: UP of Virginia, 1993.

Turner, Frank M., *Contesting Cultural Authority: Essays in Victorian Intellectual Life*. Cambridge: CUP, 1993.

—— *The Greek Heritage in Victorian Britain*. London: Yale UP, 1981.

Tylee, Claire M., *The Great War and Women's Consciousness: Images of Militarism and Feminism in Women's Writings, 1914–64*. Basingstoke: Macmillan, 1990.

Uglow, Jenny, *Elizabeth Gaskell: A Habit of Stories*. London: Faber, 1993.

U.T., 'The Eminent Professor and the Diligent Student', *The Daisy*, 3 (1890), 6.

Valpy, Richard, *Delectus Sententiarum Græcarum, Ad Usum Tironum Accommodatus*. London, 1815.

Vance, Norman, 'Horace and the Nineteenth Century', in Charles Martindale and David Hopkins (eds.), *Horace Made New: Horatian Influences on British Writing from the Renaissance to the Twentieth Century*, 199–216. Cambridge: CUP, 1993.

—— *The Victorians and Ancient Rome*. Oxford: Blackwell, 1997.

Van Thal, Herbert, *Eliza Lynn Linton: The Girl of the Period*. London: George Allen & Unwin, 1979.

Vicinus, Martha, *Independent Women: Work and Community for Single Women 1850–1920*. London: Virago, 1985.

Virgil, *The Eclogues, The Georgics*, tr. C. Day Lewis, ed. R. O. A. M. Lyne. Oxford: OUP, 1983.

Wallace, Diana, *Sisters and Rivals in British Women's Fiction, 1914–39*. Basingstoke: Macmillan, 2000.

Wallace, Jennifer, 'Elizabeth Barrett Browning: Knowing Greek', *Essays in Criticism*, 50 (2000), 329–53.

—— *Shelley and Greece: Rethinking Romantic Hellenism*. Basingstoke: Macmillan, 1997.

Ward, Mrs Humphry, *A Writer's Recollections*. London: W. Collins, 1918.

Webb, Timothy, *The Violet in the Crucible: Shelley and Translation*. Oxford: Clarendon, 1976.

Webster, Augusta, *A Housewife's Opinions*. London: Macmillan, 1879.

—— *Portraits*. London: Macmillan, 1870.

—— *Portraits and Other Poems*, ed. Christine Sutphin. Peterborough, Ont.: Broadview, 2000.

—— *The Medea of Euripides, Literally Translated into English Verse*. London: Macmillan, 1868.

—— *The Prometheus Bound of Æschylus: Literally Translated into English Verse*, ed. Thomas Webster. London: Macmillan, 1866.

West, Francis, *Gilbert Murray, A Life*. London: Croom Helm, 1984.

Wiesenfarth, Joseph (ed.), *George Eliot: A Writer's Notebook 1854–1879 and Uncollected Writings*. Charlottesville, Va.: UP of Virginia, 1981.

—— 'The Greeks, the Germans and George Eliot', *Browning Institute Studies*, 10 (1982), 91–104.

Wilkie, Brian, *Romantic Poets and Epic Tradition*. Madison: University of Wisconsin Press, 1965.

Wilkins, H. M., 'Latin Versification', *Blackwood's Edinburgh Magazine*, 76 (1854), 560–75.

Williams, Carolyn D., *Pope, Homer, and Manliness: Some Aspects of Eighteenth-Century Classical Learning*. London: Routledge, 1993.

Willis, Chris, ' "Heaven Defend Me from Political or Highly-Educated Women!": Packaging the New Woman for Mass Consumption', in Angelique Richardson and Chris Willis (eds.), *The New Woman in Fiction and in Fact: Fin-de-Siècle Feminisms*, 53–65. Basingstoke: Palgrave, 2001.

Wilson, Duncan, *Gilbert Murray, OM, 1866–1957*. Oxford: Clarendon, 1987.

Wilson, John, 'The Latin Anthology', *Blackwood's Edinburgh Magazine*, 43 (1838): 521–64.

Winterer, Caroline, *The Culture of Classicism: Ancient Greece and Rome in American Intellectual Life, 1780–1910*. London: Johns Hopkins UP, 2002.

—— 'Victorian Antigone: Classicism and Women's Education in America, 1840–1900', *American Quarterly*, 53 (2001).

Wolff, Robert Lee, *Sensational Victorian: The Life and Fiction of Mary Elizabeth Braddon*. London: Garland, 1979.

Wolfson, Susan J. (ed.), *Felicia Hemans: Selected Poems, Letters, Reception Materials*. Oxford: Princeton UP, 2000.

—— ' "Their she Condition": Cross-Dressing and the Politics of Gender in *Don Juan*', *ELH* 54 (1987), 585–617.

Wood, Christopher, *Olympian Dreamers: Victorian Classical Painters, 1860–1914*. London: Constable, 1983.

Wood, Marilyn, *Rhoda Broughton (1840–1920): Profile of a Novelist*. Stamford: Paul Watkins, 1993.

Woolf, Virginia, *A Room of One's Own*. London: Hogarth Press, 1929.

—— *A Woman's Essays*, ed. Rachel Bowlby. Harmondsworth: Penguin, 1992.

—— *Collected Essays*, iii. London: Hogarth Press, 1967.

—— *The Letters of Virginia Woolf*, ed. Nigel Nicolson and Joanne Trautmann Banks, ii. London: Hogarth Press, 1975.

Yaeger, Patricia, *Honey-Mad Women: Emancipatory Strategies in Women's Writing*. New York: Columbia UP, 1988.

Yonge, Charlotte M., *A Book of Golden Deeds of All Times and All Lands*. London: Macmillan, 1864.

—— *Aunt Charlotte's Stories of Greek History for the Little Ones*. London: Marcus Ward, 1876.

—— *Aunt Charlotte's Stories of Roman History for the Little Ones*. London: Marcus Ward, 1877.

—— *Musings Over 'The Christian Year' and 'Lyra Innocentium'; Together with a Few Gleanings of Recollections of the Rev. John Keble*. Oxford: J. Parker, 1871.

—— *My Young Alcides: A Faded Photograph* (1875). London: Macmillan, 1889.

—— *The Daisy Chain, or, Aspirations: A Family Chronicle* (1856). London: Virago, 1988.

—— *The Long Vacation*. London: Macmillan, 1895.

—— *The Trial: More Links of the Daisy Chain*. 1864. London: Macmillan, 1891.

—— *What Books to Lend and What to Give*. London, 1887.

—— *Womankind*. Leipzig: Bernhard Tauchnitz, 1878.

Young, Francis, *Mangnall's Historical and Miscellaneous Questions, Revised and Extended*. London: T. J. Allman, 1869.

Index

A Book of Golden Deeds 43
Alcestis 10
  new 189–91
Allen, Grant 81
  The Woman who did 87
Ancient Classics for English
  Readers 34
ancient history 71
Antigone 9, 44, 69, 173–4
Aristotle 23
  Poetics applied to fiction 205–6
Arnold, Mary 74
Arnold, Matthew 30, 55, 164,
  165, 173
Aspasia 10
Atalanta 89

Barrett Browning, Elizabeth 2, 3, 4,
  5, 6, 7, 8, 9, 10, 31, 33, 58, 65,
  81, 91, 190
  Aurora Leigh 2, 105, 108, 109,
    110, 112, 123, 126–8,
    132
  Casa Guidi Windows 117, 119,
    120–2, 124
  classical education 104–8
  feminine epic, modernized and
    feminized 8
  'Lady Geraldine's Courtship'
    123
  'lady's Greek' 7, 107
  Prometheus Bound 102, 103
  relationship with brother 64
  scholarly woman poet 101–4
  'the feminine of Homer' 7–10,
    113–18, 126

use of epic conventions 109,
  124
  voice as a female subject 110–11
Bassnett, Susan 32
Beale, Dorothea 3, 80, 82
Beard, Mary 6
Bible, The 149
Blackwood's Edinburgh Magazine 33
Bodichon, Madame see Leigh Smith,
  Barbara
Bodleian Library 75
Braddon, Mary Elizabeth 18
  Aurora Floyd 48
  Lady Audley's Secret 18
Bradley, Katherine 6, 31
British Museum Reading
  Room 69–70
Brittain, Vera 6, 10, 27, 52, 53,
  95, 96, 99, 192, 193, 208,
  211–19
  'the epic of the women who went
    to war' 211–19
  On Becoming a Writer 53
  Oxford Senior Local
    examination 78–9
  Testament of Friendship 219
  Testament of Youth 200, 211, 212,
    215–19
  The Dark Tide 99, 212
Brontë, Anne 4, 143
Brontë, Charlotte 6, 8, 52, 58,
  143
Brontë, Emily 143
Broughton, Rhoda 141
Browning, Robert 4, 25, 30, 33,
  36, 37, 103

Browning, Robert (*cont.*)
    *Balaustion's Adventure, including
        a Transcript from
        Euripides* 189–90
Bucolic poetry 125
Buss, Frances Mary 82
Butler, Samuel 29
    'The Humour of Homer' 28
Byron 11, 12, 32, 50, 51, 102, 109
    'drill'd dull lesson' 19–20

Caesar, Julius 35
Cambridge Ritualists 6
Cambridge University 14, 22, 24, 30
    first College for Women 81
    full membership for women 85
    Newnham College 75
    Tripos 88
Carter, Elizabeth 56, 57
Catholic Church 38
Catullus 23
Christianity 38, 43
Circe 9
Cicero 23, 35
'classical daughter' 47
    Aurora Floyd 48
    Little Dorrit 47, 51
    North and South 47
classical images in fiction 46–8
    censure 49
    exclusion 49
    frustration 49
classical training *see also* male
        mentors
    access to
        class 15
        gender 15
    access to public school
        learning 68
    aristocratic associations of 54–6
    as family duty 63–4

colleges 82
finishing school 72
formal academic
    education 70–81
gender inequalities 84
gender separation 1, 2
girls' public schools 74–81
home education 52, 57–65, 137
home student at Oxford 73
'humane aspects' of 77
male prerogative 2
masculine schooling 73
Oxbridge women's colleges 81–9
public schools 17
universities 81–9
women's 3
clergyman's daughter 57
Clough, Anne Jemima 75, 84
    Greek plays at Cambridge 92–3
Coleridge, Mary Elizabeth 6, 68,
        69, 137
    'Alcestis to Admetus' 189–91
    Medea and 188–9
Coleridge, Samuel Taylor 17, 21, 61
Coleridge, Sara 3, 60, 67, 68
Collins, Wilkie 39
    Antonina: Or the Fall of Rome 38,
        39
conversion narratives 39
Cooper, Edith 31
Cory, William 68
    'Grecian ladies' and 68–9
Cowper, Countess 31
Craik, Dinah Mulock 82

Davies, Emily 84, 88
de Quincey
    education 17
Demosthenes 23
detective stories 193, 205, 206 *see
        also* Sayers, Dorothy L

Dickens, Charles 16
  Little Dorrit 47, 51
divorce reform 164, 184
domestic incompetence 4
Donaldson, M.F. 85
'dual sense of self' 62

educational reformers 84
Electra 9
Eliot, George 2, 3, 4, 5, 6, 7, 9,
  10, 16, 25, 31, 44, 52, 58,
  70, 75, 81
  Adam Bede 173, 174, 177, 180
  Middlemarch 7, 16, 51, 70, 71,
    169, 177, 178
  novel as tragic form 170–83
  Scenes of Clerical Life 175, 178
  'The Lifted Veil' 14
  The Mill on the Floss 1, 2, 15, 16,
    84, 130, 172, 175, 176, 188,
    194, 211, 221
Elizabeth I 54
'English Sappho' 8
epic tradition in poetry 104–8, 112,
  114, 128
  woman's epic 115
Eton Latin Grammar 17, 21, 70,
  73, 136
Evans, Mary Ann 172 *see also*
  George Eliot
  Westminster Review 173

female heroism, standards for 43–4
femininity
  classical model of 199
  reconciliation with increased
    education 192–3
Fiske, John 171
Fitzgerald, Mrs Thomas 31
Ford, Ford Madox 48
Freud 194

Gaskell, Elizabeth 6, 52, 58, 70, 156
  North and South 47, 156
  'classical daughter' and 47
gender
  inequalities 84
  politics 9
  separation 1, 2, 130
Gentleman's Magazine 56, 157
girls' education *see* classical training
Girton Girl 85–6
'Girton Pioneers' 85
Gissing, George
  The Emancipated 51
Gosling Society 137
Governesses' Benevolent
  Institution 82
Gradus ad Parnassum 20
grand tour, women and the 48–51
'Greats' 23
'Grecian ladies' 69
Greek 2, 3, 5, 6, 12, 13, 14, 23, 26,
  33, 46, 52, 53, 89–91
  accents 12
  fathers teaching daughters 4
  history 34
  literature 29, 34
  mythology 6
  plays in the universities 92–4
  public schools and 17
  religion 43
  tragedies, female characters 9
  women and 132
Greek for Beginners 31
Grey, Lady Jane 55

Haldane N.M. *see* Mitchison, Naomi
Hardy, Thomas 16, 30
  A Pair of Blue Eyes 30
  Jude the Obscure 30
Harraden, Beatrice
  Ships that pass in the Night 86

Harrison, Jane Ellen 5, 6, 89–92,
    93, 200
'How to Vulgarize Homer' 29
Hecuba 9
Hemans, Felicia 8
Holtby, Winifred 217, 219
Homer 5, 8, 19, 20, 23, 111
    Iliad 13, 18, 20, 29, 117, 194
    Pope's translations 32, 196
    Victorian women writers and 193
    Odyssey 13, 28, 129
    Pope's translations 32, 33
    'the feminine of Homer' 7–10
Honour School of Literae
    Humaniores
    admission of women to, 97
Horace 11, 12, 13, 14, 23, 35
    Adam Bede 13
    Odes 13, 18
    Soracte Ode 11, 12, 13
Hughes, M.V. 77, 94
Hutchinson, Lucy
    De Rerum Natura 56

Ingelow, Jean 82

Jameson, Anna 3, 8, 33, 49
Jebb, R.C. 25, 171
Jenkyns, Richard 23
    *The Victorians and Ancient
    Greece* 5
Johnson, Samuel 56, 57
Jowett, Benjamin 25, 31
Jung 194
Junior and Senior Local
    examinations 78
Juvenal, Terence 14, 23, 35

Keats 31
    'Ode on a Grecian Urn' 32

'On First Looking into
    Chapman's Homer' 32
Kingsley, Charles 38
Kipling, Rudyard 26, 42
    Puck of Pook's Hill 26, 41

Ladies' Department of King's
    College, London 83, 93
Ladies' Educational Associations
    78
Lady's World 85
Landon, Letitia Elizabeth (L.E.L.) 8,
    109, 110
Latin 5, 12, 13, 16, 26, 33, 46,
    50, 52, 53
    fathers teaching daughters 4
    girls' public schools 76
    language 1, 2, 3, 4, 5, 6
    public schools and 17
    quantities 12
Lee, Vernon 31
Lehman, Rosamund
    Dusty Answer 99
Leigh Smith, Barbara 82, 84
Lempriere's Classical Dictionary 31, 76
Levy, Amy 6, 9, 10, 52, 69,
    79–80, 164
    'Medea'186–9
    'Xantippe' 168–70, 191
Linton, Eliza Lynn 10, 149
    *Amymone: A Romance of the Days
    of Pericles* 165–8
Literae Humaniores course *see*
    'Greats'
Livy 19, 41
Locke's System of Classical
    Instruction 172
London University 27
    full membership of women 82
Lucretius 5

Macaulay, Rose 99
Macaulay, T.B.
  Lays of Ancient Rome 40, 41, 50,
    195
Madame de Staël
  Corinne, or Italy 51
maenad image 200–1
male critics 7
  accentless 'lady's Greek' 7
male mentors, support of
  father-tutor 130, 139, 143–151
  husbands as 58–60
male relatives as 60–1, 131
  outside families 65–7
Mangnall's Questions 70, 71, 75
marriage
  rejection of 197–9
  women's education and 207
Marshall, Emma 39, 40
Martineau, Harriet 73
Marx, Eleanor 69
Maximus, Valerius 47
  daughter's devotion to father 47
Mayor, Joseph B.
  Greek for Beginners 31
Medea 9, 10, 183–9
Mermin, Dorothy 7
'Michael Field' 6, 31, 83, 200 *see
  also* Bradley, Katherine;
  Cooper, Edith
Milton 108, 110, 111, 114,
  139–42, 156
Milton's daughters 139–142
Minerva 28
Mitchison, Naomi 73, 201
Mitford, Mary Russell 33, 58, 102,
  108
Moberly, Annie 138
'Moderations' *see* 'Mods' 23
Murphy, Anna Brownell *see*
  Jameson, Anna

Murray, Gilbert 25, 26, 197
  *The Place of Greek in
    Education* 26
Musae Etonenses 20

New Women, friendships 69–70
Nightingale, Florence 3, 25, 51, 62
  Cassandra 58, 92
  grand tour and 50
novels
  brother and sister relationship
    in 131–9
  dissenters and the
    classics 155–63
  fathers and daughters
    relationship 130–1
  Victorian women writers and
    the 193–8

Ovid 23
Oxford Extension Lectures 27
Oxford Magazine 98
Oxford Movement 38
Oxford Poetry 100
Oxford University 14, 22, 24, 30, 52
  Somerville College 74, 212
  women, full membership of 27,
    199

Parr, Catherine 54
Pascoe, Charles Eyre 78, 83
Pater, Clara 84
patriarchal society, unjustness
  of 165, 168, 184, 185, 186
Penrose, Emily 97, 98
Plato 23
  Republic 25
Pope, Alexander 32, 108
Pope's Homer 8, 33
poisoned garment or jewel 178–82
Potter, Beatrice 69

prejudice
  against learned women 166, 199
Prins, Yopie 3, 6, 94
Procter, Anne Adelaide 82
Propertius 23
public schools
  Eton 14, 17
  Charterhouse 14, 30
  Harrow 13
  Rugby 17, 19, 20, 30
  Winchester 13, 17
publicity-seeking 4

Ramsey, Agnata 88
rector's daughters 143–151
Reid, Elizabeth 82
Risorgimento 117, 119
Robinson, A. Mary F. 82
  The Crowned Hippolytus 83
Romans 1
'Roman daughter' *see* 'classical
  daughter'
Roper, Margaret 54
Rose, Jonathan 28
Rossetti, Christina 109
Rossetti, Maria 64, 109
Russell, Dora,
  Medea 189

Sappho 8, 109, 111
Sayers, Dorothy L. 39, 98, 99, 193,
  201–11
  Busman's Honeymoon 211
  Gaudy Night 199, 202, 204–8,
    212
schooling, conventional
  classical 30–1
  difficulties of learning classics
    outside 30
Schreiner, Olive 69
Scott, Sir Walter 41

Secker, Thomas 56
Sellers, Eugénie 6
sewing
  Greek and 151–5, 195
  mechanical processes numbing
    intellect 170
Seymour, Jane 54
Shaw, George Bernard 26
Shelley, Mary 3, 6, 48, 49, 57, 58, 59,
    103, 221
Shelley, Percy 23, 32, 48, 59, 103
  'simultaneous daughter and son' *see*
    'dual sense of self'
Sinclair, May 52, 79, 192, 193–8
social standing 54
sonless families 62–3
Sophocles' tragedies 25
Stodart, Mary Ann 53, 114
  *Female Writers: Thoughts on their
    Proper Sphere, and their
    Powers of Usefulness* 52
Stray, Christopher 15
Swanwick, Anna 3, 9, 82, 104
  complete works of Aeschylus 34
  Oresteia 34
Syrett, Netta 76

Tennyson 8, 12, 13, 30, 36, 155
  career similarity with Elizabeth
    Barrett Browning 111
  education 17
  The Princess 81–2, 111, 123
Thackeray 14, 17, 30, 46, 52,
    171
  Vanity Fair 14, 15
Thackeray, Annie 62
  The Fritillary 100
  The Last Days of Pompeii 38, 39
Theocritus 23
Thucydides 19
  Tom Brown's School Days 19–20

tragedy, Greek
  novel and 170–83
Trollope, Anthony 12, 13, 34, 35,
  46, 151, 171
Tulliver, Maggie 6, 130
Turner, Frank M.,
  *The Greek Heritage in Victorian
  Britain* 5

universities 21–7 *see also*
  Cambridge, London and
  Oxford Universities
  Birmingham 28
  Bristol 27
  Durham 27
  Liverpool 27
University Extension Lectures 212
University of London Matriculation
  Examination 79
unwomanliness 4
  'learned women' and 199

Vance, Norman 5
verse composition 21, 55
Vestal Virgins 40
  Vestales Maximae 40
Victorian Medeas 183–9
Virgil 14, 23
  Aeneid 13, 18
    Dryden's 33
    Victorian women novelists
    and 193
  Georgics 49, 160

Wallace, Jennifer, 4
Ward, Mrs Humphry *see* Arnold, Mary
Webster, Augusta 3, 4, 10, 37, 63,
  84–5, 165
  Prometheus Bound,
    translation 36, 104
  The Medea of Euripides 9, 36
  translations of Greek tragedy
    184
Wedgwood, Julia 31
Welsh, Jane 62
Woman's World 91, 93, 94
Woolf, Virginia 5, 7, 83
  'On not knowing Greek' 7, 10,
    220–2
Wordsworth, William 17, 21
Wordsworth, Elizabeth 138
wrongs of women 164
  injustices of marriage 189
  powerlessness 185
Wuthering Heights 144, 147, 221

Yonge, Charlotte M., 2, 4, 39,
  42, 44, 63, 135–6, 137, 138
  *Aunt Charlotte's Stories of Greek
    History for the Little
    Ones* 43, 45
  *My Young Alcides: A Faded
    Photograph* 44
  *The Clever Woman of the
    Family* 137
  The Daisy Chain 2, 64, 84, 130–2,
    136, 138, 162